LIBRARIES AND NONPROFITS

LIBRARIES AND NONPROFITS

COLLABORATION

FOR THE PUBLIC GOOD

Tatiana Bryant and Jonathan O. Cain, Editors

LIBRARY JUICE PRESS
SACRAMENTO, CA

Copyright respective authors, 2020

Published in 2020 by Library Juice Press

Library Juice Press
PO Box 188784
Sacramento, CA 95822

http://libraryjuicepress.com/

This book is printed on acid-free paper.

Library of Congress Cataloging-in-Publication Data

Names: Bryant, Tatiana, editor. | Cain, Jonathan (Librarian), editor.
Title: Libraries and nonprofits : collaboration for the public good / edited by Tatiana Bryant and Jonathan Cain.
Description: Sacramento, California : Library Juice Press, 2019. | Includes bibliographical references and index.
Identifiers: LCCN 2018060483 | ISBN 9781634000574 (pbk. : acid-free paper)
Subjects: LCSH: Libraries and community--United States--Case studies. | Nonprofit organizations--United States--Case studies. | Libraries--United States--Social aspects. | Common good.
Classification: LCC Z716.4 .L465 2019 | DDC 021.2--dc23
LC record available at https://lccn.loc.gov/2018060483

Table of Contents

Acknowledgements   v

Foreword – *Nicole A. Branch*   vii

Introduction – *Jonathan O. Cain and Tatiana Bryant*   1

Case Studies

Case Study 1: Research that Reaches: Community Education on Media Health Effects – *Jill R. Kavanaugh and Kristelle Lavallee*   11

Case Study 2: Partnerships for Physical Activity: Libaries in Active Communities – *Noah Lenstra*   25

Case Study 3: Unlocking Community Advocacy: Information as a University's Key to Community Partnership – *Alejandra Nann*   39

Case Study 4: Creating an African American Arts Space with Collaborative Support from the Friends of the Missouri Governor's Mansion – *kYmberly Keeton*   53

Case Study 5: Resurfacing At-Risk Works of the Feminist Small Press – *Jane Nichols and Korey Jackson*   59

Case Study 6: An Archivist and a History-Focused Nonprofit: My Role as a Board Member for the Oregon Black Pioneers – *Natalia Fernández*   69

Case Study 7: The Japanese Cultural Center of Hawaii and Hawaii School Libraries: Partners in Educating Students About the World War II Incarceration of Japanese Americans in Hawaii – *Violet H. Harada and Jane Kurahara*   85

Case Study 8: From Campus to Community: Making the Case for Open Access by Bringing Nonprofits to Academic Libraries – *Rachel Caldwell, Melanie Allen, Ann Viera, and Alan Wallace*   103

Case Study 9: Collaborating on Science Programming – *Tracy Englert*   123

Case Study 10: Lights! Camera! Action! Librarian Collaboration with a Science Film Festival – *Amani Magid*   131

Case Study 11: Project Myanmar: Empowering Students through Maker Education – *Michael Cherry*   141

Case Study 12: Partners in Pride: Collaborating with a Community Archive to Document LGBTQ History – *Culbertson? and Lisa Lamont*   153

Case Study 13: "Doing Good": An Academic Library as a Social Change Agent – *Judith Schwartz*   167

Case Study 14: Age Mates, Play Groups, and the Community Building Blocks of Leadership for Public Housing Residents – *Roland Barksdale-Hall*   187

Case Study 15: Network Troubleshooting: Creative Partnerships
in Digital Literacy Outreach – *Sarah McFadden* 205

Case Study 16: Growing Access to Books: Supplementing
Library Services to Rural Students – *Tiffany Coulson and Barbara
Peterson* 217

Afterword – *Tatiana Bryant and Jonathan O. Cain* 241

About the Contributors 245

Index 253

Acknowledgements

We would like to thank the employees of the Urban League of Portland for partnering with us to produce the 2015 "State of Black Oregon: A Panel Discussion" event at the University of Oregon Libraries. Furthermore, thank you to all who contributed to this work and continued to push us. Let this serve as a testament to the insight, empathy, and love librarians have for their communities.

Foreword

When I entered librarianship, after nearly a decade and a half working in nonprofits, I was struck by how seamless this transition felt. While librarianship could rightly be considered a second career for me, it felt more like the logical next step of my professional trajectory. Nonprofits and libraries carry the same values and orientations: service centered on community, a commitment to the civic life our country, and a desire to provide sanctuary to those in need of it. These values drove my professional aspirations in nonprofits, and I was affirmed to find these values in librarianship. I also discovered important differences. Nonprofits and the services they provide differ substantially across communities, services, and organizational size and structure. Fundraising, while important to libraries, played a much more central role (in both positive and challenging ways) in the life of the nonprofits where I worked. While nonprofits, at their core, are accountable to those they serve and the public at large, the field as a whole lacks centralized and codified values and standards. Libraries and librarianship, on the other hand, are more narrowly focused (despite the wide variety of types of libraries) and have some core common professional values and practices. While these unifying elements have real advantages, they may also create silos within libraries and librarianship, and limit our scope and thinking about our communities.

These similarities and differences make nonprofits and libraries naturals for productive partnerships. Libraries and nonprofits are poised for mutual exchange of professional expertise, unique understanding of our communities, and a shared dedication to the public. This book—which explores these partnerships—comes at a critical time for libraries and nonprofits. Libraries are reconsidering the role of spaces and services and the changing relationships between communities and information. Nonprofits (and libraries) are pushed by social and political realities to respond to increasingly complex needs. The approaches shared in this volume point toward many possible configurations of the intersection of libraries and nonprofits and is ripe with ideas and inspiration. Here we find how we might reimagine our roles as librarians and our libraries as community collaborators.

The case studies that make up the bulk of this volume include a variety of types of libraries and nonprofits, and a range of collaborative approaches, organized around core theme areas. Public health collaborations include a nonprofit with an embedded librarian focused on media literacy and community health, and a public library partnering with individuals and agencies to increase physical activity in a rural community. Social safety net case studies include a university library bringing the traditional liaison model to a local advocacy agency. An arts and cultural collaborations study shares the approach of a library at a Historically Black University (HBCU) to open up the library as a creative space with a library arts program and an arts advisory board; another shares successful archives and small press collaborations; and another case study shares an embedded librarian's work supporting digital literacy and graphic design skills acquisition of students with disabilities through a transitional public school program. The impact of librarian partnerships for education is evident in a project that developed and implemented a comprehensive curriculum around the internment of Japanese Americans in Hawai'i.

STEM case studies provide an example of libraries supporting meaningful service learning projects through a partnership between a public library, a high school, and a local non-profit to produce and package soap for orphanages in Myanmar. Continuing this international focus, this section also shares a science film festival successfully developed and supported through a faculty-librarian partnership in

Abu Dhabi. The case studies conclude with examples of community advocacy, including literacy programming, primarily supporting dual-language families in rural communities, and a public housing library that partnered with a local AmeriCorps program to provide youth and family programming

What emerges from these examples is a mix of practical advice, blueprints for collaboration, a synthesis of the range of issues that nonprofits and libraries might address together, and perspective on how both libraries and nonprofits might reimagine their roles together. At this moment in history the connections, collaborations, and new models shared within this volume are all the more critical. Though not new concerns, over the past year our society has grappled more publicly with central concerns of our democracy—issues of social justice, civil rights, informed citizenship, and access—among others. These, too, are the central concerns of both libraries and nonprofits. The examples shared here provide fresh insight into how we might continue and build all of our respective roles in this landscape. The ghosts of our collective past—echoed in the examples in this book of the hidden (and uncovered) history of internment in Hawai'i or in the building of archives to document and acknowledge those who have historically been silenced—call for us to continue to explore these partnerships as we grapple with our current social and political reality. This book not only inspires and demonstrates powerful examples of nonprofits and libraries, it invites us to consider what critical partnerships we need to be building and sustaining next.

Nicole A. Branch
Associate University Librarian for Learning & Engagement
Santa Clara University, Santa Clara, California

Introduction

Jonathan O. Cain and Tatiana Bryant

On February 28, 2018, the *New York Times* published a story related to a topic that had recently dominated media conversation across politics, social policy, and healthcare. The article, "Once It Was Overdue Books. Now Librarians Fight Overdoses" was part of the developing coverage of what would come to be known as the U.S. "opioid epidemic." While news relating to the epidemic had been covered during the previous year, this article was notable for mainstream coverage of the "first responders"—it highlighted the critical role that libraries and librarians are playing in delivering services to those affected by the epidemic. The article quotes Middletown Thrall Library director Matt Pfister stating that it would be "easier to call the police, to wait for E.M.S," about his library's decision to make an active intervention combatting the loss of life linked to opioid abuse.[1] It also is illustrative of the level of attention that libraries as institutions and library workers are receiving around the delivery of life-changing services. This led the Secretary of Health and Human Services to create a grant program allowing public libraries in High Intensity Drug Trafficking Areas (HIDTAs) to purchase naloxone rescue kits and provide training for employees to use naloxone rescue

---

1. Annie Correal, "Once It Was Overdue Books. Now Librarians Fight Overdoses," *New York Times*, February 28, 2018, https://www.nytimes.com/2018/02/28/nyregion/librarians-opioid-heroin-overdoses.html.

kits.[2] This act tacitly acknowledges that public libraries are on the front lines of government service delivery.

The *New York Times* article is not the first news story to illustrate the close relationship between libraries and emergency services. In June of 2017, *American Libraries* ran a feature called "Saving Lives in the Stacks," illustrating the ways that public libraries have become first responders to drug overdoses.[3] It is not just one or two libraries engaged in this work—the American Library Association (ALA) highlighted the critical interventions that libraries have taken in response to the opioid epidemic, even hosting a live webinar called "The Opioid Epidemic and Libraries: An American Libraries Live Webcast" in late 2017.[4] This webinar concretizes the library as a stakeholder, even though when we think of drug addiction treatment we often think of government social service providers or nonprofit organizations as service deliverers. An article in *Nonprofit Quarterly*, "Nonprofits Facing Challenges in Opioid Battle," discusses how active the nonprofit sector has been in addres-sing the growing issue of opioid addiction in the United States.[5] The article presents a myriad of collaborations and instances of overlap between multiple government agencies and nonprofits seeking solutions. The recent social and political attention paid to opioid abuse, its cost in human lives, and the toll it takes on communities and the ways communities and governments have chosen to respond to the crisis provides but one example of the ways that libraries and nonprofits continue to operate in similar domains.

---

2. Sean Maloney, "Maloney Introduces Life-Saving Librarians Act to Stop Heroin and Opioid Overdose Deaths," October 31, 2017, https://seanmaloney.house.gov/media-center/press-releases/maloney-introduces-life-saving-librarians-act-to-stop-heroin-and-opioid.

3. Anne Ford, "Saving Lives in the Stacks," *American Libraries*, June 21, 2017, https://americanlibrariesmagazine.org/2017/06/21/saving-lives-in-the-stacks/.

4. American Library Association, "The Opioid Epidemic and Libraries: An American Libraries Live Webcast," press release, December 5, 2017, http://www.ala.org/news/press-releases/2017/12/opioid-epidemic-and-libraries-american-libraries-live-webcast.

5. Anna Berry, "Nonprofits Facing Challenges in Opioid Battle," *Nonprofit Quarterly*, June 14, 2017, https://nonprofitquarterly.org/nonprofits-facing-challenges-opioid-battle/.

Libraries have operated as the catch-all for critical services in communities—serving as community centers, early and continuing education centers, job training locations, e-government touch spots, and increasingly as deliverers of critical social services, financial literacy, and public healthcare support. Libraries constitute a significant channel for generating social impact because they "have a role in creating community by providing a place for people to connect. The library is also the logical provider of information on community events and organizations, which brings people together in other areas."[6]

Libraries should fulfill a role for everyone. That versatility extends beyond pleasure reading, foundational education, and job training. From early on, libraries have been proponents of assimilation, social betterment, and advancement in their communities. Libraries continue to serve new immigrant communities. In 2007 the American Library Association (ALA) adopted a resolution in support of immigrant rights. This builds on earlier work: in 1924, the ALA published "The Polish Immigrant and His Reading," by Eleanor Ledbetter as a part of the series "Library Work with the Foreign Born."[7] Libraries have benefited from hiring culturally representative librarians from the communities which they serve, which has helped them to promote and deliver services. For example, an early initiative to recruit "young women from ethnic enclaves" resulted in the hiring of the first Puerto Rican librarian in the New York Public Library (NYPL). Pura Belpré began working for NYPL in the 1920s and made a tremendous impact on NYPL's services to library users from non-English speaking and multilingual communities.[8] In this capacity she offered both Spanish and English language story times across the city and, noting there were

---

6. Jeanetta Drueke, "Researching Local Organizations: Simple Strategies for Building Social Capital," *Reference & User Services Quarterly* 45, no. 4 (2006): 327–333.

7. American Library Association "New Immigrants," http://www.ala.org/tools/atoz/new-immigrants.

8. Neda Ulaby, "How NYC's First Puerto Rican Librarian Brought Spanish to the Shelves," NPR.org, September 8, 2016, https://www.npr.org/2016/09/08/492957864/how-nycs-first-puerto-rican-librarian-brought-spanish-to-the-shelves.

no children's books in Spanish available, published one called *Perez y Matina*. The work of Belpré illustrates the impact that libraries continue to have in community-building. Belen Garcia highlights the impact on these types of actions when referring to how hard it was to reach out to Spanish-speaking children, stating "their parents didn't let them come to the library because they thought the library was only English."[9]

A 2007 ALA study shows that this is both a continuing challenge and an area of concentration for libraries.[10] The Urban Libraries Council highlighted the case of the Providence Public Library (PPL) and the issue of attracting immigrant families to the libraries. The PPL was actively reaching out to the children of immigrant families because of the "positive and statistically significant relation between children's services in public libraries and early reading success at schools."[11] In an effort to increase early childhood literacy, the library cultivated a partnership with the Providence Children's Museum to create the Chace Children's Discovery Library. Unfortunately, language was thought to be a barrier to getting immigrant families to patronize the museum. As a result, the PPL developed the Discovery Guide Program with the intention to "increase the number of immigrant families who view the Library as a free family fun and educational destination resulting in their overall increased use of Library's resources and programs; and (ii) equip immigrant adults with transferable work skills, increased language and literacy skills and an established US work history."[12] This program was designed to hire graduates from the Rhode Island Family Literacy Initiative (a literacy program at the PPL) to serve as Discovery Guides

---

9. Ibid.

10. American Library Association, Office for Research and Statistics, "Serving Non-English Speakers in U.S. Public Libraries," (Chicago: ALA, 2007), http://www.ala.org/aboutala/offices/diversity/nonenglishspeakersreport.

11. Urban Libraries Council, "Immigrant Outreach by the Library's Adult Literacy Students," accessed March 27, 2020, https://www.urbanlibraries.org/innovations-old/2013-innovations/civic-community-engagement/immigrant-outreach-by-the-librarys-adult-literacy-students.

12. Urban Libraries Council, "Immigrant Outreach by the Library's Adult Literacy Students," accessed March 27, 2020, https://www.urbanlibraries.org/innovations-old/2013-innovations/civic-community-engagement/immigrant-outreach-by-the-librarys-adult-literacy-students.

and as advocates for the library to the community by recruiting new families to the library to engage with social service providers.[13]

The nonprofit sector also operates multidimensionally. Nonprofits fulfill roles as service providers, advocacy organizations, expressive organizations (organizations that "give expression to various causes, such as civil rights, environmental protection and the right to life"[14] and community-building groups.[15] The National Council of Nonprofits, a nonprofit advocacy and education association, illustrates the breadth of these entities as well as their level of impact in stating that one "would be hard-pressed to find anyone who has not been touched in some way by a nonprofit organization, whether they knew it or not."[16] This is not a surprise considering the long-lasting relationship between government, citizens, residents, and nonprofit institutions in the U.S in particular.

Boris and Steuerle argue that "A glance into history quickly reveals that devolution of service responsibilities to the nonprofit sector—whether from federal or state governments—has been occurring for decades. A driving force behind many recent changes in the size and scope of the nonprofit sector has been the use of charities and nonprofit institutions as intermediaries or contractors in providing the services government finances."[17] Vernis et al. highlight the development of this role, stating "One of the most outshining changes produced in nonprofits is the increase in their social claim role. Citizens gathered in consumer associations, environmental organizations associations and human rights organizations raise a loud voice to protest against unfair situations often caused by international organizations and business

---

13. Ibid.

14. Lester M. Salamon, *America's Nonprofit Sector: A Primer*, 3rd ed. (New York: Foundation Center, 2012).

15. Thomas P. Holland and Roger A. Ritvo, *Nonprofit Organizations* (New York: Columbia University Press, 2008).

16. National Council of Nonprofits, "Nonprofit Impact in Communities," September 22, 2014. https://www.councilofnonprofits.org/nonprofit-impact-communities.

17. Elizabeth T. Boris and C. Eugene Steuerle, *Nonprofits & Government: Collaboration & Conflict* (Washington, DC: The Urban Institute Press, 2006).

companies, or by private or public interests."[18] As we can see, the nonprofit sector fills a specific role between the government and the public.

We can make a similar claim about libraries, as they also fill the role of service provider for communities. However, libraries occupy a slightly different niche, often operating as hubs for community activity and information delivery as well as a physical community space to receive materials, services, and information. Nonprofits and libraries fulfill complementary and supplementary roles in society. Their goals are so aligned that it seems only natural that they would ally in addressing the issues that affect their communities.

The initial inspiration for this project was generated from personal connections the editors have in libraries and with leading, studying, and supporting the nonprofit sector. Through our work we visualize the connections between these two fields and witness the impact they have on communities. With a projected 116,867 libraries of all types operating within the United States,[19] it is a rare individual who has never been impacted by a library supporting educational, government, or other administrative functions.

Understanding how these two fields can intersect and strengthen each other is crucial. Both libraries and nonprofits provide vital cultural and social services to vulnerable communities. In recent years, shrinking support for social spending in the U.S. has made their work more indispensable in supporting the needs and sustaining the health of individuals and communities. With the trend of government fiscal priorities skewing towards a reduction of social spending for nearly two decades (and looking unlikely to abate anytime soon), it seems more crucial than ever for service-focused organizations to understand each other, the work that each does, and the possibilities that exist for collaboration.

As the nonprofit sector is seen as a primary delivery mechanism for critical social services, it is important for organizations to form

---

18. Alfred Vernis, Maria Iglesias, Beatriz Sanz, and Angel Saz-Carranza, *Nonprofit Organizations: Challenges and Collaboration* (New York: Palgrave Macmillan, 2006).

19. American Library Association, "Number of Libraries in the United States," accessed March 27, 2020, http://libguides.ala.org/numberoflibraries.

partnerships with cultural and community agents. Kenneth Anderson Taylor of the Bush School of Government and Public Service at Texas A&M University points out, "Nonprofits, such as medical research institutions, houses of worship and shelters for sexual abuse victims, usually fill gaps between what the government and private sector do. A large share of them serves communities with great needs, a population that is disproportionately made up of people of color."[20] However, the leadership overwhelmingly is not.

While not a solution for the problem that Anderson explores with nonprofit leadership, collaborating with entities that have a proven track record of being embedded in their communities is a step toward making sure that the right sets of services are being offered and delivered. Leading With Intent asserts, "At the most fundamental level, who serves on a board impacts how it functions and the decisions it makes" and that the "blind spots created by a lack of racial and ethnic diversity are particularly concerning, as they may result in strategies and plans that ineffectively address societal challenges and inequities, or even reinforce them."[21]

Nonprofits and Libraries: Collaboration for the Public Good is an exploration of connections between libraries and nonprofits. This book seeks to highlight how these institutions operate similarly to address the needs of their respective communities, but also showcases how these organizations recognize that common ground and the will to work together to address their missions and challenges. This collection of case studies explores connections created between the libraries and nonprofits. The volume is unique in that practitioners serve as case study authors, giving them the opportunity to highlight the novel nature of their collaborations, including needs, goals, challenges, and successes. This book also provides a framework for best practices for

---

20. Kenneth Anderson Taylor, "Too Many Nonprofit Boards Lack Diversity: It's a Problem that Can be Fixed," *Chicago Tribune*, accessed March 27, 2020, http://digitaledition.chicagotribune.com/tribune/article_popover.aspx?guid=febd185f-9578-41ca-b95c-49790d5137a1.

21. BoardSource, "Leading with Intent: 2017 Index of Nonprofit Board Practices," (Washington, D.C.: BoardSource, 2017).

working collaboratively with external partners. As there is no shortage of problems facing communities and seemingly a reduction in the re-sources that are available to the organizations addressing these issues, *Libraries and Nonprofits* seeks to offer instructive insights into how libraries have collaborated with external partners to address community issues.

We hope readers learn more about the phenomenal work that libraries and nonprofits are collaborating on throughout the U.S, and that they are inspired to seek creative solutions to issues that exist in their own communities. Moreover, we hope that readers will find a valuable and encouraging model to apply to work in libraries, nonprofits, and in communities.

Bibliography

American Library Association. "New Immigrants." http://www.ala.org/tools/atoz/new-immigrants.

American Library Association, "Number of Libraries in the United States," accessed March 27, 2020, http://libguides.ala.org/numberoflibraries.

American Library Association. "The Opioid Epidemic and Libraries: An American Libraries Live Webcast." Press release, December 5, 2017. http://www.ala.org/news/press-releases/2017/12/opioid-epidemic-and-libraries-american-libraries-live-webcast.

American Library Association, Office for Research and Statistics. "Serving Non-English Speakers in U.S. Public Libraries." Chicago: ALA, 2007, http://www.ala.org/aboutala/offices/diversity/nonenglish-speakersreport.

Berry, Anna. "Nonprofits Facing Challenges in Opioid Battle." *Nonprofit Quarterly*, June 14, 2017. https://nonprofitquarterly.org/nonprofits-facing-challenges-opioid-battle/.

BoardSource. "Leading with Intent: 2017 Index of Nonprofit Board Practices." Washington, D.C.: BoardSource, 2017.

Boris, Elizabeth T., and C. Eugene Steuerle. *Nonprofits & Government: Collaboration & Conflict*. Washington, DC: The Urban Institute Press, 2006.

Correal, Annie. "Once It Was Overdue Books. Now Librarians Fight Overdoses." *New York Times*, February 28, 2018. https://www.nytimes.com/2018/02/28/nyregion/librarians-opioid-heroin-overdoses.html.

Drueke, Jeanetta. "Researching Local Organizations: Simple Strategies for Building Social Capital." *Reference & User Services Quarterly 45*, no. 4 (2006): 327–33.

Ford, Anne. "Saving Lives in the Stacks." *American Libraries*, June 21, 2017. https://americanlibrariesmagazine.org/2017/06/21/saving-lives-in-the-stacks/.

Holland, Thomas P., and Roger A. Ritvo. *Nonprofit Organizations: Principles and Practices*. New York: Columbia University Press, 2008.

Maloney, Sean. "Maloney Introduces Life-Saving Librarians Act to Stop Heroin and Opioid Overdose Deaths." October 31, 2017. https://seanmaloney.house.gov/media-center/press-releases/maloney-introduces-life-saving-librarians-act-to-stop-heroin-and-opioid..

National Council of Nonprofits. "Nonprofit Impact in Communities." September 22, 2014. https://www.councilofnonprofits.org/nonprofit-impact-communities.

Salamon, Lester M. *America's Nonprofit Sector: A Primer*. 3rd ed. New York: The Foundation Center, 2012.

Taylor, Kenneth Anderson. "Too Many Nonprofit Boards Lack Diversity: It's a Problem that Can be Fixed." *Chicago Tribune*. Accessed March 27, 2020. http://digitaledition.chicagotribune.com/tribune/article_popover.aspx?guid=febd185f-9578-41ca-b95c-49790d5137a1.

Ulaby, Neda. "How NYC's First Puerto Rican Librarian Brought Spanish to the Shelves." NPR.org, September 8, 2016. https://www.npr.org/2016/09/08/492957864/how-nycs-first-puerto-rican-librarian-brought-spanish-to-the-shelves.

Urban Libraries Council. "Immigrant Outreach by the Library's Adult Literacy Students." Accessed March 27, 2020. https://www.urbanlibraries.org/innovations-old/2013-innovations/civic-community-engagement/immigrant-outreach-by-the-librarys-adult-literacy-students.

Vernis, Alfred, Maria Iglesias, Beatriz Sanz, and Angel Saz-Carranza. *Nonprofit Organizations: Challenges and Collaboration*. New York: Palgrave Macmillan, 2006.

Case Study 1

Research that Reaches: Community Education on Media Health Effects

Jill R. Kavanaugh and Kristelle Lavallee

Abstract

In our digital age, individuals, families, and communities are recognizing the profound impact that media and technology have on our lives. While often engaged with and adopted in order to facilitate everyday tasks, media and digital devices also elicit concerns about how they affect our learning, physical health, social connections, and mental well-being. As the wealth of content sensationalizing, assessing, and addressing these concerns can be overwhelming, and the ability to discern science from opinion proving more and more difficult in an era of "fake news," individuals and organizations are recognizing the need for these issues to be understood and addressed.

In order to fulfill this need, the nonprofit Center on Media and Child Health (CMCH) began almost two decades ago at Boston Children's Hospital, providing trusted resources to help communities understand the impacts that media have on education, health, and society. As an interdisciplinary research center, CMCH employs scientists, clinicians, academics, and other media experts in order to nurture children's health and development in today's media-saturated environment.

Central to CMCH's mission are the content strategist, Kristelle Lavallee, and librarian, Jill R. Kavanaugh, who work closely together to provide the latest and most credible evidence for community outreach in the form of presentations, workshops, and other resources. Organizations reach out to CMCH for guidance and expertise in order to address specific areas of concern such as cyberbullying, problematic interactive media use, violent media, and social media's effects on relationships. While CMCH has a global presence online, CMCH's local community outreach spans throughout New England, ranging from clinical audiences (Southcoast Health, Holy Family Hospital); schools (elementary through high school); government agencies (Massachusetts Departments of Public Health, Connecticut Commission on Children); and community health centers (Fenway Health, Martha Eliot Health Center).

This case study will outline CMCH's successful collaborative outreach process, beginning with the first request from a concerned community group, to the crafting of research-based messages, to a tailored presentation, and any resulting follow-up. This overview will provide valuable insight into the collaboration between librarianship and outreach within this unique nonprofit research institution.

Case

This case study is based on the Center on Media and Child Health (CMCH), a nonprofit interdisciplinary academic research center operating under the umbrella of the Division of Adolescent and Young Adult Medicine at Boston Children's Hospital. This case study will highlight the collaboration between the Center's embedded librarian and content strategist, who formed a collaboration in order to address how to best translate academic research into useful and easy-to-understand presentations for diverse audiences.

Background

The mission of the Center on Media and Child Health (CMCH) is to nurture children's health and development in media-rich environments. Founded in 2002 by pediatrician and former Hollywood filmmaker, Michael Rich, MD, MPH, CMCH focuses on how media, such as TV, movies, video games, mobile apps, social media, and music, exist as powerful environmental health influences. The Center's projects, research, and outreach initiatives strive to bring better understanding of how media positively *and* negatively influence children's and adolescents' development in areas including sleep, sexual behaviors, substance use, academic performance, physical activity, nutrition, social skills, and time management. In response to these findings, CMCH creates research-based resources for helping children and adolescents foster healthy, balanced, and mindful media use.

Today's advancing technology and the increasing ubiquity of media have made it essential for parents, clinicians, and caregivers to understand the role of media in the lives of children. Recent research shows that 96.6% of children under the age of four use mobile devices.[1] Tweens aged eight to twelve average six hours per day of screen time, and adolescents average nine hours per day.[2] Additional data reports find that 92% of youth are online every day with 24% reporting a near "constant" connection.[3] As concerns mount over how these technologies affect children's academic achievement, social skills, physical health, and mental well-being, various educators, parents, clinicians, and community groups are turning to skilled experts and research-based institutions such as CMCH for advice, tools, and resources for raising children in today's digital world.

The Center's dedicated and diverse staff, along with outside collaborators, student interns, postdoctoral researchers, and other associates, share a passion and dedication to its mission. The work supporting the Center's mission falls largely within three categories: investigation, translation, and innovation. Investigation encompasses CMCH's own and collaborative research projects examining the positive and negative

---

1. Hilda K. Kabali, Matilde M. Irigoyen, Rosemary Nunez-Davis, Jennifer G. Budacki, Sweta H. Mohanty, Kristin P. Leister, and Robert L. Bonner, "Exposure and Use of Mobile Media Devices by Young Children," *Pediatrics* 136, no. 6 (2015): 1044-50.

2. Vicky Rideout, "The Common Sense Census: Media Use by Tweens and Teens," Common Sense Media, https://www.commonsensemedia.org/sites/default/files/uploads/research/census_researchreport.pdf.

3. Amanda Lenhart, "Teens, Social Media & Technology Overview 2015," Pew Research Center, http://www.pewinternet.org/files/2015/04/PI_TeensandTech_Update2015_0409151.pdf.

effects that media have on children's health. The Center also compiles scholarly literature from the field in a comprehensive, searchable database. CMCH takes this wealth of scientific knowledge and translates it into practical, actionable guidance for our audience, which includes parents and caregivers, through in-person presentations, publications, blogs, curricula, and other forms of outreach. CMCH's stakeholders differ from the audience, in that they provide both funding and visibility, and the team works in conjunction with them to satisfy their audience's needs. Finally, CMCH is continuously innovating, both in research design and creative ways of using media tools to support and enhance children's health and development.

Drawing on all three areas of the Center's core work are the presentations given by selected team experts. These talks, workshops, and lectures are tailored by subject, audience, and venue, and contain the latest relevant research and grey literature to inform and educate the public and selected groups about media and child health. These presentations often provide the Center with additional networks for disseminating its resources and helps to foster communities where additional thought and conversations around media health issues often lead to actionable change.

Collaborator: Content Strategist

The field of media and child health is supported by thousands of studies across many disciplines. This research is often seen as too abstract or removed for the general public to understand and implement; thus, CMCH engaged a content strategist to translate the science into resources that are both practical and accessible for diverse audiences.

The content strategist's work involves creating practical health resources, educational curricula, child media use guides, social media messages, and a variety of other resources that revolve around informing and educating key audience groups about children's media use and subsequent effects on health. Central to the content strategist's objectives is the diffusion of this work to a broad audience. To that end, the content strategist must also oversee the Center's dissemination efforts, through in-house publications, public and closed presentations, and the the outreach efforts of CMCH partnerships and collaborative endeavors.

Collaborator: Librarian

Since the inception of the Center fifteen years ago, CMCH has consistently earmarked funding for a full-time, embedded librarian. One of the founding commitments of the Center was "to develop, maintain, and make available a comprehensive, up-to-date library of the 'state of the knowledge' on media and their effects on children and adolescents"—a database project undertaken by the Center's first librarian.[4]

In addition to this database (currently called the CMCH *Database of Research*, but soon to be relaunched as *Mediatrics*), the CMCH librarian provides direct research support in the form of literature searches and citation management services for the various projects at the Center. Specifically, the librarian provides research support for the content strategist's presentations.

Objectives

The main goal of the collaboration between the content strategist and the librarian is to ensure that all presentations are informed by the best available evidence on media health effects and delivered in a format that is accessible and beneficial to the audience. Due to the rapidly-changing nature of media and technology, the body of literature expands frequently, and monitoring emerging research is a major crucial task performed by the librarian. The librarian receives notifications from reputable peer-reviewed journals in the fields of medicine, public health, computer science, social science, psychology, and many others, indicating when new articles have been published. From there, the librarian reviews these new articles, and evaluates them based on a set of criteria, including the author's credibility in the field of media and

---

4. Michael Rich, and Brandy E. King, "Center on Media and Child Health: Scientific Evolution Responding to Technological Revolution," *Journal of Children and Media* 2, no. 2 (2008): 183-88.

health; the study's design and rigor; the relevance of the article; how well-supported the data and outcomes are within the field; and the funding source. In addition to traditional scholarly literature, the librarian also reviews grey literature from authoritative research groups, nonprofits, and occasionally market research, in order to provide the team with a wider breadth of coverage. Articles that meet the criteria are then passed along to the team and incorporated in both research and outreach projects.

To meet this goal, the content strategist and librarian operationalized a streamlined workflow with a series of clearly defined action steps that allows each to participate fully in almost every aspect of the creation of a presentation. The process is as follows:

1. A stakeholder contacts CMCH requesting a presentation, and the content strategist and the stakeholder work together to identify clear topic areas and objectives to meet their audience's needs.
2. The content strategist and librarian work together to identify key topic areas for research.
3. The librarian conducts a literature review of relevant and recent research.
4. The librarian and content strategist synthesize the relevant research findings into main points that serve the stakeholder's objectives.
5. The content strategist creates and integrates the research-based points into a comprehensive presentation for the primary audience.
6. The librarian reviews the presentation, ensuring that the data points used are the most relevant, up-to-date, and accurate.
7. The content strategist presents the material to the stakeholder's audience.
8. After the presentation, the stakeholder provides feedback (positive or negative) that is then incorporated into future presentations.

This process is both multidisciplinary and interdisciplinary[5] as both the content strategist and librarian tackle the issue from their respective disciplines, but also integrate their perspectives and knowledge to create presentations that diverge from each other significantly. In fact, the field of media effects has always been multidisciplinary,[6] which is reflected within these presentations and the Center itself.

Stakeholders

The funding for each presentation varies: some stakeholders provide a donation to the Center, some presentations have been written into awarded research grants, and others are provided pro-bono. While CMCH's community outreach is both national and international, with various team members presenting around the world, the content strategist is responsible for presenting mostly locally, in Boston, Massachusetts, and throughout New England. Each request is evaluated by the content strategist who passes along all viable requests to the Center's director for final approval.

CMCH attracts a variety of stakeholders; subsequently, the Center receives requests for talks, lectures, panel participation, workshops, and other types of presentations from a variety of public, private, professional, and community groups, including:

- **Clinical and healthcare professionals.** This group includes physicians, nurses, and social workers. These presentations occur in a clinical setting (e.g. Southcoast Health, Holy Family Hospital), and continuing education credits or other credentials are often offered to attendees.

---

5. Sidath Gunawardena, Rosina Weber, and Denise E. Agosto, "Finding That Special Someone: Interdisciplinary Collaboration in an Academic Context," *Journal of Education for Library and Information Science* (2010): 210-21

6. David S. Bickham, Jill R. Kavanaugh, and Michael Rich, "Media Effects as Health Research: How Pediatricians Have Changed the Study of Media and Child Development," *Journal of Children and Media* 10, no. 2 (2016): 191-99.

- **Educators.** This group includes teachers, administrators, and education specialists. These presentations are often held within school settings (e.g. Keene State College, Worcester Technical High School). Attendance may be optional or mandated by teachers' unions, and continuing education credits are often provided to attendees.
- **Parents.** This group includes parents and caregivers. These presentations are often held in community health centers, (e.g. Fenway Health, Martha Eliot Health Center), as well as public institutions such as schools and museums (e.g. Belmont High School, Museum of Jewish Heritage). These talks are meant to educate and inform parents and caregivers about specific areas of concern related to children's media use, or to provide a general overview and suggest best practices for their child or teen.
- **Government.** This group includes government officials, policy makers, and invited or interested civilians. These presentations are often held within designated public arenas (e.g. the Boston Public Library, Connecticut General Assembly). These events are often mandatory for relevant government officials and may also be broadcast on local public access TV.

Intervention

Requests for presentations are often crafted around an identified need. Typically, organizations and groups are looking for expert information, practical resources, solutions to an existing problem, or preventative steps regarding a known media concern. Prior to creating or preparing for a particular event, the content strategist works with the organizer to identify the goals they hope to accomplish, and tailors messages and resources in order to meet those outlined goals. These objectives are meant to have a profound and direct influence on professional or community audiences; examples of intervention outcomes include:

- Educating clinicians and other healthcare professionals about how to recognize and address media health issues within their patient populations. Often these presentations contribute directly to medical education by meeting requirements for Continuing Education Unit (CEU) credits for nurses or Continuing Medical Education (CME) credits for physicians.

- Bringing awareness to community groups about the benefits and risks associated with children and adolescent populations using a variety of different types of media. These presentations can be focused on specific health and/or safety concerns or present a general overview. They also offer practical advice and resources for addressing and preventing the negative outcomes associated with media use. Often, the group leader will take the relevant resources noted in the presentation, such as CMCH's age-based healthy media use tip sheets, and make them available to the larger group. This can include creating a link to CMCH resources that is accessible through the group's website, or physically downloading and printing them to distribute.
- Addressing a specific media-related problem within a school or adolescent employment setting. These presentations outline the health concerns, policies, and legal ramifications surrounding a particular media issue. Suggestions for resolution and prevention are also offered. This information is used to inform changes in school or corporate policy. This can include best practices for employee's social media use, as well as acceptable device use while in class or on the job.
- Assisting and informing policy makers wanting to craft and revise legislation for educational institutions. The information in these presentations is used when policy makers want to create or revise practices around media and technology use. This includes designating funding for educational technologies for public schools and managing regulations for safe technology use in public.[7]

---

7. Gail Lavielle, "Lavielle & Commission on Children Host Forum Exploring Technology's Effects on Student Learning," http://www.cthousegop.com/lavielle/2015/11/24/lavielle-commission-on-children-host-forum-exploring-technologys-effects-on-student-learning/.

Outcomes

The ongoing success of the partnership between the librarian and content strategist is due to several factors. First, the individual expertise of both collaborators; second, their commitment to the Center's mission; and third, the success of the presentations they present. Both the librarian and the content strategist have diverse educational and professional backgrounds; the librarian has a library and information science degree, and the content strategist has a graduate degree in developmental psychology. Additionally, the librarian comes from an international background and has experience working in social development within the government, and the content strategist draws on her experience working as an educator and children's media producer.

Both the librarian and the content strategist bring a shared devotion to and passion for the underlying mission of CMCH—to provide evidence-based information on media health effects, as opposed to taking an advocacy-based stance. Individuals who strongly align with the vision and mission of an organization (i.e. affective commitment) contribute highly to organizational performance,[8] which is certainly the case with the content strategist and librarian at CMCH.

The success of the collaboration between the librarian and content strategist is tied directly to the success of the presentations they create. Many of the organizations the content strategist presents to have in-house assessments, which ask attendees to note if and what they learned from the presentation, and whether they felt that the information and knowledge gleaned was presented well and worth their time. This kind of feedback is often analyzed by the group organizers who then provide feedback to the content strategist. This feedback is reviewed by both the content strategist and the librarian, who take it under consideration and adjust subsequent presentations accordingly.

One notable example was a presentation crafted by the librarian and content strategist addressing a social media problem at a local public

---

8. Bhavesh S. Patel, Lorne D. Booker, Hazel Melanie Ramos, and Chris Bart, "Mission Statements and Performance in Non-Profit Organisations," *Corporate Governance* 15, no. 5 (2015): 759-74.

school. The content strategist spoke to the school's community of parents, administrators, and students, and directly addressed the school's issues within the presentation. Based on research, data, and examples used in the presentation, the school's administration changed its policy regarding digital devices and the use of social media applications.

Another measure of success is the resulting communication from presentation attendees, noting praise, criticism, and follow-up questions that often come via email, or through the Center's *Ask the Mediatrician*® web portal, where users are able to anonymously ask a media health-related question. If allowed, sign-up sheets for CMCH resources are distributed following each presentation. Although not a formal metric, the Center gauges interest in its resources following each presentation; for example, CMCH often receives an increase in subscription requests for its publications. Each new subscription following a talk is an anecdotal indicator of the success of the presentation.

Additionally, success is informally assessed by word-of-mouth referrals, as well as repeat invitations to annual events. This includes receiving requests for additional presentations from the same group as well as receiving new invitations from groups who were given recommendations from past presentation attendees. While informal in nature, these "follow-up" and "piggy-back" requests are noted and help the content strategist and librarian better understand what works well and what changes need to be made.

Reflections

The partnership between the content strategist and librarian continues to serve the Center's mission, providing a direct link between science and practice that is accessible to key stakeholders and audiences. While the outlined steps forged from the collaboration have proven to be successful, challenges are inevitable and must be handled regularly.

As with many nonprofit organizations, funding is always a challenge. CMCH prides itself on offering free resources and services for the benefit of the general public, not just the privileged. As such, the content strategist is often asked to speak by community groups and professional organizations with limited or no financial resources available for the costs associated with the endeavor (e.g. staff time, travel expenses, and honoraria).

Additionally, because both the content strategist and the librarian work to craft each presentation to fit the needs of a particular audience and imbue it with the most accurate and up-to-date research, the amount of time needed from both can be difficult to obtain. Schedules at the Center are often intense, with many members of the team working on a number of projects simultaneously. Finding the time for both the librarian and the content strategist to dedicate to the creation of a presentation is often a challenge and must fit in with CMCH's ongoing work and existing project timelines.

Overall, the partnership was and is successful, based on the reception of the presentations. Given the range of audiences, it can be a challenge to adapt our content and style, compelling the content strategist and the librarian to evaluate each presentation individually.

Most importantly, this collaboration highlights the benefits of having an embedded librarian in the Center. The founder and team have created a supportive environment that prioritizes the need for an in-house librarian. Together, the librarian and the content strategist have developed an efficient method for researching and creating presentations on media health effects. As an integral part of upholding the Center's mission, the partnership will continue as long as society is interested in how media and technology affect the health and lives of children and adolescents.

Bibliography

Bickham, David S., Jill R. Kavanaugh, and Michael Rich. "Media Effects as Health Research: How Pediatricians Have Changed the Study of Media and Child Development." *Journal of Children and Media* 10, no. 2 (2016): 191-99.

Gunawardena, Sidath, Rosina Weber, and Denise E. Agosto. "Finding That Special Someone: Interdisciplinary Collaboration in an Academic

Context." *Journal of Education for Library and Information Science* (2010): 210-21.

Kabali, Hilda K., Matilde M. Irigoyen, Rosemary Nunez-Davis, Jennifer G. Budacki, Sweta H. Mohanty, Kristin P. Leister, and Robert L. Bonner. "Exposure and Use of Mobile Media Devices by Young Children." *Pediatrics* 136, no. 6 (2015): 1044-50.

Lavielle, Gail. "Lavielle & Commission on Children Host Forum Exploring Technology's Effects on Student Learning." http://www.cthousegop.com/lavielle/2015/11/24/lavielle-commission-on-children-host-forum-exploring-technologys-effects-on-student-learning/.

Lenhart, Amanda. "Teens, Social Media & Technology Overview 2015." Pew Research Center. http://www.pewinternet.org/files/2015/04/PI_TeensandTech_Update2015_0409151.pdf.

Patel, Bhavesh S., Lorne D. Booker, Hazel Melanie Ramos, and Chris Bart. "Mission Statements and Performance in Non-Profit Organisations." *Corporate Governance* 15, no. 5 (2015): 759-74.

Rich, Michael, and Brandy E. King. "Center on Media and Child Health: Scientific Evolution Responding to Technological Revolution." *Journal of Children and Media* 2, no. 2 (2008): 183-88.

Rideout, Vicky. "The Common Sense Census: Media Use by Tweens and Teens." Common Sense Media. https://www.commonsensemedia.org/sites/default/files/uploads/research/census_researchreport.pdf.

Case Study 2

PARTNERSHIPS FOR PHYSICAL ACTIVITY: LIBRARIES IN ACTIVE COMMUNITIES

Noah Lenstra

Abstract

This case study examines how, over a five-year period, a small-town public library partnered with nonprofits to increase public access to opportunities to engage in active lifestyles. Partnerships discussed include efforts that led to the creation of a community garden, a walking group, and free yoga and tai chi classes. After providing an analytical description of these partnerships, the chapter concludes with a reflection on how libraries, and public libraries in particular, can productively partner with nonprofits to contribute to fostering active lifestyles for all.

Introduction

Over the last fifteen years, public libraries have increasingly developed programs and services that increase access to opportunities to engage in active lifestyles. These programs and services include such things as exercise classes, StoryWalks®, play-based programs, and many others.[1] These programs frequently emerge through partnerships with local nonprofits, including community action agencies and healthy advocacy

---

1. As evidenced by the Let's Move in Libraries: Movement-Based Programs in Public Libraries project website, accessed May 22, 2017, http://www.letsmovelibraries.org/map/.

groups, among others.² This chapter discusses how, through community partnerships, one public library developed a series of programs focused on fostering active lifestyles. The lessons from this case study illustrate how, through partnerships, libraries can positively impact population health in new ways.

In 2011, Natalia Tuchina became the new library supervisor at the Walkertown Branch Library, which is part of the Forsyth County Library System in the Piedmont region of North Carolina. Walkertown is a small town of 4,675. Over time, the town has increasingly become an exurb of nearby Winston-Salem, which has a population of a quarter million people. Nonetheless, the town retains a small-town feel and community. Walkertown, like many small towns in America, lacks free spaces in which to learn about and to practice physically activities.³

In her new role at the Walkertown Library, Natalia sought to work closely with the small community. Reporting on her hire, a local newspaper reported that Natalia wanted "to make the Walkertown library a community center…a place for people to get together for educational and recreational programs."⁴ To achieve this goal, Natalia formed multiple partnerships with local and regional nonprofits. These partnerships have grown over time; as area agencies see one nonprofit partner with the library, they then think of forming a collaboration as well.

Partner Overview

The first partnership Natalia entered into after becoming library supervisor consisted of a collaborative effort to create a community garden next to the library (**Figure 1**). Natalia said the garden emerged at the

---

2. Noah Lenstra, "Let's Move! Fitness Programming in Public Libraries," *Public Library Quarterly* 36 (2017): 11-12, http://dx.doi.org/10.1080/01616846.2017.1316150.

3. Anush Yousefian, Erika Ziller, Jon Swartz, and David Hartley, "Active Living for Rural Youth: Addressing Physical Inactivity in Rural Communities," *Journal of Public Health Management and Practice* 15, no. 3 (2009): 223-231.

4. Ryan Gay, "From Russia to Walkertown," *Kernersville News*, April 19, 2011.

Figure 1. Community Members Farming at the Walkertown Library Community Garden. The Library is the Building Behind the Raised Beds. Photograph by Natalia Tuchina. Used with permission of the Walkertown Branch Library.

library because "the community wanted it."[5] Shortly after she started the position as library supervisor, community members wrote her a letter requesting a community garden. One of the community members who wrote the letter recalled that the genesis of the garden emerged from an informal group of people "who share an interest in community gardening" and "were looking for more affordable, local, and healthier options for feeding ourselves and our families….gardening is an excellent form of exercise and stress relief."[6] Natalia passed this letter along to the library administration, who subsequently approved the initiative. In early 2012, twelve raised bed gardens were installed on the library property. Individuals and families could "check out" one of the raised beds for the summer.

---

5. This and subsequent quotes from Natalia Tuchina come from interviews the author did with her in Winter 2017.

6. Don Dwiggins, "A Community Garden Grows in Walkertown," *Forsyth County News*, June 7, 2012, https://www.co.forsyth.nc.us/article.aspx?NewsID=17684.

The partnership worked well because it was driven by the interests of community members who had organized themselves around the idea of forming a community garden at the public library. One member of this group stated that "the library plays a vital role in community activities," a sentiment that led them to turn to the library with their idea. This fact illustrates one method for forming collaborations for the public good through libraries: by working to cultivate and sustain the sentiment that the library "plays a vital role in community activities," librarians create the conditions in which community groups come to them with ideas for impactful partnerships.

Case

The garden is administered by the local community. An informal group of local citizens provides all of the labor needed to keep the community garden going year after year. According to Natalia, there are two other gardens in public libraries in North Carolina, "but they are maintained by staff, not by the community." In addition to partnering with local gardeners for this initiative, the library has also partnered with a nonprofit medical center. Through this partnership, the library has hosted a series of classes on topics such as how to grow tomatoes, spring gardening, how to cook and eat fresh produce, and other more general programs about how to live a healthier lifestyle and maintain one's weight. The community group that led to the formation of this garden has also extended the partnership to local businesses, which have donated hardware and supplies for local gardeners to use at the library. Based on the success of the library's community garden, a nearby middle school started its own community garden.

The community partnerships involved in creating the community garden brought the library to the attention of others in the community interested in health and wellness. In the summer of 2012, a local man came to the library and said that he would "like to help the community" by offering free Tai Chi classes there. The man lived across the street from the library and was well known in the local community. As a result, when he offered classes at the library in 2012 and 2013 as many as forty individuals participated in a given week.

As a grassroots partnership between the library and a volunteer Tai Chi instructor, the classes emerged with minimal oversight from the county library system. This situation changed in early 2013 when lawyers from Forsyth County learned that Tai Chi classes were being offered at one of its facilities. The county government insisted that participants start signing hold harmless waivers, which was not a problem. More damaging to the partnership was the county's insistence that any individual leading physical activity classes in a county library have at least $1,000,000 in insurance coverage. The amount required was so high because the county government considered Tai Chi to be a form of martial arts.

The man offering Tai Chi at the library was doing so as a volunteer, and as a result he did not have the coverage required, nor could he afford to purchase it. Natalia remembered that the man said to her at the time "'You know I am giving my time to do these free classes that otherwise cost $65-$120, and you are asking me to pay for the insurance? That is not fair.' And I said 'I understand completely,'" but Natalia was constrained by the new requirement. As a result of this constraint, the partnership, and the free Tai Chi classes, ended. This incident illustrates how grassroots partnerships can be blocked by larger institutional regulations, which may limit the types and forms of partnerships that libraries can undertake with individuals and institutions working on a nonprofit basis.

A more sustainable partnership formed around offering exercise classes at the library emerged around the same time that the Tai Chi classes were ending. A local woman seeking certification as a yoga instructor approached Natalia with the idea of offering free yoga classes at the library. Through her affiliation with the national nonprofit Yoga Alliance, this woman had—and has—the insurance coverage required by the county government. She initially offered monthly classes, but since the classes proved to be so popular, she now offers approximately four classes a month, with some in the late afternoon and others in the early evening. The different time slots appeal to different audiences.

To sustain the partnership, Natalia has worked with the local government to find ways to fund the classes on an ongoing basis. As a library administrator, Natalia has learned that it is "hard to keep volunteers" because "they run out of gas or energy." To make the yoga classes a sustainable part of the library, Natalia approached the municipal government in the town of Walkertown to see if they would pay the volunteer a small amount as compensation for her time. Natalia said she did this work not because the yoga instructor insisted on it—she was happy to continue to volunteer her time even after she achieved certification—but because she thought it was the right thing to do.

Based on the success of the yoga and Tai Chi partnerships, Natalia started thinking about how to build this type of programming at her library. Like many small and rural communities throughout the United States, the town of Walkertown does not have a recreation center.[7] Recognizing this gap in public community services, Natalia decided to have the library start filling this role. Natalia went to the municipal government and said "You don't have a recreation center. We have the space. Can we work together?" The town government initially only wanted to provide the library with funding for arts-related programming, but after Natalia explained how successful and impactful health-related programming had been, the town government decided to also fund these types of services at the library.

Through this inter-governmental partnership,[8] the library is able to provide the volunteer yoga instructor with a small amount of

---

7. Active Living Research, "Promoting Active Living in Rural Communities," *Active Living Research Briefs* September 2015, https://activelivingresearch.org/sites/default/files/ALR_Brief_RuralCommunities_Sept2015.pdf; Anush Yousefian, Erika Ziller, Jon Swartz, and David Hartley, "Active Living for Rural Youth: Addressing Physical Inactivity in Rural Communities," *Journal of Public Health Management and Practice* 15, no. 3 (2009): 223-231.

8. In North Carolina, public libraries are generally funded at the county level. So, the Walkertown Public Library, although based in Walkertown, is in fact funded entirely at the county level. As such, this initiative constituted an inter-governmental partnership between Forsyth County and the Town of Walkertown.

compensation. This payment is less than what she earns elsewhere when she teaches yoga, but is enough to maintain the partnership and to prevent burn-out or fatigue. Through this arrangement with the municipal government, Natalia said that "we kind of assumed the role [of town recreation center], and we are happy about that. Because as people come to programs [like yoga] they check out books, and vice versa. When people come to look at the book or the magazine or a DVD they see this [monthly calendar and flyers] and then they see" all the recreational programs that the library has (**Figure 2**).

Figure 2: Flyer Used to Advertise Yoga Programs at Walkertown Branch Library in January 2017. The Library Actually has Mats Available if Participants Forget to Bring One, or Do Not Own One. Flyer used with permission of the Walkertown Branch Library.

Based in part on the success of the yoga and garden programs, in August 2014 a local woman approached Natalia with the idea of starting a walking club at the library. Natalia enthusiastically supported the idea. A library walking group was something that Natalia had been thinking about after she learned from her mother (who lives in St. Petersburg, Russia) about the increasing popularity of Nordic trekking pole walking groups there, especially among older adults. A walking group that calls itself WOW: Walkers of Walkertown started meeting at the library. The group gathers at the library twice a week at 9 a.m. to go on walks together. Up to a dozen people go walking on a given day. Even on hot or rainy days three to five people will usually go out walking. Regulars in the group have formed a Facebook group to coordinate on days of inclement weather. After the walk, the group will talk about healthy lifestyles and cooking at the library. Two of the regulars have also started participating in the community garden.

Over time the walking group has been supported and sustained through a partnership with a regional YMCA. An instructor from the YMCA will occasionally join the group to show participants how to step properly, and how to hold the trekking poles, if one chooses to use them. Some walkers use trekking poles, some use more conventional walking sticks, and some just go out walking (**Figure 3**). The group is open to all. This partnership with the regional YMCA works well because the instructor lives in Walkertown. Since Walkertown does not have a YMCA facility, he cannot work in Walkertown, but he identified a need for the services one would expect of a YMCA in the community where he lived. Thus, he worked with the library to develop the walking group to extend the YMCA's services into Walkertown.

Around the same time that the walking group began, the library was approached by a local nonprofit senior center, the Shepherd's Center of Greensboro, with the idea of hosting a series of Matter of Balance® classes at the library. For three weeks in 2014, and again in 2015, staff from the Shepherd's Center came to the library and led eight to ten participants through a series of chair-based exercises focused on how to maintain one's balance, and how to move around while staying grounded. Shepherd's Center approached the Walkertown Library with this idea because there was no other natural site for such a movement-based class in Walkertown. Unlike the partnership with the YMCA, the Shepherd's Center partnership did not endure over time. One reason for this difference may relate to the fact that none of the partners lived in Walkertown; they all drove thirty minutes from Greensboro to lead the programs and then returned to Greensboro after the programs ended.

Figure 3: WOW: The Walkers of Walkertown, a Community Group Formed at the Library That has been Sustained and Supported in Part through a Partnership with a Regional YMCA. Photograph by Natalia Tuchina. Used with permission of the Walkertown Branch Library.

Lacking a local person to sustain the partnership over time, the collaboration led to a finite series of classes on balance for older adults at the library. On the other hand, the success of these series of classes led the Forsyth County Library system as a whole to partner with Shepherd's Center on a broader programming series focused on better meeting the needs of older adults throughout the county.

Assessment

The principal way Natalia assesses the success of these partnerships is through tracking the number of individuals who participate in programs. Since the community garden program started in 2012, all twelve raised beds have been checked out and used productively every summer. Related gardening programs co-sponsored with a nonprofit medical center have also been well attended. The Matter of Balance® classes were also at capacity each time they were offered. **Figure 4** illustrates recent participation patterns in yoga and walking programs at the library. Natalia says that participation sometimes ebbs and flows, especially during holiday seasons and during periods of inclement weather, but in general all of these programs have been popular.

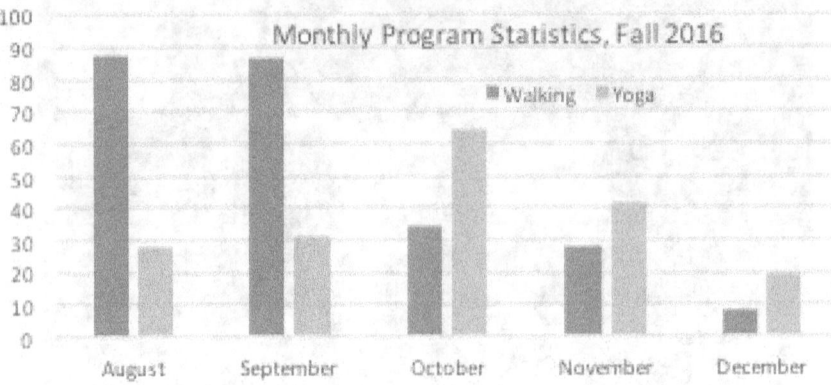

Figure 4: Participation Patterns in WOW: Walkers of Walkertown and Yoga Programs Offered at the Walkertown Branch Library in Fall 2016.

In addition to quantitative evidence on the impact of programming, Natalia also more informally collects stories of participants. She is an astute observer of what goes on in the library, as well as in the broader community of Walkertown, and adjusts her policies and practices based on what she sees. Demonstrating the popularity of these programs fulfills multiple needs. It communicates to stakeholders in the county government that these types of active programs are valued in the local community. It also communicates to the community, as well as to potential partners, that the library can and does play an important role in terms of population health and wellness.

Reflection

The examples discussed in this chapter illustrate how, through partnerships with nonprofit individuals and institutions, public libraries can branch into new territory such as providing opportunities for community members to engage in active lifestyles. This chapter also shows how such partnerships build on each other. After the initial partnership began—the community garden—other individuals and institutions increasingly perceived the library as a natural partner in efforts focused on encouraging physical activity among the residents of Walkertown. A yoga instructor, a Tai Chi instructor, a regional senior center, a medical center, and a YMCA all came to Walkertown Public Library with ideas about partnerships that could positively impact the health of the local community. The success of these partnerships in part can be attributed to Natalia's enthusiasm for these types of programs. She sees these types of recreational programs as important for her community and for her library. For instance, Natalia personally vacuums the carpeting of the library's community room prior to every yoga class because it is important to her that everyone enjoys their experience in the class.

Nevertheless, not all of these partnerships have been sustained over time. The grassroots momentum that led to the start of Tai Chi classes at the library had to confront the bureaucratic structures created by a county government wary of lawsuits. The nonprofit instructor could not afford to pay for the mandated insurance coverage, and as a result the partnership ended. This cautionary tale should remind librarians thinking about embarking on partnerships focused on improving population health that there exist valid concerns about liabilities that may emerge from injuries sustained in those activities, either by participants or instructors.

Nonetheless, being open to ideas for new partnerships has been crucial to the emergence of these programs. At a broader level, these partnerships emerged because Natalia maintains an open mind about what public libraries are for. As she said when she became the branch supervisor in 2011, she sees public libraries as community centers. Community centers fulfill multiple community needs: informational, recreational, artistic, and many more. Being open to taking the library in new directions has been an important element in the emergence of these programs. Not all public libraries, especially in communities the size of Walkertown, have such a robust array of opportunities for patrons to engage in physical activities. These programs emerged because Natalia saw supporting healthy, active lifestyles as an important role of the library in its community, and because she was excited about forming and sustaining partnerships with nonprofit individuals and institutions to achieve that goal.

Although not all public libraries have as many programs as Walkertown Branch Library, this library is by no means an isolated case. Directly contributing to physical activity by providing opportunities for people to engage in healthy movement at the library is an emergent role for many public libraries. Stepping into this role can be supported by partnerships with nonprofit institutions and individuals that have experience in this domain. In my research, I have identified other small-town public libraries in the region around Walkertown which have also developed similar programs. In Jefferson, North Carolina (population 1,611) the library partners with a local yoga group seeking a place to meet. This partnership led to the creation of weekly yoga classes at the library that are open to all, and that are advertised as library programs. In Mount Airy, North Carolina (population 10,388) the library partners with a local senior center to provide ongoing Tai Chi classes for individuals with arthritis. There is evidence that these types of partnerships are also emerging in diverse communities throughout North America.[9]

Bibliography

Active Living Research. "Promoting Active Living in Rural Communities." *Active Living Research Briefs* September 2015. https://activelivingresearch.org/sites/default/files/ALR_Brief_RuralCommunities_Sept2015.pdf.

Dwiggins, Don. "A Community Garden Grows in Walkertown." *Forsyth County News*, June 7, 2012. https://www.co.forsyth.nc.us/article.aspx?NewsID=17684.

Gay, Ryan. "From Russia to Walkertown." *Kernersville News*, April 19, 2011.

Lenstra, Noah. "Let's Move! Fitness Programming in Public Libraries." *Public Library Quarterly* 36 (2017). http://dx.doi.org/10.1080/01616846.2017.1316150.

---

9. Lenstra, 2017.

Lenstra, Noah. "Let's Move in Libraries: Movement-Based Programs in Public Libraries." http://www.letsmovelibraries.org/.

Yousefian, Anush, Erika Ziller, Jon Swartz, and David Hartley. "Active Living for Rural Youth: Addressing Physical Inactivity in Rural Communities." *Journal of Public Health Management and Practice* 15, no. 3 (2009): 223-231.

Case Study 3

Unlocking Community Advocacy: Information as a University's Key to a Community Partnership

Alejandra Nann

Abstract

In February of 2016, a librarian at the University of San Diego's Copley Library began the library's relationship with Bayside Community Center as their dedicated liaison. She met with the Bayside Community Advocates to discuss the information needs of the different leadership academies. The library liaison then worked with a small committee of other Copley librarians to brainstorm relevant activities to fulfill these needs with any interested members of the leadership academies. This case study will illustrate Copley Library's role in cultivating a productive relationship with Bayside Community Center. It will discuss the library's initiatives in educating and supporting community members of the leadership academies through workshops, library tours, and other informational meetings to help them formulate and accomplish advocacy goals aligned with Bayside Community Center's mission and vision.

Background

Partnerships between institutions and their local community are nothing new. Many institutions, including academic libraries, are continually working toward partnerships with their local communities. Research indicates why academic institutions, including libraries, should collaborate with their community, detailing benefits and challenges that go hand in hand with these external partnerships. It is critical for institutions to have a role within their communities other than to provide financial assistance.[1] Hosting relevant workshops and meeting with community members to discuss projects are examples of beneficial sessions for community members. Challenges include finding a time that is amenable to community members' work and family schedules and creating a workshop to assist various learning styles.

Crafting a partnership with the surrounding community is often influenced by the library's mission, vision, and strategic plan. Plenty of academic libraries include outreach as a broad theme so that librarians can use their level of expertise to help their community partner, whether it is by teaching information literacy instruction sessions, creating subject guides, or providing access to various library resources.[2] Academic librarians extend their resourceful disposition outside of the university by working with neighboring libraries and producing various forms of outreach.[3] Further, institutions use their strategic plan as a starting point to encourage faculty and librarians to participate in these initiatives to improve the way the university and community interact and collaborate on several levels.[4] Often, academic librarians desire to help others beyond their immediate patrons. Although there are plenty of assumptions as to who should dedicate time to community partnerships, it is important to note that academic librarians, regardless of whether they work in private or public institutions, work toward a positive relationship with the external community.[5]

---

1. Meagan M. Ehlenz, "Neighborhood Revitalization and the Anchor Institution," *Urban Affairs Review* 52, no. 5 (September 2016): 715.

2. Tina Schneider, "Outreach: Why, How and Who? Academic Libraries and Their Involvement in the Community," *Reference Librarian* 39, no. 82 (September 2003): 203.

3. Ibid., 204.

4. Iona R. Malanchuk and Marilyn N. Ochoa, "Academic Librarians and Outreach Beyond the College Campus," *Southeastern Librarian* 53, no. 3 (Fall 2005): 26.

5. Nancy Courtney, "Unaffiliated Users' Access to Academic Libraries: A Survey," *Journal of Academic Librarianship* 29, no. 1 (January 2003): 3.

Challenges can come in many forms when developing partnerships. There are arguments that point out obvious reasons that institutions may forego long-term or large-scale partnerships. Academic librarians' first priority is their students, faculty, and staff, so it can be challenging to find time, resources, and a case for building and maintaining community partnerships. One key challenge to take into consideration is time commitment. As with any new project, creating a partnership with a community takes a lot of planning. Getting to know the community and coming up with an appropriate plan to see even small transformations or long-term results takes time.[6] Another challenge is limited resources such as space allocation, resource-sharing, and the use of computer terminals; this can be discouraging to many academic libraries, and the question about how to create space for the community remains unanswered.[7] Turnover at an institution can cause setbacks with partnerships, while many members remain in their community long-term.[8] Although community partnerships require a considerable time commitment, the benefits outweigh the challenges, which gives academic libraries and institutions as a whole momentum to continue their work.

Academic libraries' resources can be considered more vast and thus more helpful than what one would find at a public or school library.[9] In order to make these types of partnerships work between an academic library and a community, it is important to solidify plans based on the needs and wants of the community and what the library and its resources can offer them.[10] Creating goals, pathways, and support helps stabilize

---

6. Howell S. Baum, "Fantasies and Realities in University-Community Partnerships." *Journal of Planning Education and Research* 20, no. 2 (June 2016): 243.

7. Jack Hang Tat Leong, "Community Engagement—Building Bridges between University and Community by Academic Libraries in the 21st Century." *Libri: International Journal of Libraries & Information Services* 63, no. 3 (September 2013): 223.

8. Thomas G. Basler, "Community Outreach Partnerships," *Reference Services Review* 33, no. 1 (February, 2005): 34.

9. Nancy Courtney, "Unaffiliated Users' Access to Academic Libraries: A Survey." *Journal of Academic Librarianship* 29, no. 1 (January, 2003): 7.

10. John-Bauer Graham, "Outreach Programs Beyond the Immediate University Community," *Library Management* 26, no. 3 (May, 2005): 114.

and reassure both partners that it is possible to maintain a solid foundation.[11] It is evident that it is part of the process to struggle and face challenges while maintaining the flexibility to create new plans in order to manage a successful and dynamic partnership.[12]

Project Overview

The University of San Diego (USD) is located in Linda Vista, California, a small and incredibly diverse community in San Diego County. In 2016, USD established itself as an anchor institution in Linda Vista, with a desire to partner and collaborate with local organizations, schools, and groups to better serve the community. More specifically, USD began collaborating with Bayside Community Center—a catalyst for advocacy within the Linda Vista community. Bayside's mission seeks to "improve quality of life through services, education, and advocacy."[13] The Center created two leadership academies to engage the community and guide members into positions of advocacy for the Linda Vista community. Librarians at Copley Library, USD's university library, identified and offered ways to support the educational programs developed by Bayside Community Center.

Copley Library's Dean invited Bayside Community Center's Executive Director as well as an active community member to a December 2015 library department meeting to discuss the various ways USD and Bayside could be collaborating. After the meeting, the Dean appointed Nann (Electronic Resources and Serials Librarian) to be their liaison and created a small committee of librarians to assist in developing the purpose and goals for this partnership. The committee included the Head of Technical Services and the Head of Reference.

---

11. Howell S. Baum, "Fantasies and Realities in University-Community Partnerships," *Journal of Planning Education and Research* 20, no. 2 (June, 2016): 234.

12. Ibid., 242.

13. Bayside Community Center, "About Bayside," http://www.baysidecc.org/about-bayside/.

Overview of Copley Library

The University of San Diego (USD) is a Roman Catholic Private Liberal Arts Institution. Copley Library is the University's main library. It serves the undergraduates, graduates, faculty, and staff of USD. The library includes the Dean of the University Library, fifteen library faculty, two part-time librarians, two administrators, and fourteen library assistants. The collection contains 500,000 volumes, 187 databases, about 67,000 e-journals, and over 140,000 ebooks. Copley Library's five-year strategic plan includes five key themes that are imperative to the library's success: research and scholarship, collections, community, environment, and technology. Community, in particular, is a key theme that truly resonates with the way the library has collaborated and worked with the community members of Bayside Community Center.

Overview of Bayside Community Center

Bayside Community Center is located one mile from USD and serves the Linda Vista community. Since its establishment in 1932, the purpose of the community center has been to help community members revitalize their family life as well as the community. Currently, the community center focuses on specific areas that affect Linda Vista: food security, educational empowerment, and health and wellness.[14] The center created leadership academies, including the Resident Leadership Academy (RLA) and the Cooperative Leadership Academy (CLA), and there are a number of branches for each of these academies, including the Youth RLA and the Vietnamese RLA. These academies help their members become advocates for the Linda Vista community.

Purpose of the Partnership

The main purpose of the partnership between Copley Library and Bayside Community Center was to assist the center in their advocacy work to improve the Linda Vista Community. As the librarians learned

---

14. Ibid.

more about Bayside and the current collaborations between different departments on campus and the community center, they realized that there were certain components that were missing. Active partnerships included faculty members who created assignments that embedded their students into the community. The librarians believed it was important to use this opportunity to think creatively about how they could support the CLA. Members of the CLA were auditing courses at USD that correlated to the kinds of activism they were doing within Linda Vista, which included leadership and nutrition courses. The library committee decided to create short-term goals for the first year by identifying the kinds of services and resources the library could offer. The librarians decided it was best to offer several introductory workshops on issues that were complementary to their community and advocacy work and also to provide evidence to show why using libraries, both public and academic, were critical to their community work.

Stakeholders

As an anchor institution, the President and Provost fully supported Copley Library's commitment to supporting and assisting the Bayside Community Center. Both individual faculty and a number of departments across campus have created partnerships within Bayside Community Center programs and Linda Vista to strengthen the connection between the community and the university. The Dean of the University Library played an active role in the growth of the partnership with Bayside Community Center by providing library access and financial support. CLA members were allowed to create library accounts and the liaison received funding for events.

The first year of this partnership focused on RLA and CLA. The Resident Leadership Academy was developed into a ten-session course that would help enrolled members learn skill sets to successfully advocate for health and wellness across Linda Vista. In 2016, Bayside established a Youth RLA that included ten students from two Linda Vista high schools in order to educate them about the successes and challenges of their community. In 2014, the graduates of the RLA, also known as Linda

Vista Leaders in Action, pushed for more education, knowledge, and training in order to continue their advocacy. Through the collaboration between Linda Vista and USD, they established the CLA, which would continue the momentum. USD also began offering tuition-free USD courses, that were relevant to their community work, to CLA members.

Outreach and Collaboration

In the spring of 2016, the Dean and committee members met to brainstorm and develop a plan to contribute to the CLA. The liaison and a member of the committee set up a meeting during CLA's regular hours to discuss their role in Linda Vista and what they wanted to accomplish, both short-term and long-term. The members expressed an interest in learning about different tools that would help them build on their knowledge of the community and how they could continue their advocacy work. They also wanted to learn about how the library could help them succeed while they audited USD courses. The CLA members' community work and USD course work required them to have the appropriate skill set and confidence to present on their work during their class or have the capability to speak with stakeholders and grassroots leaders about their efforts that affect the community.

The first step was to introduce the CLA members to Copley Library and provide them with information about how librarians can assist them in their efforts. The Dean offered the members visitor library cards so they could check out books from Copley Library. Copley also allows access to library materials, computer terminals, and study spaces to visitors and other community members. The liaison invited CLA members to the library during one of their weekly meetings for a tour of the library and an instruction session on using the library catalog and navigating some of the relevant online resources available to them while working in the library. Further, the liaison developed several workshops for the CLA based on the feedback they gave her during the introductory meeting. Some of these instruction sessions included internet privacy and security, using Google Scholar, social media for professionals, using the San Diego Circuit, and developing research skills. These workshops were taught by several librarians who had expertise in these different areas. In addition, the liaison scheduled a tour at the newest public library in San Diego to give the CLA members an idea of how public library resources, services, and features could also assist them in their community and advocacy work.

The liaison also worked with Bayside to embed two library workshops into the Youth RLA summer program. For their community involvement project, the leadership academy asked the library to focus on land use that pertains to Linda Vista, including successes, challenges, and possible future plans to improve the way land is utilized in Linda Vista. The first workshop included a tour of Copley Library along with an instruction session on how to develop research strategies, use search engines, and find credible and reliable sources. The second workshop was held at Bayside, in which a librarian from the Bayside committee focused on their community involvement project related to land use. He discussed several resources that would help the students complete their plan using trustworthy resources to back up their project. In an effort to begin working with more RLA groups, the liaison met with the Vietnamese RLA to discuss their goals as members of the Vietnamese community within Linda Vista. This group asked to attend an instruction session on finding informational resources relevant to food security and safety.

Many former RLA graduates have joined CLA to demonstrate their commitment to Linda Vista. Several generations of RLA members, including the inaugural RLA and Vietnamese RLA have continued to audit courses at USD to learn about leadership, food security, and safety. In Spring 2017, several CLA members took a five-week course on nutrition. Their final project included researching and presenting information on a specific topic related to nutrition that would be beneficial to their families and Linda Vista. Keeping in mind the various learning styles and levels of education in this diverse CLA group, the liaison created a subject guide. The guide included basic research tips as well as websites to find helpful information for their presentation at the end of the program. The liaison met with them to show them how they could use search engines to find reputable sources, including government websites that provide policies and outlines on how to access healthy food, create a food budget, and the importance of food safety, among other important nutrition and wellness topics.

Outcomes

The efforts of the Copley Library and Bayside Community Center partnership have been successful as evidenced by the continued interest of the community and requests for more training and education to improve their community work. For example, the liaison has participated in other aspects of Bayside Community Center such as joining the steering committee for the One Linda Vista two-day forum that occurred on May 3-4, 2017. Additionally, the members of the community always invite and welcome Copley Librarians to attend RLA graduation ceremonies, CLA presentations, annual festivals, and events organized by Bayside Community Center. The enthusiasm shared by Copley Library and the community members encouraged a more effective partnership. During the first year, the liaison worked closely with the Community Advocate Coordinator, the Community Advocate, and the Executive Director of Bayside to extend collaborations beyond the different leadership academies.

Reflection

When the Dean discussed the partnership with the potential members of the Bayside Committee, she offered the Electronic Resources and Serials Librarian the liaison position, it was for a couple of reasons. At USD, librarians are tenure-track faculty and must meet the four criteria of Copley Library's Appointment, Reappointment, Rank, and Tenure (ARRT) Criteria to earn tenure. The work with Bayside fell within the third and fourth criteria. The third criterion is dedicated to university and public service, while the fourth criterion is based on the support of the mission and vision of the university.

In USD's Envisioning 2024 Strategic Plan, six pathways were created in order to provide a more cohesive plan to develop a better university community by 2024. One particular pathway, serving as an anchor institution, encourages the continued efforts made by USD faculty, staff, and students to reach out to the community. Most recently, the USD community became more engaged with Linda Vista by way of the Bayside Community Center, the K-12 schools in the area, and various Linda Vista organizations.[15] The Mulvaney Center for Community Awareness and Social Action, as well as the Changemaker Hub, are two centers where community engagement frequently occurs between the Linda Vista community and USD faculty, staff, and students/

Another of the themes in the Copley Library 2016-2020 Strategic Plan is community. One particular action item listed under the community goal is the development of an outreach plan that integrates Copley Library into both the university and the local community.[16] Given the lack of partnerships in the past with Bayside Community Center, it was important to bridge the gap and discover ways to collaborate to better support community engagement and activism.

Some of the biggest challenges the library committee faced while working with the Bayside Community Center was trying to figure out where this assistance would fit in. Although Bayside has managed to work with several constituencies on campus, their small staff were most likely overwhelmed by the various efforts created. After speaking to the members of CLA, it was evident that assistance in research skills was crucial in order for them to do well in USD classes and community involvement. In addition, because most of Copley's licenses to online databases only allow USD faculty, staff, and students to access content remotely, it was critical to point out other credible sources such as government websites, open access content, and public library resources that would be beneficial to their advocacy. Furthermore, working with community members and gauging their learning styles was challenging.

---

15. University of San Diego, "Pathways to 2024: Anchor Institutions," http://www.sandiego.edu/envisioning-2024/pathways/anchor-institution.php.

16. University of San Diego, Copley Library, "Copley Library Strategic Plan, 2016-2020," http://www.sandiego.edu/library/documents/strategic-plan-complete.pdf.

The members' educational backgrounds ranged significantly. There were members of the community who were very savvy on their tablets but unfamiliar with basic computer programs such as Microsoft Word, while there were others who had little to no experience using the internet or computers.

Future Plans

Fortunately, there is continued interest in the partnership between Copley Library and Bayside Community Center from both groups. The liaison continues to collaborate with Bayside Community Center to generate ideas for future success and the sustainability and growth of the current partnership. Some ideas include:

1. Working with the Linda Vista Public Library to develop programs to better assist current projects.
2. Creating an online repository using Google Docs or a wiki to house notes taken from various meetings with stakeholders and grassroots leaders in order to foster a more cohesive and transparent partnership with USD.
3. Working with faculty members who allow CLA students to take their course.
4. Building on the current subject guide to include Bayside's main areas of concern: food security, educational empowerment, and health and wellness.

Feedback from community members remains positive. However, it is imperative for the library committee to discuss ways to review and evaluate the effectiveness of the partnership. One idea is to survey community members who have collaborated with Copley Library and ask them how the library has improved their advocacy work. Finally, the most important question to include in the survey is to ask them what the library can do to expand the partnership and what additional programs they need in order to continue their work to improve the Linda Vista community.

Bibliography

Bayside Community Center. "About Bayside," n.d. http://www.baysidecc.org/about-bayside/.

"Anchor Institution - Envisioning 2024 - University of San Diego." https://www.sandiego.edu/envisioning-2024/pathways/anchor-institution.php.

Basler, Thomas G. "Community Outreach Partnerships." *Reference Services Review* 33, no. 1 (2005): 31–37.

Baum, Howell S. "Fantasies and Realities in University-Community Partnerships." *Journal of Planning Education and Research* 20, no. 2 (2000): 234–246.

———. "Fantasies and Realities in University-Community Partnerships." *Journal of Planning Education and Research* 20, no. 2 (December 1, 2000): 234–46. https://doi.org/10.1177/0739456X0002000208.

Courtney, Nancy. "Unaffiliated Users' Access to Academic Libraries: A Survey." *Journal of Academic Librarianship* 29, no. 1 (January 1, 2003): 3–7. https://doi.org/10.1016/S0099-1333(02)00387-7.

———. "Unaffiliated Users' Access to Academic Libraries: A Survey." *Journal of Academic Librarianship* 29, no. 1 (January 1, 2003): 3–7. https://doi.org/10.1016/S0099-1333(02)00387-7.

Ehlenz, Meagan M. "Neighborhood Revitalization and the Anchor Institution: Assessing the Impact of the University of Pennsylvania's West Philadelphia Initiatives on University City." *Urban Affairs Review* 52, no. 5 (September 1, 2016): 714–50. https://doi.org/10.1177/1078087415601220.

Graham, John-Bauer. "Outreach Programs beyond the Immediate University Community." *Library Management* 26, no. 3 (April 2005):113-122.

Leong, Jack Hang Tat. "Community Engagement–Building Bridges between University and Community by Academic Libraries in the 21st Century." *Libri* 63, no. 3 (2013): 220–231.

Malanchuk, Iona R., and Marilyn N. Ocha. "Academic Librarians and Outreach Beyond the College Campus." *Southeastern Librarian* 53, no. 3 (2005): 11.

Schneider, Tina. "Outreach: Why, How and Who? Academic Libraries and Their Involvement in the Community." *The Reference Librarian* 39, no. 82 (2004): 199–213.

University of San Diego, Copley Library. "Copley Library Strategic Plan, 2016-2020." 2015. https://www.sandiego.edu/library/documents/strategic-plan-complete.pdf.

Case Study 4

CREATING AN AFRICAN AMERICAN ARTS SPACE WITH COLLABORATIVE SUPPORT FROM THE FRIENDS OF THE MISSOURI GOVERNOR'S MANSION

kYmberly Keeton

Introduction

How should we create a partnership with community constituents for a university library arts program and space? A recent trend in academic libraries involves reimagining library spaces as creative incubator spaces for their university communities. Many academic libraries that are venturing into "libraries as creative spaces" lack the necessary funding to recreate themselves in this way. Inman E. Page Library, a Historically Black Colleges and Universities (HBCU) academic library at the Lincoln University of Missouri, also lacked funding support for such initiatives. In order to design creative spaces for research and scholarship, a plan was formed to establish an arts program that was innovative and accessible, but did not require university funding. In order to gain buy-in for this project within the university and community, I determined the time had come to reach out to nonprofits within the city to help move it forward.

Within a few short months an arts program was created for the university library entitled "The Arts At Page Library." First, in order to gain buy-in from the university, an art-library advisory committee was formed which included faculty members, students, and professionals to help make administrative decisions regarding the program and future space within the library. Approaching the community was the next important step. Rebecca Gordon, Executive Director of the Friends of the Governor's Mansion, in Jefferson City, Missouri, was asked to become a committee member and she accepted with enthusiasm. With her expertise in leadership, preservation, history, fundraising, and museums, it was critical to have her help with this initiative. Furthermore, it set a precedent that an African American academic library art advisory committee and a non-profit institution in the state of Missouri could collaborate to achieve something for the benefit of their community.

Library Overview

Founded in August 2016, The Arts At Page Library is a library arts program and space located at Inman E. Page Library, Lincoln University of Missouri. The art program was designed to expose students, faculty, and the community to culture and arts at an HBCU academic library. Through the leadership of the Arts Library Coordinator, the Advisory Arts Committee, and Student Docents, The Arts At Page Library is a premier space that provides creative educational programming, physical and online exhibitions, access to an African American art book collection, library art tours, and an academic library for research and lecture series.

In January 1997, Lincoln University of Missouri opened a new library. The Jefferson City community joined with Lincoln University alumni, faculty, and staff to raise $443,000 in cash and pledges toward the completion of the approximately $11 million dollar structure. The 80,000 square foot, state-of-the-art library is four times larger than the old facility. Inman E. Page Library serves as the primary educational resource center of Lincoln University of Missouri, supporting the curricula and research needs of the institution through the development of pertinent library collections and the provision of services designed to facilitate access to information. The facility has a seating capacity of approximately 450 and contains over 200,000 volumes.[1]

---

1. Lincoln University of Missouri, "Inman E. Page Library History," https://www.lincolnu.edu/web/inman-e.-page-library/about-us/history.

Partner Overview

Friends of the Missouri Governor's Mansion (FMGM), formerly Missouri Mansion Preservation (MMP) is the "official non-profit supporting organization of the Missouri Governor's mansion." Their mission is the "preservation of the Missouri Governor's Mansion, its history, and its historical treasures..."[2]

Case

Our objective was to build an art docent program and a professional mentorship program with FMGM in Jefferson City. The goals of the collaboration were to design a network of community constituents who would help create a university arts library program and back its mission in the community. Our stakeholders included the University Library Administration and Community Constituents, and we gained significant buy-in from the Missouri Governor's Mansion. Meeting with Rebecca Gordon, Executive Director of the Friends of the Governor's Mansion, helped jumpstart this project. Gordon's influence as a committee member and her mentorship led to the Mayor of Jefferson City accepting an invitation to join as the Honorary Board Chair for the arts library advisory committee. This then led to my appointment to the Jefferson City Cultural Arts Committee.

The major issue in this process was gaining buy-in from the university administration. Gordon was familiar with city and university politics and she helped strategize with me on how to approach stakeholders to obtain approval for the project. In addition, at stakeholder meetings we articulated our vision of what docent work would mean for students and how their work as interns would benefit the Governor's Mansion, the arts program, and our ongoing partnership. Staying open to new strategies and ideas generated from the university and the community's needs and developing sound partnerships helped propel this project to the next level. The Advisory Arts Committee and the docent internship

---

2. Friends of the Missouri Governor's Mansion, "Missouri Governor's Mansion Preservation Projects Wishlist," https://www.missourimansion.com/images/870/document/fmgm2018_370.pdf.

are now implemented and the first two students have been approved to work for the next two semesters. Each partner brought their own unique experiences, professional connections, ideas, and suggestions to make this work.

Reflection

I met Rebecca Gordon, Executive Director of Friends of the Governor's Mansion—Missouri on a flight returning home from a conference. We immediately clicked while talking about the cultural makeup and need for diversity and the arts in the state capital. From that point on, I knew that I needed her in my professional network. After several meetings it became clear to me that forming a partnership was the way to make this project work and have a major impact at the university and in the community. Gordon assured me that she would help me navigate meeting new people and building buy-in from city constituents. However, there were challenges getting this project off the ground and everything did not work out as planned. Many issues derived from the university administration. Trying to gain buy-in for an advisory board and a gallery space was challenging due to lack of funding and the support from the administration in academic affairs, who had their own vision and goals for the library. I was able to counter this challenge by showing how the project would benefit the university and introduce the administration to the nonprofit partners. I believe starting a partnership with the Friends of the Governor's Mansion was critical to gaining buy-in and aligning all of the stakeholders.

Though the art gallery did not come to fruition, we were able to design an Arts Library Advisory Board and have the Mayor of Jefferson City, Missouri serve as the Honorary Board Chair. In addition, we formed and initiated a successful Docent Internship Program for students interested in the arts and public service through this partnership between the Inman E. Page Library and The Friends of the Governor's Mansion—Missouri.

Bibliography

Friends of the Missouri Governor's Mansion. "Missouri Governor's Mansion Preservation Projects Wishlist," n.d. https://www.missourimansion.com/images/870/document/fmgm2018_370.pdf.

Lincoln University of Missouri. "History—Library—Lincoln University." Accessed June 28, 2020. https://www.lincolnu.edu/web/library/about/history.

Case Study 5

RESURFACING AT-RISK WORKS OF THE FEMINIST SMALL PRESS

Jane Nichols and Korey Jackson

Abstract

Independent, feminist publishing saw a renaissance from the 1970s through the 1990s. Small presses arose out of the women's movements in response to the persistent, long-standing under-representation of published works by women authors. Self-funded and incorporated as non-profits, most relied on volunteers and grew as their title lists grew. The rise of corporate publishing and chain bookstores partially supported the goals and success of the feminist press by making dominant voices of the feminist press more readily available, but leaving other voices behind. Many feminist publishers either closed their doors or became an imprint of a larger publisher. Fast forward to the early twenty-first century and we see that the presses that survived, such as Calyx Press, Inc., are undergoing a transformation to attract a new generation of readers and writers and to publish content in both print and electronic formats. The authors of this case study describe our partnering on a project as one piece of Calyx's transformation. The partnership and project are designed to buttress Calyx as it strengthens its place in the contemporary landscape of feminist publishing.

Introduction

Independent, feminist publishing saw a renaissance from the 1970s through the 1990s, in part due to the rise of feminist small presses which gave voice to under-represented women authors. As self-funded non-profits, many relied on grants and volunteer labor to grow their capacity and their title lists. Over time, many either closed their doors or were bought out by larger publishing companies. Fast forward to today and we see that surviving feminist presses are experimenting with new ways to ensure their continued work, to attract new audiences, and to publish content in both print and electronic formats. In this case study, we share an approach undertaken by Calyx Press in partnership with Oregon State University Libraries and Press (OSULP) to reinvigorate Calyx.

Project Overview

OSULP and Calyx Press partnered to implement our National Endowment for the Humanities/Carnegie Mellon grant-funded project to resurface out-of-print titles by digitizing and making them available as ebooks under a Creative Commons license. Twenty-six titles from Calyx's backlist were selected for their representation of the breadth of feminist concern.

Digitization of feminist publications like this has the potential to attract new and returning generations of readers as well as scholars interested in the emergent forms of twentieth- and twenty-first century feminist art and writing. Looking to the future, we are hopeful that the collection will take its place alongside similar efforts to aggregate and disseminate at-risk work of feminist authors and scholars.

The project started when we responded to the National Endowment for the Humanities (NEH) and the Andrew W. Mellon Foundation joint call for proposals to its "Open Books" program. Intended for academic presses, successful proposals were granted funds to digitize academic monographs that were effectively out of print and no longer available due to a lack of demand or being out of stock. We felt Calyx could be eligible for this grant because its literary works have been used in academia, typically in Women and Gender Studies courses, and because the call was not exclusive to academic presses. As we discussed our approach to and reasons for responding to the call, we landed on the concept of resurfacing titles from the feminist small press knowing that the Calyx titles we wanted to digitize, while technically still available in print, in practice were not available due to their limited stock and the press's limited ability to promote them.

As a collaboration, this project combines Calyx's personnel and longstanding independent lens and feminist literary connections with OSULP's dedicated infrastructure and personnel. Calyx's managing editor, one of three project co-directors, manages communications with authors, contributes marketing and promotional savvy, and provides overall project guidance. Along with two project co-directors' dedicated time and labor, the library brings its publishing, marketing, institutional repository, metadata, and project management experience to bear on this project. Our project complements similar efforts, such as the digitization of the feminist magazine *Spare Rib* (1972-1993) by the British Library and JISC, a non-profit that supports digital technologies in research and education, bringing forth previous feminist understandings to new audiences.

Overview of OSU Libraries and Press

OSU Libraries and Press, committed to reshaping the landscape of scholarly communication, supports projects like this that work to make content openly and freely available. The library maintains an active institutional repository, consults with faculty members about their rights as authors, contributes to major international organizations such as the Library Publishing Coalition and Knowledge Unlatched, and has built a joint digital archive and exhibit space with the University of Oregon (Oregon Digital). Since 2007, OSU Press has been an administrative part of the library and the University Librarian also holds the position of Press Director. In 2013, the library dedicated its Gray Family Chair for Innovative Services (the Gray Family Chair) position to the theme of digital publishing (the Chair is a term-limited position and takes on a different theme each term). With this theme established, the library began supporting a number of digital publishing projects, including the digitization of the OSU Press backlist, creation of various web-based digital works, and supporting new open access journals.

Partner Overview: Calyx Press, Inc.
Calyx has nurtured women's creativity for over forty years by publishing art and literature by women. Calyx's body of literature is deeply personal and political. It presents feminist critiques of race, class, colonialism, and sexuality politics in the U.S. and globally. As a whole, this literature represents an important voice expanding generational understanding of the feminist movement.

Project Objectives
As their most aspirational goal, OSULP and Calyx wanted to surface at-risk works of the feminist independent nonprofit press. Such works effectively are out of print, yet retain their place within the body of independently published feminist literature of the late 1970s through the 1990s. Our collaboration was in part motivated by the affordances a grant offers and in part spurred by a new generation seeking to support feminist literature and publishing.

Grants create capacity for each partner to work on projects they otherwise wouldn't. For OSULP, the project supported our goal to explore the bounds of our digital publishing program while enacting our land grant mission. At the time we launched our partnership, Calyx sought to re-establish its footing as a publisher of book-length works of poetry and prose. Worried about having to close its doors, partnering with OSULP was one of several strategies undertaken to expand its footprint.

Stakeholders
With support from the OSU Libraries University Librarian, two staff members were encouraged to partner with Calyx to apply for the NEH/Mellon grant: the Gray Family Chair for Innovative Library Services and a teaching and engagement librarian with liaison responsibilities

for departments in the Humanities and Social Sciences (the librarian). The latter has served in various positions on Calyx' board of directors prior to this project, lending additional tacit knowledge and connection to the project.

The librarian approached the director of Calyx about the project. After establishing her interest, they teamed up with the Gray Family Chair; over the course of several meetings, they scoped the project, and wrote and submitted the grant. Because Calyx is a small press, no further buy-in was needed; the director holds the authority and judgement to decide whether and to what extent to participate in this type of effort. The University Librarian's encouragement was the only buy-in the library staff needed to participate.

Funding primarily came from the NEH/Mellon grant; we were awarded $96,437. The majority off-set time spent on the project by the Calyx director, the librarian, and the Gray Family Chair. A portion of the grant was allocated to pay for a person to create marketing materials and to purchase e-ISBNs. A nominal amount was used for printing promotional and other materials. To off-set royalties that authors could have made from the sale of their books, each title was allocated $500.

Intended Audiences

While Calyx exists to publish literature by women for women and anyone interested in or advocating on behalf of issues that women face, the NEH Mellon project focused on publishers of academic works largely intended for students and faculty at higher education institutions. Recognizing that many scholarly monographs published since 1923 are not in the public domain, NEH Mellon supports making them openly available for these audiences and the public at large. These twin audiences of education institutions and the public matched our intention of bringing Calyx's works to a new generation of scholars and the public.

Interventions

As we considered whether the authors would be open to this project's open access ethos, we recognized that we would be asking authors who may have been under- or unpaid for their creative endeavors to forego compensation. To counter this, we included a small stipend in the grant for authors as a nominal compensation.

Readers of the ebooks created will be able to access them for free. We hope that this will inspire some to purchase print copies from existing stock or as available through print on demand, as well as spur word-of-mouth promotion of the titles.

We established a relationship with the University of Chicago Press BiblioVault Distribution Center (CDC) for high-quality scanning and conversion to ebook format. This necessitated securing and sending clean print copies of each book to the center. We supplied the CDC with e-ISBNs that we had purchased and reviewed the files after conversion to epubs to check for errors.

For an annual fee, the CDC distributes the ebooks to vendors such as Amazon, Barnes and Noble, and iBooks, and to catalogs such as HathiTrust. We were able to choose this route with ongoing financial support from OSU Libraries and Press. Calyx staff will also make the ebooks available on the Calyx web site. We are working with the service manager for OSU Libraries' ScholarsArchive, our institutional repository, to ingest the epub files for preservation and for providing an additional point of access.

Impact

Beyond preserving literature from the independent, feminist press, we are hopeful that our efforts to make this at-risk feminist literature more visible will spur new research into these primary sources to better understand how they contributed to feminist activism of the twentieth century and their continued impact on feminism today. Title selections were made for their literary value, their value to scholarship, and their value to the classroom. Selected titles form a literary navigation of identity politics and feminist critiques of race, ethnicity, class, colonialism, and sexuality politics in the U.S. and globally in the late twentieth- and early twenty-first centuries. As a whole, the titles are positioned to expand generational understandings of feminist critiques.

Titles include the 1990 National Book Award Winner *Forbidden Stitch: An Asian American Women's Anthology*, *Indian Singing* (Tremblay), and *Killing Color* (Sherman) which address the dual consciousness of women of color in the United States. Supported by a feminist press, the authors explore their complex identities to push against mainstream publishing. The collection also contains selections from international authors, including the first U.S. publications of Nobel Prize-winner Wislawa Szymborska, both in their original language and in English translation. The collection addresses the variety of ways in which women are embodied. Voices represented here address issues of motherhood, caretaking, and death (*Florilegia*), youth and the struggles of coming to adulthood in a female body (*Present Tense: Writing and Art by Young Women*), sexuality (*Femme's Dictionary*), faith (*Raising the Tents*), homelessness (*Natalie on the Street*), and aging in a culture that reveres youth (*Women and Aging*).

Some of the most powerful works in this collection explore the legacy and geo-political impact of U.S. colonialism. Particularly interested in how colonial dominance affects women in marginalized ethnic groups, these texts offer a personal lens through which readers can bear witness to the pain of cultural upheaval. Topics cover the illegal overthrow of the Hawai'ian government (*Light in the Crevice Never Seen*), unrest in south Asia (*Black Candle: Poems about Women from India, Pakistan, and Bangladesh*; *Storytelling in Cambodia*), and diaspora (*Going Home to a Landscape: Writings by Filipinas*).

What did each partner bring to the collaboration to make it a successful partnership?
As we discussed the overall project, we hoped to rely on each partner's strengths. Calyx brought a rich body of literature and relationships with authors without whom the project cannot proceed, both for their support of the concept and their willingness to make their publications open and freely available, foregoing royalties earned from the sale of these ebooks. Calyx's forty-year reputation as a publisher of quality

literature advancing social justice and giving voice to under-published female authors lends a timely mission to the project.

In practical terms, Calyx's managing editor and editorial assistant, both part-time employees, provide hands-on work. For example, the managing editor has taken the lead on contacting authors and reviewing their contracts. Some authors have been easy to reach and quick to lend their support. For others, distance, both in time and geographically, necessitated extra care for locating, reaching out to them, and ascertaining their interest and ability to participate. For a few who are no longer living, we are negotiating with their estates to include their work(s).

We measure our success in a couple of ways. OSU, like many land-grant higher education institutions, values community partnerships and employees' efforts to establish and sustain partners are supported. Being the recipient of a competitive national grant is considered a form of success by both organizations, in part because it confers recognition and in part because the funding enables each to engage in work they may not otherwise do. Our partnership is considered successful.

Reflection

We pursued this partnership and project to explore the bounds of digital publishing. Working on this project ties into OSU's land grant mission to serve the state as well as the institution's goal of contributing to the state's economy. The project aligns with the libraries' mission and goal to make information (of all kinds) accessible, to advance open content, and to enact the values of diversity and inclusivity.

We faced common challenges that many projects encounter. Time constraints were the most pervasive. Each partner had several competing projects and deadlines. Due to this we realized after the fact that we should have structured the grant so that we could have hired someone on a temporary basis to drive and complete the work.

An unanticipated time-consuming task was locating, organizing, and reading Calyx' book contracts with authors and finding their contact information. A primarily paper-based office for much of its history, the contracts in question first needed to be dug out of more than twenty years of inconsistently filed papers. Once found, we checked the contracts to learn whether there were any barriers to reprinting the texts and making them openly available. While contact information was kept in a Rolodex, and to some extent online, contacting authors became more complex when we learned that the information was out-of-date or incorrect. In some cases an author was no longer living, which required us to contact their estate and added time and extra steps to this process.

To date we consider this a successful partnership; although our progress is slow, we are continuing to move forward. Four books are digitized, we are mocking up a web page that will feature the project, and we are beginning to link to the ebooks from both the Calyx and OSU Libraries websites. We are revising our plans for distributing the ebooks to vendors such as Amazon, Barnes and Noble, and other popular ebook sites, along with entities such as HathiTrust.

The partnership will continue until this project is complete. After that our focus will turn to ongoing tasks such as maintaining the websites and the relationship with BiblioVault, as well as ongoing promotional activities. At that point, we can take stock of each partners' capacity to work on future projects. We knew going into the partnership that at least one co-principle investigator, whose endowed position has a fixed length of employment, would possibly have to end their participation. Given this and the likelihood of other changes, it's too early to predict if there will be additional projects.

The Calyx partnership motivated us to accept a similar collaboration with another community organization. We worked with the Oregon Jewish Museum and Center for Holocaust Education (OJMCHE) to create a digital companion to two monographs published with OSU Press, *Embracing a Western Identity: Jewish Oregonians, 1849–1950* and *The Jewish Oregon Story 1950-2010*. The companion highlights photos selected from the OJMCHE collection. It is hosted on Scalar, an open-source platform supporting born-digital, media-rich publishing developed by the Alliance for Networking Visual Culture. Scalar supports multiple reading paths, both linear and non-linear. Mirroring each book's structure, visitors see the landing page and can then navigate the site by book and book chapter. Taking a non-linear path, readers can launch one of the visualizations (grid, radial, media, or tag) to follow the people, places, and dates which tell the stories of Jewish Oregonians. Our hope was to increase the visibility of the books and their carefully chosen photos. As an exploratory project, we understand that the site may be ephemeral; what is enduring is the knowledge gained on both sides during the site's creation, which each organization can carry forward into future projects.

Case Study 6

AN ARCHIVIST AND A HISTORY-FOCUSED NONPROFIT: MY ROLE AS A BOARD MEMBER FOR THE OREGON BLACK PIONEERS

Natalia Fernández

Abstract

In this case study, the author describes and reflects upon her role as archivist serving on the board of directors for the history-focused nonprofit, the Oregon Black Pioneers (OBP). The author shares information about the OBP, how her relationship with the organization began, the purpose as well as the goals of her role as a board member, and her work with and contributions to the organization. She concludes the case study with reflection regarding her service to the OBP and a set of recommendations for serving on the board of a history-focused nonprofit organization.

Introduction

While Oregon's African American population may only account for 2% of the total population in the state, the communities' histories from across the state, seen through both their struggles and accomplishments, are rich, diverse, and worthy of documentation, scholarly research, exhibition, and celebration. Despite the exclusion laws and slavery faced in the nineteenth century, and the economic and social discrimination of the twentieth century that continues into the twenty-first, African Americans have lived in thirty-two of Oregon's thirty-six counties since 1788.[1] In the last decade alone, there have been a variety of stories presented in documentaries, books, and articles featuring African American early pioneers, families kept as slaves, loggers, cowboys, sailors, and "firsts" in a number of schools and professions.[2] There is a continued need to document these stories for inclusion in museums and school curriculums. The Oregon Black Pioneers is a nonprofit history and education-based organization that seeks to do just that. As an archivist who curates an archive that seeks to collect and preserve the histories of traditionally underrepresented groups, partnering with an organization like the Oregon Black Pioneers is an incredible opportunity for collaboration. This case study is an example of how an archivist can share their expertise with a statewide nonprofit history and education-based organization, and also includes recommendations for other archivists and librarians interested in developing relationships with similar organizations.

Within the archival profession, archivists seek out opportunities to work with underrepresented communities and can offer to fill an important role in assisting community-based archives and organizations. In its "Core Values Statement and Code of Ethics," the Society of American Archivists, the nation's oldest and largest national professional association dedicated to the needs and interests of archives and archivists, states that "[archivists] seek to build connections to

---

[1]. "Blacks in Oregon," Last modified September 30, 2015, https://oregonencyclopedia.org/articles/blacks_in_oregon/#.WURINrpFwfW.

[2]. While a detailed history of Oregon's African American communities is beyond the scope of this article, the author encourages readers to seek out resources if interested in learning more. The following list contains examples of the resources that showcase the types of histories mentioned: *The Logger's Daughter*, an Oregon Experience documentary episode; "The Unwanted Sailor: Exclusions of Black Sailors in the Pacific Northwest and the Atlantic Southeast" by Jacki Hedlund Tyler, published in the *Oregon Historical Quarterly*; *Red, White, and Black: A True Story of Race and Rodeo* by Rick Steber; *Breaking Chains: Slavery on Trial in the Oregon Territory* by Gregory Nokes; *A Light in the Wilderness* by Jane Kirkpatrick; *Images of America: African Americans of Portland* by Kimberly Moreland; and *Perseverance: A History of African Americans in Oregon's Marion and Polk Counties* by Gwen Carr. The Oregon Encyclopedia, https://oregonencyclopedia.org/ also has a variety of entries regarding African American history in the state.

under-documented communities to support…[the] formation of community-based archives."[3] Thirty years prior to SAA's statement, in his seminal article, "Archival Strategies for the Post-Custodial Era," the archivist F. Gerald Ham made a call to the profession for archivists to see themselves beyond the role of "custodian" of records and to use a "post-custodial" approach in which they "encourage and assist other institutions and organizations such as local historical societies, public libraries, municipalities, voluntary associations, businesses, and so forth, to share [the] responsibility" of maintaining the historical record.[4] More recent articles reflect the partnerships and collaborative work that archivists are doing with community-based archival organizations, from the archivists' perspective.[5] In a 2016 research study in which the authors report the results of a series of qualitative interviews with academic members of one ethnic community regarding their responses to one community archives, they explain that community archives enable and empower "communities [to] make collective decisions about what is of enduring value to them, shape collective memory of their own pasts, and control the means through which stories about their past are constructed."[6] While they note that more research like theirs needs to

---

3. "SAA Core Values Statement and Code of Ethics," http://www2.archivists.org/statements/saa-core-values-statement-and-code-of-ethics.

4. F. Gerald Ham, "Archival Strategies for the Post-Custodial Era," *American Archivist* 44:3 (1981): 212.

5. A sample of articles within the archival literature pertaining to collaborations with community-based archives, including case studies and more theoretical reflections, include: Terry Cook, "Evidence, Memory, Identity, and Community: Four Shifting Archival Paradigms," *Archival Science* 13 (2013): 95–120; Dominique Daniel, "Documenting the Immigrant and Ethnic Experience in American Archives," *American Archivist* 73:1 (2010): 82–104; Andrew Flinn, Mary Stevens, and Elizabeth Shepherd, "Whose Memories, Whose Archives? Independent Community Archives, Autonomy, and the Mainstream," *Archival Science* 9 (2009): 71–86; and Cristine Paschild, "Community Archives and the Limitations of Identity: Considering Discursive Impact on Material Needs" *American Archivist* 75:1 (2012) 125-142. Also recommended is the book edited by Jeannette Bastian and Ben Alexander, *Community Archives: The Shaping of Memory* (London: Facet, 2009).

6. Michelle Caswell, Marika Cifor, and Mario H. Ramirez, "'To Suddenly Discover Yourself Existing': Uncovering the Impact of Community Archives." *American Archives* 79:1 (2016): 61.

be conducted, they conclude that community archives can have important impacts on the communities that they represent.[7] Notably, the authors define community archives broadly as organizations that have "community members dedicated to shaping the collective memory of a community's past," and include 501(c)(3) nonprofit organizations, with archival projects as a part of their larger community organization, within their definition.[8] The Oregon Black Pioneers is an example of one such community archives.

Partner Overview

The Oregon Black Pioneers (OBP) is an all-volunteer organization based in Salem, Oregon; it was founded in 1993 and incorporated in the State of Oregon in 1994 as a nonprofit.[9] It is recognized as an IRS 501(c)(3) organization, and while it does not offer memberships, it does solicit contributions. Throughout its twenty-five-year history, the OBP has conducted research, given presentations, curated exhibits, written books, partnered with school districts and historical organizations to educate Oregonians about African-Americans' contributions to the state's history, and established a small archives. The organization's vision is to be the premier resource for Oregon's African American culture and heritage. Its mission is to research, recognize, and commemorate the culture and heritage of African Americans in the State of Oregon. The OBP's eleven-member board of directors, a small group of volunteers, and special advisors comprise the entire organization. The OBP has no paid staff, and the board includes a small group of dedicated individuals with self-taught historical research experience. Around the time that the chair of the board development committee reached out to me, the OBP was in the process of seeking to expand its membership

---

7. Caswell, "'To Suddenly Discover," 76.

8. Caswell, "'To Suddenly Discover," 62.

9. "Oregon Black Pioneers," Last modified October 23, 2017, http://www.oregonblackpioneers.org/blog/home/.

to include community members and professionals with more experience in education, fundraising, and archival work.

My relationship with the OBP began in 2013, when the organization was in the process of planning a 2015 exhibit with the Oregon Historical Society, the state's historical society located in Portland. The OBP exhibit team requested to use materials from one of the collections within the Oregon Multicultural Archives (OMA), which I curate and direct at the Oregon State University's Special Collections and Archives Research Center.[10] The mission of the OMA is to assist in preserving the histories and sharing the stories that document Oregon's African American, Asian American, Latino/a, and Native American communities. The archives' diverse collections reflect the ways in which these communities have contributed to the identity of the state of Oregon. Over the course of the next couple of years, the OBP and I continued to develop our relationship. I further assisted the exhibit team with its requests, attended the 2015 exhibit opening, and participated in other events hosted by the organization. I saw these activities as a part of my professional work to develop relationships to support communities and organizations, specifically within the African American community. In the summer of 2015, when the OBP recruited me to serve as a member of the organization's board of directors, I saw the opportunity to further extend my support and deepen the relationship. Since the mission of the OMA is to assist communities in sharing and preserving their stories, and the OBP strives to be the premier resource for Oregon's African American culture and heritage information, we share a very similar purpose and the collaboration was a good match. It is because of my professional position, and the knowledge and skills I could bring to the OBP, that I was asked to join the board. As a part of my position with the OMA, I have collaborated with various organizations and community groups, including a nonprofit, on specific projects; however, prior to my work with the OBP, I had not served on the board of directors for

---

10. "Oregon Multicultural Archives," Last modified Oct 31, 2017, http://guides.library.oregon-state.edu/oma.

a nonprofit organization. My previous experience collaborating with a nonprofit organization involved a project with the Oregon Chinese Consolidated Benevolent Association to create an online exhibition featuring a set of documents pertaining to Oregon's disinterment history.[11] After learning more about the mission of the organization and the purpose of my role, I joined the OBP board in the summer of 2015, and I am currently nearing the completion of my three-year term.

About the Oregon Black Pioneers Board of Directors

The structure of the OBP is such that board members are very active participants in the day-to-day activities that promote the organization's mission. Members serve on at least one of its five committees, if not more; these include positions related to the program committee, virtual museum, marketing and communications, board development, and fundraising. The program committee has a number of sub-committees for exhibit curation, collections management, as well as research and education. As part of my application to serve on the board, I listed my skills and areas of expertise. Based on a combination of the board's needs and what I could offer, I was assigned to serve on the program committee's various sub-committees. At the time of writing this article, the board consisted of twelve board members and five special advisors; notably, the OBP also retains a grant writer who is paid through awarded grant funding. During my time on the board, the number of members has remained about the same; however, there has been turnover of about a third of the membership, with some members joining and then recusing themselves from service for a number of reasons. Board members include retired individuals, along with professionals in a variety of fields; all bringing their special skills in their areas of expertise.

When I joined the board, no archivist had ever served as a member; however, the OBP had a number of partnerships with archival

---

11. A detailed description of this project can be found in a 2013 article the author co-wrote: Natalia M. Fernández and Cristine N. Paschild, "Beyond a Box of Documents: The Collaborative Partnership Behind the Oregon Chinese Disinterment Documents Collection," *Journal of Western Archives* 4:1 (2013): 1-16.

repositories. One of the OBP's most important long-standing partnerships is with the Oregon Historical Society (OHS). The OHS was founded in 1898 and is a private museum with a research library and archives. The OHS has hosted three OBP exhibits in 2011, 2013, and another in 2015; the museum will be hosting the next OBP exhibit in 2018. In addition, the organization also collaborates with OHS on public programming, both in conjunction with exhibits and as opportunities present themselves. The museum also physically stores a number of large artifacts on behalf of the OBP. The OBP has a storage space in Salem, but it does not meet archival and museum standards, so larger and more valuable pieces are not stored there. The OBP also has a similar relationship with the Willamette Heritage Center (WHC) in Salem. The WHC is a private 501(c)(3) nonprofit organization that was formed through the merger of the Mission Mill Museum and the Marion County Historical Society. It currently houses an OBP artifact that it has included in exhibits with OBP permission. It was in part through these relationships that OBP members increased their knowledge about archival repositories and the work of archivists.

The Purpose and Goals of My Role as an OBP Board Member

When my term as board member began in the summer of 2015, the Oregon Black Pioneers was in the process of reviewing its 2014-2016 strategic plan. The plan was comprised of seven strategies, each with various goals. The strategies included building capacity through board development, building a framework for taking OBP's programs and services to the next level, establishing both a virtual museum and a program for the Historic African American Properties, developing a marketing and communications plan, increasing funds and resource development, and, lastly, assessing the organization's financial management process. The plan not only laid out the organization's strategies and goals, it also included work plans for each strategy. These work plans listed the objectives, actions, timelines, and the assigned lead contact to ensure the goals' completion. As a board member, my role was to assist the OBP in accomplishing its strategic goals, and to, in turn, support its mission and vision. Of the seven strategies, my skills and expertise best fit with Strategy II, which was to "build a framework for taking OBP's program and services to the next level." The goals for this strategy included establishing program administration and a presentation program, re-establishing the OBP research program, as well as developing an exhibit curation and publishing plan. I also considered the amount of time and resources I was able to dedicate to the board and decided that, rather than over-committing, I would select specific action items and projects that seemed most realistic to accomplish. In addition, I thought about my own professional goals and how my role with the OBP would help me achieve them. Having never served on a nonprofit board before, I wanted to learn more about the management of this type of organization. For example, I was curious about the financial and legal aspects, the fundraising challenges and strategies, and the overall structure of how a board functions. However, my interest was not in the particulars of these aspects of the board. For me, the process of determining my service commitment to the OBP was a combination of balancing what the organization needed and what I was capable of offering. In conversations with members of the board, I began my role as a board member as part of the program committee with a special focus on collections, specifically the organization's archival and research materials. However, during these two and a half years, I have worked with the OBP on a variety of projects, mostly in support of the organization's exhibit and public programing endeavors.

Before describing the projects themselves, it is important to explain the logistics of serving on the OBP board, specifically the time commitment. The board has monthly in-person Saturday morning meetings at the Salem office, but there is a conference call option. I live about an hour from Salem. For the first year, I made the effort to meet in person because I wanted to show my commitment to the organization and use the meetings as an opportunity for more casual and personal conversations with fellow board members. Though the meetings were only about two hours, it was a four-hour commitment for me including travel time; on workdays, I could use a state vehicle for travel, but on the weekend, I was using my personal vehicle. As I became more comfortable with my role and realized my physical presence was not always required, I began attending more meetings via conference call, which saved me both time and money. On average, the program committee meets once every two months, and those meetings are usually conference calls. On occasion, I have met in Salem or Portland with other board members as part of my program committee duties. While there are some weeks in which the only OBP related work I do is check my OBP email—the organization uses Gmail—there are other weeks when my commitment is more time intensive, such as when working on an exhibit de-installation or organizing collections at the storage unit. My monthly commitment averages about twelve hours; however, depending on the type of projects I am working on, the time commitment increases as needed. There are board members, especially those who are retired or others who have decided to take on more responsibility, who work many more hours per month than I do. My work and time commitment has remained focused on the activities and projects that best support the OBP's program and services.

My Work as an OBP Board Member

My position as the curator and archivist for the Oregon Multicultural Archives overlaps and supports my role as an OBP board member, and vice versa. The skills I have gained in my position with the OMA, such as collection development, exhibit curation, community outreach, and event planning, are all applied to and strengthened through my work with the OBP. In addition, as part of my role with the OBP, the new knowledge I have gathered on topics such as fundraising, board recruitment, and considerations for the development of a museum, has been useful in helping me to understand the broader archives and museum profession and how the OMA fits into it.

My work with the OBP has included exhibit installations/de-installations, assistance with organizing the OBP's collections, and co-leading a number of public programming initiatives. Within just a few months of joining the board, one of my first projects was to assist in the de-installation of the exhibition, "A Community on the Move," hosted by the Oregon Historical Society during the first half and into the fall of 2015. In early October of that year, I led the development of a more streamlined system to track the exhibit panels, artifacts, and props, and assisted with the physical de-installation. I also drafted the necessary documents to enable the organization to loan out a set of the panels to another institution.

The next year, 2016, marked my first full year on the board. My projects included collections storage and organization, exhibit-related work, and a number of public programing initiatives. Various members of the program committee formed a collections team to address how best to organize the many types of materials owned by the organization; these materials include artifacts with historical value, artwork, administrative archives, props, exhibit stands and panels, and supplies. In the winter of 2016, the team met a number of times to review the materials and remove unneeded content; we also physically moved and consolidated the collections into one large storage unit. In the early spring of 2017, the team gathered again to add shelving to the storage unit and to arrange the collections by type for easier access and use by members of the board. Our next project is to create a collection inventory.

In 2016, the OBP was also beginning the planning and curation for the 2018 exhibit, "Racing to Change: Oregon's Civil Rights Years," which would be at the Oregon Historical Society from January to June 2018. The exhibit showcased the civil rights movement in Oregon, focusing on the years between 1960 and the early 1980s. The OBP developed a community-based advisory group that includes members of the board, OHS staff, staff from other Portland archival repositories, and community members. I served as a member of the group, as well as the lead for the public programming committee. The advisory group met with an interpretive planner a number of times throughout the year to develop the exhibition plan. The program committee also met to set the groundwork for six programs to take place while the exhibit was open. As the committee lead, I delegated the program planning details to other board members, who served as co-leads for the six events, while I managed the programming as a whole. In the months leading up to the exhibit, the committee met and communicated more frequently to finalize the program details.

My role as board member with the OBP has also involved co-leading a number of public programming initiatives. In May of 2016, I co-led a bus tour for about thirty-five community members. We traveled together to five historic locations in the Willamette Valley associated with Oregon's African American history. The daylong bus tour, *Back Roads to Black History*, engaged participants in learning about Oregon's black pioneers. We began the day at Portland's Unthank Park and then traveled to the Salem Pioneer Cemetery, the Mt. Union Cemetery in Philomath, the Eliza and Hannah Gorman House in Corvallis, and the Helvetia Community Church in Hillsboro. We concluded the tour with a reception at the Abbey Creek Winery in North Plains. The OBP used a $1,500 grant from Oregon Humanities and collaborated with a number of partners to organize and fund the tour. In October of that year, the OBP participated in the Oregon Archives Crawl in Portland. The event featured dozens of archival repositories, museums, and history-based organizations. I, along with a fellow board member, served as OBP representatives, staffing a booth with information about the organization as part of the event. In addition to the previously mentioned work, as an OBP board member I also participate in a number of smaller projects and discussions. As examples, in May of 2016, I offered my institution as a site to host the OBP annual meeting in Corvallis, and I have offered my knowledge and perspective as part of the organization's in-depth conversations and report regarding the future of an OBP museum. My main projects for my last year on the board included a collections inventory and collaboration with the OBP virtual museum committee to create an online museum, as well as continued planning for an exhibition in my role as lead for the programing committee.

Reflection

As with any partnership, taking some time to reflect on the collaboration can be helpful to strengthen the relationship. While I initially had trepidations about serving on the board, now looking back, I see that my concerns about service to the OBP focused on two elements: how it complemented my role as the curator of a multicultural archive with a focus on community collaboration and how my service fit into my institution's goals as a land grant university that prides itself on outreach to communities and organizations beyond the university.[12] These considerations continue to be relevant, however. By playing to my strengths, knowing my limitations in terms of what I can offer to the board, along with clear communication to the board, I have been able to maintain that balance and level of commitment. In addition, it has also been incredibly rewarding to see the positive impact of the OBP for audiences beyond the reach of the OMA. While the intended audience of the OMA goes beyond the Oregon State University community and reaches scholars and community members from all over the state, the OBP's intended audience is much more far-reaching, especially in its focus on the K-12 community. For example, the OBP exhibits draw hundreds of students to engage with Oregon's African American history, and the books published by the OBP are now incorporated into various school curriculums. Students within K-12 schools are beyond the scope of the OMA, but I recognize and enjoy seeing the power of history reach that audience.

It is often difficult to balance paid work with a service position, and my main challenge in this collaboration, which I have expressed to the other board members, has been in managing my role as board member and my full-time position as an archivist. With that said, the collaboration between myself, in my professional position, and the OBP in my role as board member, has evolved to one between the OBP and myself as an individual. I made a personal commitment to ensuring that I would

---

12. "Oregon State University Mission Statement," last modified in 2017, http://leadership.oregonstate.edu/trustees/oregon-state-university-mission-statement.

serve the full three years of my term and accomplish my OBP projects to the best of my abilities, and I have done so. Although there is no formal assessment of the relationship as a whole, after three years of ongoing conversations with board members and feedback on programs we have implemented, I have concluded that my service to the OBP has proved fruitful for both myself and my personal goals, as well as for the organization's overall mission. As a result of these experiences serving on the board of a nonprofit history-based organization, I have developed the following set of recommendations listed below.

Recommendations for Serving on the Board of a History-Focused Nonprofit Organization

- Research the mission and vision of the organization to determine whether it is an organization you want to be a part of and support.
- To better assess the work of the organization, and most importantly, how you work together, develop a professional relationship with members of the organization before committing to serve on the board.
- If possible, assess the working environment of the organization to determine if the interpersonal relationships between existing members are successful and positive. This may be accomplished through participation and observation at the organization's events and activities, as well as asking for recommendations from others who have collaborated with the organization.
- If the organization has a strategic plan, read it thoroughly, especially the timeline, and ask yourself, "How do I fit in and where can I offer my skills and expertise?" Also, discuss how the organization's members see you fitting in and where.
- Be clear about what you can and want to offer, without overcommitting your time.
- Reflect upon your own professional goals and how your service with the organization can help you achieve them; a service commitment to a nonprofit can be mutually beneficial.

- Before committing to serve, determine how this service fits into your job duties and what kind of support your institution will offer. Have a frank discussion with your supervisor and any others who need to be informed of your commitment.
- Periodically reflect and assess your commitment to the organization. As needed, discuss your concerns with members of the organization to determine if the relationship continues to be mutually beneficial.
- Know that it is okay to say "no" to requests that are beyond your capacity and/or time commitment. Also, know that you can resign your service prior to the end of your term or request a leave of absence.

Future Plans and Final Thoughts

For my last year of service, my role on the board was to focus on exhibit public programming organization and implementation, the collections inventory, and a collaboration with the virtual museum committee to assist in the development of the OBP virtual museum. In addition, I also continued my participation in the discussions regarding the broader issues facing the organization, as well as provided assistance to other OBP endeavors. However, as I look toward the future of possibilities, I also take the time to look back to all the OBP has accomplished thus far. In May of 2017 and during the second year of my service on the board, the University of Oregon presented the OBP with the George McMath Historic Preservation Award.[13] Since 2009, this award has celebrated a leader who has made significant contributions to historic preservation in the state of Oregon. While this is not the first time the organization has been recognized for its contributions and work, it is notable that for this particular preservation award the OBP was the first organization, rather than an individual, to receive the award. For decades, the OBP board of directors has worked tirelessly and passionately to research, preserve, and make accessible the history of African Americans in Oregon. To

---

13. "Oregon Black Pioneers Awarded the 2017 George McMath Historic Preservation Award," last modified May 15, 2017, http://www.oregonblackpioneers.org/blog/preservation/oregon-black-pioneers-awarded-the-2017-george-mcmath-historic-preservation-award/.

single out a specific individual would negate the role of the board of directors, as well as all the volunteers, advisors, and collaborators, who work together in support of the organization's mission. While the award was to recognize and celebrate the organization's past work, during the ceremony the OBP president spoke about present endeavors and future plans, and I was honored and humbled to know that I was included as a part of her words. As one of many within a committed group of individuals, ultimately, I see myself as a member of the board that helps to ensure the Oregon Black Pioneers' mission to research and educate Oregonians about African-Americans' contributions to Oregon's history as it moves forward and continues on into the future.

Bibliography

Caswell, Michelle, Marika Cifor, and Mario H. Ramirez. "'To Suddenly Discover Yourself Existing': Uncovering the Impact of Community Archives." *American Archivist* 79, no. 1 (2016): 56-81.

Ham, F. Gerald. "Archival Strategies for the Post-Custodial Era." *American Archivist* 44, no. 3 (1981): 207-216.

Millner, Darrell. "Blacks in Oregon." *Oregon Encyclopedia*. Last modified September 11, 2017. https://oregonencyclopedia.org/articles/blacks_in_oregon/#.WURINrpFwfW.

Oregon Black Pioneers. "Oregon Black Pioneers." Last modified October 23, 2017. http://www.oregonblackpioneers.org/blog/home/.

Oregon Black Pioneers. "Oregon Black Pioneers Awarded the 2017 George McMath Historic Preservation Award" Last modified May 15, 2017. http://www.oregonblackpioneers.org/blog/preservation/oregon-black-pioneers-awarded-the-2017-george-mcmath-historic-preservation-award/.

Oregon Multicultural Archives. "Oregon Multicultural Archives." Last modified October 31, 2017. http://guides.library.oregonstate.edu/oma.

Oregon State University. "Oregon State University Mission Statement" Last modified in 2017. http://leadership.oregonstate.edu/trustees/oregon-state-university-mission-statement.

Society of American Archivists. "SAA Core Values Statement and Code of Ethics" (2011). Last modified September 23, 2016. http://www2.archivists.org/statements/saa-core-values-statement-and-code-of-ethics.

Case Study 7

THE JAPANESE CULTURAL CENTER OF HAWAII AND HAWAII SCHOOL LIBRARIES: PARTNERS IN EDUCATING STUDENTS ABOUT THE WORLD WAR II INCARCERATION OF JAPANESE AMERICANS IN HAWAII

Violet H. Harada and Jane Kurahara

Abstract

This case study focuses on the work of the Japanese Cultural Center of Hawaii (JCCH) in establishing an educational partnership with secondary school librarians and teachers in the state. A critical component of this nonprofit agency's work has been to educate students in the public and private schools about a little-known aspect of World War II history: the incarceration of over 2,000 Japanese and Japanese Americans in seventeen detention and imprisonment sites on various islands in Hawaii. While little has been chronicled in U.S. textbooks about the World War II incarceration of Japanese Americans on the continental U.S., even less has been published on similar experiences in Hawaii. This case study describes the work of volunteers at the JCCH, who developed a range of resources and units that teachers and librarians in secondary schools might incorporate into the curriculum. The authors detail the organization and content of the instructional resources produced, recount the professional training offered to collaborative teams of school librarians and classroom teachers working with students, and reflect on lessons learned as the JCCH team currently considers future options.

Introduction

Over the past twelve years, the Japanese Cultural Center of Hawaii (JCCH) has established a partnership with secondary school librarians and teachers in the state to educate students about the internment experience of Japanese Americans in Hawaii during World War II. The authors detail the development of this curriculum partnership that began in 2005 and that continues through the present. They describe the organization and content of the instructional resources produced, elaborate on the professional training offered to collaborative teams of school librarians and classroom teachers working with students, chronicle the implementation of the curriculum, and reflect on the results in terms of insights and actions on the part of the JCCH resource developers and the school partners. In addition, they discuss challenges faced in the development and outreach aspects of this project and the best practices discovered in fostering partnerships between nonprofit organizations and schools. To understand the significance of this initiative, the authors first introduce the broader context of the internment episode in U.S. history.

The Historical Context

The bombing of Pearl Harbor on December 7, 1941 led to President Franklin Roosevelt signing Executive Order 9066 that sanctioned the mass incarceration of over 100,000 Japanese Americans on the West Coast of the U.S.[11] The act was described by a federal commission as "a grievous episode in American history caused by race prejudice, war hysteria, and a failure of political leadership."[2] To this day, there has been no evidence of a single documented case of sabotage or espionage by an ethnic Japanese in the U.S during World War II. The damning

---

1. Commission on Wartime Relocation Internment of Civilians, United States, *Personal Justice Denied* (Seattle, WA: University of Washington Press, 1997), 459.

2. Ibid.

fact was that the *Nisei* (first generation of ethnic Japanese born in the U.S.) and the *Issei* (immigrant generation) were presumed guilty because of their racial affiliation.[3] In Hawaii, selective rather than wholesale internment occurred because the Japanese community in the Territory of Hawaii comprised almost forty percent of the entire population and the military government realized mass incarceration would have crippled the Hawaiian economy.[4] In addition, the territory was under martial law. According to the National Park Service, "the best estimate for the number of people of Japanese ancestry incarcerated from Hawaii is approximately 2,356."[5] Those arrested were almost entirely Japanese immigrant generation males. Later detainees included American citizen *Kibei*, Japanese Americans who had been born in the U.S. but raised and educated in Japan.

While books and articles have been published about the imprisonment of Japanese Americans in the continental U.S., comparatively little has been written about the internment situation in Hawaii. In the last few years, however, the secrecy surrounding the Japanese internment experience in Hawaii came to an end, thanks largely to the research efforts of the JCCH and the faculty and students at the University of Hawaii-West Oahu. Jeff Burton, the principal author of an overview of incarceration sites on the continental U.S., worked with the JCCH in obtaining a grant from the U.S. Department of Interior to complete an archaeological overview of the Japanese American incarceration sites in Hawaii. The researchers identified at least seventeen detainment centers and internment camps on Oahu and neighbor islands.[6]

---

3. Robert K. Gordon, "Casualties of History," *New Republic* 189 (1983): 12

4. Burton, Jeffery F., and Mary M. Farrell. 2007. "World War II Japanese American Internment Sites in Hawaii," Trans-Sierran Archaeological Research and Japanese Cultural Center of Hawaii Research Center, http://www.densho.org/assets/media/Burton-HawaiiInternmentSitesOverview2007.pdf , 1.

5. National Park Service, *Honouliuli Gulch and Associated Sites: Final Special Resource Study and Environmental Assessment* (Washington, D.C.: United States Department of the Interior, 2015), 10.

6. Ibid., xiii.

Of these sites, Honouliuli Internment Camp emerged as the most visible remnant of this dark period in U.S. history. It was the largest of the sites built to incarcerate Japanese Americans and Prisoners of War that opened in 1943 and closed in 1946.[7] Although it lay in the Ewa Plains in southern Oahu only a few miles from Pearl Harbor, the towering monkey pod trees and overgrown brush created a tropical jungle that shut out the rest of civilization. The Hawaiian name, Honouliuli, meant "blue harbor" or "dark bay."[8] This site also had another name that was not so idyllic: Japanese Americans, who were interned there during World War II, referred to it as *"Jigoku Dani,"* or "Hell Valley."[9] Honouliuli was literally forgotten until a local television station contacted the JCCH in 1998 for help in finding the site. The query motivated a JCCH staff associate to initiate an investigation. The watershed moment occurred when a three-hour exploratory expedition on the Ewa Plains resulted in the discovery of the former facility.[10] Since discovering the site in 2002, the JCCH has worked with Hawaii's congressional leaders and community supporters to preserve the site as a national monument. In 2015, their efforts were rewarded when President Barack Obama signed a proclamation recognizing the site as a national monument to be managed by the National Park Service.[11]

Partner Overviews

Japanese Cultural Center of Hawaii

---

7. Jane Kurahara, Brian Niiya and Betsy Young, "Finding Honouliuli: The Japanese Cultural Center of Hawaii and Preserving the Hawaii Internment Story," *Social Process in Hawaii* 45 (2014): 17.

8. Jeffery F. Burton et al., "Hell Valley: Uncovering a Prison Camp in Paradise," *Social Process in Hawaii* 45 (2014): 44.

9. Ibid.

10. Kurahara, Niiya and Young, "Finding Honouliuli," 17.

11. "Presidential Proclamation—Establishment of the Honouliuli National Monument," The White House, Office of the Press Secretary, last modified February 24, 2015, https://obamawhitehouse.archives.gov/the-press-office/2015/02/24/presidential-proclamation-establishment-honouliuli-national-monument.

The Honolulu Japanese Chamber of Commerce (HJCC) initiated the Japan-Hawaii Cultural Center project, "The Dream," in 1986 to preserve the legacy of the pioneers who came to Hawaii from Japan.[12] In 1987, the Cultural Center was incorporated under state law as a non-profit corporation to develop, own, maintain, and operate a Japanese cultural center in Hawaii.[13] As an independent entity, the mission of the newly created JCCH was to perpetuate the history, heritage, and culture of the evolving Japanese American experience in the state. Today, the JCCH coordinates a range of activities including educational programs for all ages, cultural festivals for the public, and historical and cultural events and services for local and visitor audiences. The physical facility located in Honolulu includes exhibition galleries, a gift shop, a martial arts studio, a teahouse, meeting and event spaces, and offices. Of special significance to their preservation and education goals, the JCCH also houses a resource center and an education center. These two centers are described more fully here.

Tokioka Heritage Resource Center
The resource center focuses on archival collections detailing the Japanese American experience in Hawaii. Its resources include oral histories, manuscripts, diaries, letters, drawings, photographs, and paintings.[14] The center has a collection of over 5,000 books in English and Japanese that deal primarily with local Japanese history but also includes information about Japanese Americans on the continental U.S. as well as the culture and history of Japan.[15] In addition, the center contains vertical files of news clippings and pamphlets, two-dimensional artifacts, and both print and digital versions of back issues of the *Hawaii Herald*, the oldest

---

12. "History," Japanese Cultural Center of Hawaii, accessed May 29, 2017, https://www.jcch.com/history.

13. "History."

14. "Tokioka Heritage Resource Center," Japanese Cultural Center of Hawaii, accessed May 29, 2017, https://www.jcch.com/tokioka-heritage-resource-center.

15. "Tokioka Heritage Resource Center."

newspaper in the English language serving the local Japanese community.[16] Staffed by a collections librarian with assistance from volunteers, the resource center's primary materials have served as a significant source for researching the Hawaii internment story.

Honouliuli National Monument JCCH Education Center

The most recent addition to the JCCH facilities is the Honouliuli National Monument JCCH Education Center, which officially opened in October 2016.[17] The center provides students, teachers, and the community with opportunities to learn about the new national monument, its history, and its lessons for the future. It features photos of the Honouliuli Internment Camp, artifacts from the internees, oral history videos, and virtual tours of the Honouliuli National Monument.[18] Key partners in bringing this center to fruition were the Freeman Foundation, a philanthropic grant-funding organization which targets historic preservation; Monsanto Hawaii, an agricultural corporation which donated the land where Honouliuli is situated; and JTB Hawaii, Inc., a travel service and events planning company.[19]

Partnership with Schools in Hawaii

The JCCH alliance with the system of public schools in the state has been a vital partnership committed to educating Hawaii's young people about the internment story. According to the Hawaii DOE'S Strategic Plan for 2017-2020, there are nearly 300 K-12 public and charter schools on the islands of Hawaii, Maui, Kauai, Molokai, Lanai, and Oahu.[20] In addition, there are over a hundred private schools located on the various

---

16. Ibid.

17. "Honouliuli Education Center," Japanese Cultural Center of Hawaii, accessed May 29, 2017, https://www.jcch.com/honouliuli-education-center.

18. Ibid.

19. bid.

20. "Strategic Plan 2017-2020," Hawaii State Department of Education and Board of Education, accessed May 29, 2017, http://www.hawaiipublicschools.org/DOE%20Forms/Advancing%20Education/SP2017-20.pdf.

islands which are loosely organized under the Hawaii Association of Independent Schools. While the JCCH has largely targeted the secondary public schools, the organization has also reached out to interested private schools.

An important goal of the JCCH has been to educate students in the public and private schools about the incarceration of over 2,000 Japanese and Japanese Americans in the detention and imprisonment sites on various islands in Hawaii. Recognizing the need for school children to learn about this tragic episode, a cohort of JCCH volunteers under the leadership of Jane Kurahara and Betsy Young undertook the challenge of developing materials to engage young citizens in investigating the multilayered issues related to internment, including civil rights, civil liberties, and civic engagement. These volunteers were retired educators, doctors, lawyers, and other professionals who were committed to the educational goals of the JCCH.

The alliance with the Hawaii DOE was established by Kurahara and Young, both retired school librarians with strong professional networks in the DOE state offices. They reached out to key content-area educational specialists in social studies and language arts to discuss how best to make curriculum resources available to the public schools. Serendipitously, the state specialists were revising state content standards and agreed to incorporate benchmarks dealing specifically with the Hawaii internment experience in the social studies objectives. We elaborate on the impact of this decision in the following pages, including the funding received to support the development and dissemination of resources at JCCH.

Case

Forging the Educational Alliance
While work with teachers and librarians can be traced back to an internment workshop conducted in 1999, a major educational effort began in 2005 when the Hawaii DOE established new learning standards in the social studies curriculum for grades 9 and 10 that explicitly mentioned

the study of the removal and incarceration of Japanese Americans in World War II.[21] To implement these standards, the schools required teaching and learning resources for both faculty and students. When the DOE acknowledged that such materials were sparse, the JCCH volunteers seized this opportunity to create the needed curriculum resources. They produced discovery boxes, designed curriculum units, coordinated field experiences for high school students, and developed training sessions for instructors.

Recognizing the value of instructional team building, JCCH welcomed teachers and librarians working as partners in developing learning plans and projects for students. Toward this end, priority was given to such teams attending training sessions together. While teachers possessed the content knowledge, librarians contributed skills in working with primary and secondary resources and online searching for and evaluation of information. In a few instances, librarians also assumed leadership roles in recruiting teachers for the JCCH training and coordinated with JCCH volunteers to offer training sessions in their schools and communities.

The curriculum development effort of the JCCH volunteers over the past twelve years is described below in five overlapping phases. Some of this information has been documented by Kurahara, Niiya, and Young in a 2014 article on finding Honouliuli;[22] however, most of it comes from informal notes and reports kept by one of this chapter's authors (Kurahara), who has been a key member of the educational team.

Phase 1: Internment Discovery Boxes

Capitalizing on the rich repository of primary print sources and artifacts available in the Tokioka Heritage Resource Center, one of the volunteers, Betsy Young, took the lead in creating internment discovery boxes to provide students with hands-on experiences. In 2006, Young and team developed five discovery boxes in the form of suitcases that contained

---

21. Kurahara, Niiya and Young, "Finding Honouliuli," 34.
22. Ibid., 16-42.

both primary and secondary sources and lesson plans.[23] Three of the boxes were housed at museums on the Big Island of Hawaii, Maui, and Kauai, and the remaining boxes were kept at the JCCH. The contents of each suitcase included materials covering pre-war factors and the incarceration experience with sufficient copies of these resources for a classroom. A school could borrow a discovery box for one week. With assistance from Hawaii DOE state level specialists in social studies and Hawaiian studies, the JCCH volunteers trained personnel in using the discovery boxes.

While the boxes were popular, the volunteers discovered shortcomings with this mode of instruction. For one, teachers and librarians said there was too much material in a box. They indicated that it was overwhelming to teach all the concepts represented by the various items in each box. In addition, having only five discovery boxes meant that the demand outstripped the supply. Also, schools tended to study the same topics at the same time of the school year, which compounded the dilemma.

Phase 2: Resource Folders

The JCCH volunteers realized that they had to streamline their efforts. They received feedback through an intensive one-day focus session with teachers and several informal exchanges with both teachers and librarians. With input from classroom teachers and librarians who had used the discovery boxes, they sifted through the suitcases and identified the most critical topics and resources. This more compact set of materials was compiled into a resource folder entitled, "World War II Hawaii Internees' Experiences."[24] In 2007, with a grant from the Honolulu Chapter of the Japanese American Citizens League and supplemental funds from various units in the Hawaii DOE, the JCCH provided two hard copies of the folder to seventy public high schools. In addition, "Silent

---

23. Ibid., 35.
24. Ibid.

Suffering," a DVD on aspects of the internment episode produced by the Hawaii DOE Teleschool Unit was also enclosed with the folders.

The folder included sections about pre-World War II perceptions and actions, the treatment and effects of internment, and the issues faced by Japanese Americans during and after the war.[25] Within each section, primary and secondary sources were organized around critical questions such as the following: What were the public's perceptions of Japanese Americans before the war? Why were the Japanese interned? What can be done to protect people's civil rights so that racially discriminatory incarceration will not happen again?[26] The resources in the folders ranged from government reports and archival photographs to transcriptions of interrogations and letters from the internees in both English and Japanese.[27] According to Kurahara, following up on the actual usage of the folders was difficult. The JCCH group were dependent on the availability of the state specialist in social studies to assist with the collection of usage data; however, changes in specialists and shifting priorities within the Hawaii DOE have been barriers to greater collaboration on data collection.

Phase 3: Curriculum Units

Social studies teachers in grades 9 and 10 appreciated the resource folders. However, they were stymied in developing instructional units that specifically addressed the learning objectives in three critical courses: Modern History of Hawaii, U.S. History, and Participation in Democracy. Recognizing this need, the JCCH volunteers undertook an ambitious project to design units that might be used in these courses. In 2007-2008, they solicited the assistance of Hawaii DOE curriculum experts. The JCCH received funding from Education through Cultural and Historical Organizations (ECHO) to contract with four social studies teachers as unit designers and a former state assistant superintendent of curriculum

---

25. Ibid.
26. Ibid.
27. Ibid.

to oversee the project.[28] The curriculum units focused on studying the complex issues of racism and bigotry through the lens of the World War II incarceration. In addition, nine teachers were contracted to review the units and six others to test them in their classrooms. A limited number of hard copies were made available on request and the units were also accessible online through a website located at http://www.hawaiiinternment.org/. Publicity regarding the website was handled through the Hawaii DOE's communication channels. School librarians also promoted the units with their respective social studies departments.

The units focused on a range of topics including the events leading up to the bombing of Pearl Harbor; reasons for the internment on the continental U.S. as well as in Hawaii; the short- and long-term economic, political, and social repercussions of the internment; and the military involvement of Japanese American soldiers in the 442nd Regimental Combat Team. A constructivist, inquiry-based approach framed the lessons: students were involved in scenarios that dealt with the arrest and the interrogation of Japanese Americans and their lives in the camps. The scenarios provoked deep discussions about the reasons for historical actions and the consequences of these acts. Students chose how they wanted to demonstrate their understanding: they could write letters, craft poems, illustrate scenes, create dramas, or develop timelines. Historical empathy was a crucial underlying target for all the lessons. Students gained a thoughtful appreciation of historical events through activities that fostered compassion as well as cognitive engagement. Extending beyond issues of civil liberties, students also tackled a range of topics dealing with social justice and environmental sustainability in today's world. In one instance, students worked on an action plan addressing the global issue of water pollution in Third World countries. Unwilling to limit themselves to a plan on paper, the students created their own campaign to raise funds for an international clean water project. They publicized the project using posters distributed in the community and held a bake sale that netted several hundred dollars.

---

28. Ibid., 36.

The JCCH volunteers also conducted training workshops on several islands. Two teachers, who had used the curriculum units in their classrooms, participated in these sessions. They described what they had done and how the students responded. Workshop participants responded positively to these shared classroom experiences and the student work samples provided.

Phase 4: Place-Based Learning
In 2011-2012, the JCCH formed an alliance with the National Park Service to launch tours of the Honouliuli internment site. Some of the tours were conducted for the public by the National Park Service. With funds from the Japanese American Confinement Sites grant program, the JCCH offered special tours for teachers, librarians, and students. The grant was used to subsidize bus transportation for over 800 students, teachers, and librarians from twelve public and private high schools to participate in tours of Pearl Harbor as well as Honouliuli.[29] These students had already studied the JCCH units and the tours served as extended enrichment experiences.

Serving as tour guides, the JCCH volunteers engaged the school groups in exploring the remnants of the camp that included the shells of a few wooden buildings, segments of rock walls and fences, concrete slabs where the mess hall had stood, and post holes indicating where the guard towers had once been situated. The volunteers augmented this on-site experience with displays of photographs and maps as well as excerpts from stories and poems written by the internees. The volunteers noted,

> Although the site looks very different from the World War II period, upon being engulfed in the isolation, heat, humidity, and mosquitoes, the sense of place of what the internees called *"Jigoku Dani"* (Hell Valley) became very real to them [school children], not just something out of a textbook.[30]

---

29. Ibid.
30. Ibid.

Importantly, students capitalized on this experience as a springboard to examine other issues of human rights and social justice in their local communities. Some of the exemplary outcomes were showcased at a culminating event held at the JCCH in April 2013. In one example, students attending a school near a large homeless community created a short film that documented a tour of the homeless site located on a beach and featured interviews with the leaders of that community. The film left viewers feeling new empathy for the young homeless parents when they described themselves as "houseless" and not "homeless" because they were still together as families.

Phase 5: Continuing Outreach and Virtual Expansion
In the last few years, the JCCH volunteers have continued to publicize the resources available to the schools and have conducted workshops for teachers and librarians throughout the state. Some schools have also taken advantage of the tours available in the JCCH Historical Gallery and the Honouliuli Education Center. Other schools have invited volunteers to visit their campuses and work directly with the students. Kurahara notes that, since 2014, JCCH volunteers have met and interacted with over 1,300 students in secondary schools. During these classroom sessions, the teams capitalize on firsthand accounts of the internees to make the World War II experiences come alive for teenagers. They perform re-enactments of the arrest and interrogation of the internees and the poignant family visiting days at the camps. By having students read aloud some of the poems written by the internees, the teams find students expressing compassion for the prisoners' lonely and desperate existence.

In 2014, the JCCH assembled and distributed curriculum packets to all public, private, and charter high schools in the state. The packets contained a DVD of the documentary film, "The Untold Story: Internment of Japanese Americans in Hawaii" along with an accompanying lesson. The packet also included the earlier mentioned resource folders with flash drives of the contents, reduced facsimiles of exhibit panels, and copies of the autobiography of Otokichi Muin Ozaki, who was interned at eight different camps in Hawaii and on the continent. The

JCCH developers publicized the packets at teacher institute meetings throughout the state.

While on-site visits have been effective opportunities to work directly with students, the JCCH volunteers are keenly aware that busy teachers and librarians need resources that are accessible at the point of need. Presently, the online repository located at http://www.hawaiiinternment.org/ contains not just the curriculum units and digital copies of the folders, but also an essay on the internment period in Hawaii's history, finding aids, a chronology of the internment, samples of internment-related collections from the Tokioka Heritage Resource Center, and a thirty-minute version of the DVD, "The Untold Story: Internment of Japanese Americans in Hawaii." Discussion is underway about making the website a more interactive venue where teachers and librarians can contribute content and provide feedback. This might involve the creation of a blog that would allow for productive professional exchanges and conversations.

Reflection

The JCCH's major effort in the last twelve years has been to design and implement the various initiatives described in this chapter. At the same time, the volunteers want to devise stronger measures to evaluate the impact of their efforts. As one of the group's leaders, Kurahara acknowledges that data on actual use of the curriculum resources in schools have been limited. A possible strategy for data collection might be more focus group sessions with teachers and librarians. These sessions would aid the JCCH in identifying ways to improve current efforts and to shape future initiatives. In addition, information workshops at state library conferences and the institute days planned by the state teachers' union might provide other opportunities to seek feedback on present and future options.

The volunteers are also realistic about the extent to which teachers have time to use these resources. With the many demands placed on educators to meet curriculum and testing requirements, teachers are hard pressed to devote large portions of class time to single episodes in

U.S. history. For this reason, the volunteers are contemplating how the existing curriculum units might be broken into meaningful segments. Teachers and librarians who are familiar with the resources would serve as invaluable consultants for this purpose.

Final Thoughts

The JCCH partnership with teachers and librarians in Hawaii's schools is a crucial alliance to enlighten students about a neglected chapter in U.S. history. Since Honouliuli has become a national monument, the JCCH has entered into a cooperative agreement with the National Park Service to provide an educational interpretation of the site. The work conducted thus far underscores the importance of studying the past to thoughtfully understand the present and responsibly shape actions for the future. One of the students, who studied the plight of the internees and visited the Honouliuli site, wrote the following letter to the editor to the *Honolulu Star-Advertiser* on March 14, 2013:

> Seeing the remnants of the building [at Honouliuli] and hearing true stories of families who went through this traumatic experience taught me that we must stand up to social injustices. As American citizens, we are promised many things through the Constitution, but the most important thing we are promised is our freedom. Let my generation never force its citizens into situations where their rights to freedom are completely forgotten. May my generation never make these same mistakes.[31]

By putting human faces on our nation's history, the JCCH alliance with schools sends the message that history will continue to repeat itself unless we tell the real stories and stand up to racism and bigotry wherever it exists.

Acknowledgments

The authors wish to acknowledge the JCCH volunteers who have contributed countless hours to the various initiatives mentioned in this

---

31. Keala Parker-Lee, letter to the editor, *Honolulu Star Advertiser*, March 13, 2013.

chapter. In alphabetical order, they are: Penny Atcheson, Ann Berman, Lester Goto, Randolph Hara, Linda Harada, Tatsumi Hayashi, Marilyn Higashide, Cheryl Humiston, Melvin Inamasu, Katherine Kiyabu, Gale Kobayashi, Lloyd Nakamura, Ellen Okazaki, John Okutani, Claire Sato, Amy Shimomura, Ella Tomita, and Betsy Young. The authors extend special thanks to Brian Niiya, who served as JCCH staff member and program director for many of these initiatives, and to Carole Hayashino, president and executive director of the JCCH, for her tireless efforts in seeking funding for these various projects.

Bibliography

Burton, Jeffery F., and Mary M. Farrell. "World War II Japanese Internment Sites in Hawaii." Tucson, AZ: Trans-Sierran Archaeological Research, 2007. http://www.densho.org/assets/media/Burton-HawaiiInternmentSitesOverview2007.pdf .

Burton, Jeffery F., Mary M. Farrell, Lisa Kaneko, Linda Maldonato and Kelley Altenhofen. "Hell Valley: Uncovering a Prison Camp in Paradise." *Social Process in Hawaii* 45 (2014): 43-79.

Commission on Wartime Relocation Internment of Civilians, United States. *Personal Justice Denied.* Seattle, WA: University of Washington Press, 1997.

Gordon, Robert K. "Casualties of History." *New Republic* 189 (1983): 11-14.

Hawaii State Department of Education and Board of Education. "Strategic Plan 2017-2020." Accessed May 29, 2017. http://www.hawaiipublicschools.org/DOE%20Forms/Advancing%20Education/SP2017-20.pdf.

Japanese Cultural Center of Hawaii. "History." Accessed May 29, 2017. https://www.jcch.com/history.

___. "Honouliuli Education Center." Accessed May 29, 2017. https://www.jcch.com/honouliuli-education-center.

___. "Tokioka Heritage Resource Center." Accessed May 29, 2017. https://www.jcch.com/tokioka-heritage-resource-center.

Kurahara, Jane, Brian Niiya, and Betsy Young. "Finding Honouliuli: The Japanese Cultural Center of Hawaii and Preserving the Hawaii Internment Story." *Social Process in Hawaii*, 45 (2014): 16-42.

National Park Service. *Honouliuli Gulch and Associated Sites: Final Special Resource Study and Environmental Assessment.* Washington, D.C.: United States Department of the Interior, 2015.

Parker-Lee, Keala. "Letters to the Editor." *Honolulu Star Advertiser*, March 13, 2013.

The White House, Office of the Press Secretary. "Presidential Proclamation—Establishment of the Honouliuli National Monument." Last modified February 24, 2015. https://obamawhitehouse.archives.gov/the-press-office/2015/02/24/presidential-proclamation-establishment-honouliuli-national-monument.

Case Study 8

FROM CAMPUS TO COMMUNITY: MAKING THE CASE FOR OPEN ACCESS BY BRINGING NONPROFITS TO ACADEMIC LIBRARIES

Rachel Caldwell, Melanie Allen, Ann Viera, and Alan Wallace

Abstract

Every October since 2009, many (mostly academic) libraries around the world celebrate Open Access (OA) Week to improve awareness and adoption of open access publishing. At the University of Tennessee (UT) Libraries, which serves two campuses in Knoxville with a combined 1,531 faculty and 5,913 graduate students, low attendance at campus OA Week events was discouraging to librarians. In summer 2016, fall 2016, and spring 2017, UT Libraries offered workshops for nonprofit organizations in the Knoxville community. After the workshops, participants were invited for brief, on-camera interviews in which they were asked about why public access to research matters. This case study will present the development of the workshop, how the workshop changed over the course of a year, responses from campus partners to the videos presenting nonprofit organizations' research needs, participants' feedback from the workshops, and future plans for this outreach. It will, overall, demonstrate how academic libraries can contribute to building productive relationships between campuses and larger communities, and simultaneously provide campus researchers with compelling, personal reasons to advocate for open access.

Introduction

Who is the audience for scholarly research in the form of peer-reviewed articles? Academic researchers mainly write for other researchers in their discipline, but their findings could help many people outside of academia make more informed decisions using data and evidence.[1] Unfortunately, access to academic journals is a privilege for a limited audience, since much of the research literature is reserved for those affiliated with institutions that pay subscriptions to scholarly journals.

In response to this inequity, the Open Access (OA) movement has encouraged scholarly authors to publish openly rather than in journals available only behind a subscription paywall. In particular, during Open Access Week—an annual celebration organized by the Association of Research Libraries' Scholarly Publishing and Academic Resource Coalition (SPARC)—academic librarians are especially encouraged to plan events related to the benefits of open publishing.[2] However, these librarian-led programs targeting faculty and graduate students typically reach only a small number of authors on any given campus.

Recent OA Week promotions at the national level have incorporated videos with personal stories of what non-academics can do when they have access to research. For example, one of SPARC's promotional videos featured high school student Jack Andraka, who developed a new diagnostic tool after comparing many peer-reviewed articles on pancreatic cancer.[3] With this approach in mind, a group of librarians at the University of Tennessee (UT), led by their scholarly communication librarian, decided to focus their OA Week outreach efforts on local nonprofit organizations (NPOs), inviting NPO staff to participate

---

1. Jillian West and Stephanie Chernitskiy, "Turning Research into Action: A Dialogue with Decision-Makers (Part One)," *Policies for Action* (May 16, 2017), http://www.policiesforaction.org/blog/turning-research-into-action-a-dialogue-decision-makers-part-one.

2. Scholarly Publishing and Academic Resources Coalition, "International Open Access Week," accessed April 24, 2017, http://www.openaccessweek.org.

3. Scholarly Publishing and Academic Resources Coalition, "How Open Access Empowered a 16-Year-Old to Make a Cancer Breakthrough," accessed June 23, 2017, http://www.openaccessweek.org/video/how-open-access-empowered-a-16-year-old-to-make-cancer-breakthrou.

in a workshop called Accessing Academic Research (AAR). NPOs learned how to search for and access academic research and, at the end of the workshop, participants were invited to share their own stories of how access to research matters to their organization and clients. Librarians plan to use these stories in training events, newsletters, and campus outreach materials, presenting research authors with compelling local narratives about the value of open access.

Background

Academic libraries in the United States have a long record of outreach to off-campus community groups broadly defined.[4] Stangl notes that "elements of outreach exist in early discussions," citing a symposium held in 1967.[5] Schneider finds evidence of outreach as far back as 1958 and states that "the principles of librarianship have endured over the years; issues of access to information, responsibility of the academy to the public, and creating useful partnerships continue to play a large role in our profession."[6]

These principles were present in the AAR workshops offered by librarians with assistance from students in the School of Information Sciences (SIS) at the University of Tennessee (UT). Since 2016, UT librarians have offered three stand-alone workshops for NPOs in Knox County and surrounding communities in East Tennessee. Librarians covered the following topics:

---

4. Tina Schneider, "Outreach: Why, How and Who? Academic Libraries and their Involvement in the Community," *Reference Librarian* 39 (2004): 199-213; Nancy Courtney, ed., *Academic Library Outreach: Beyond the Campus Walls* (Westport, CT: Libraries Unlimited, 2009); William Miller and Rita M. Pellen, eds., *Libraries Beyond Their Institutions: Partnerships that Work* (Binghamton, NY: Haworth Press, 2006).

In anticipation of more research in this area, we created a Zotero public group with all the citations from our literature reviews for this chapter: https://www.zotero.org/groups/librariesandnonprofits.

5. Angela M. Stangl, "Academic Library Outreach: A Framework," Paper presented at the annual meeting for the BOBCATSS Symposium, Barcelona, Spain, January 29-31, 2014, https://proceedings.bobcatsss2014.hb.se/article/view/302.

6. Schnieder, Tina.

- An introduction to peer-reviewed literature and subscription databases
- An overview of open access, paywalls, and subscription access
- Strategies for searching library databases, such as building a good search string with keywords, finding synonyms, and identifying academic jargon and subject headings
- Domain-searches in web browsers for finding data and government reports
- Google Scholar
- Access options for participants after the workshop

During the workshop, time was reserved for one-on-one research consultations with librarians. Participants were also notified that they may request up to twenty articles from journals to which the library has a subscription in the six months following the workshop, provided at no cost to the NPOs. At the end of the workshop, participants were invited to take part in brief, video-recorded interviews about their thoughts on public access to research.

The AAR workshop was similar to two NPO-centered academic library outreach efforts reported in the library literature, though at least one researcher over a decade ago anticipated that many more academic libraries might offer such programs.[7] Given the size of the nonprofit sector, similarities between libraries and nonprofits, the commitment of universities to measure community engagement, the longstanding breadth and depth of partnerships between different types of libraries, and the education needs of nonprofit professionals and of library school students, evidence of only two other outreach efforts seems low. This may indicate that academic library outreach to nonprofits in an orchestrated manner is under-reported.

---

7. Roger Durbin and Jo Ann Calzonetti, "Academic Meets Corporate: Science and Technology Library Services in the Corporate World," *Science & Technology Libraries* 24 (2003): 73-86; Romelia Salinas and Richard Chabrán, "Preparing Ethnic Non-profits for the 21st Century," in *Libraries Beyond their Institutions: Partnerships that Work* (Binghamton, NY: Haworth Press, 2005), 121-136; Russell A. Cargo, "Made for Each Other: Nonprofit Management Education, Online Technology, and Libraries," *Journal of Academic Librarianship* 26 (2000): 15-20.

This supposition is substantiated to a degree by two recent cases of nonprofit outreach by academic librarians. In 2016, the library at Simon Fraser University and a Canadian foundation sought to "provide leaders in charitable and non-profit organizations in British Columbia with access to the latest research and knowledge in their fields" via a pilot called the Community Scholars Program.[8] And in 2017, Crumpton and Bird reported preliminary results from two studies for the project Real Learning Connections.[9] The project trains library and information science (LIS) students to serve as bridges between libraries and NPOs while also refreshing librarian practitioner skills.

In one of the Real Learning Connections studies titled "What Do Community Organizations Need from Libraries?", students interviewed NPO staff to answer this research question: "How can libraries engage with other community organizations, especially nonprofits, to support their needs with the unique skills offered by librarians?" Five skills NPOs identified as needs with which libraries could help included "teaching research skills."[10] Crumpton and Bird conclude that "deeper research could further explore the opportunities and benefits of library/nonprofit collaboration."[11]

Similarly to Crumpton and Bird, an important partner in UT's AAR workshops was the group of SIS students who assisted library workshop leaders. Though students have had only an informal role in the workshops to date, a group of SIS students will have the opportunity to commit to involvement over the course of a year starting in fall 2017. For their culminating project, these students will lead drop-in

---

8. Simon Fraser University Library, "The Community Scholars Program," last modified June 15, 2017, http://www.lib.sfu.ca/about/overview/services-you/community-scholars.

9. Michael Crumpton and Nora Bird, "Connecting Libraries and Learning with Community Organizational Needs," presented at the Annual Meeting of the Association for Library and Information Science Education Conference, Atlanta, Georgia, January 18, 2017, https://libres.uncg.edu/ir/uncg/f/M_Crumpton_Connecting_2017.pdf.

10. Ibid.

11. Ibid.

sessions for NPOs that have previously participated in a workshop and seek further research consultations.

Additional AAR partners included the university library and NPOs. UT is a land-grant university with a library system made up of three campus libraries serving approximately 28,000 students and over 1,500 faculty.[12] Distinct from Memphis in the western part of the state and Nashville in the center, Knoxville is an Appalachian community in East Tennessee. NPOs in East Tennessee serve a community of thirty-three counties, 21% of which are considered economically "distressed" counties and 40% of which are economically "at-risk" counties, though Knox County and most of its immediate neighboring counties are considered economically "transitional" counties.[13] The land-grant mission of the university and the economic conditions of East Tennessee make both outreach to NPOs and advocacy for open access to research a natural fit for the university library.

Case

The AAR workshop had two objectives: to demonstrate how academic libraries can contribute to building productive relationships between campus and the larger community, and to provide university researchers with compelling reasons to share their work openly.

The first objective is in support of UT's quality enhancement plan (QEP), which focuses on experiential learning. The QEP involves students in projects and "useful partnerships" that solve a real-world problem or directly affect a community, typically mediated through a credit-bearing course.[14] With renewed campus attention on community

---

12. The University of Tennessee, Knoxville, Office of Institutional Research and Assessment, "UTK 2016-17 Fact Book," https://oira.utk.edu/factbook/admissions.

13. Tennessee. Department of State, "The Three Grand Divisions," in *Tennessee Blue Book 2013-2014* (Nashville, TN: Secretary of State, 2013): 625, http://www.tennessee.gov/sos/bluebook/; Appalachia Regional Commission, "County Economic Status and Distressed Areas per County in the Appalachian Region, FY 2017," https://www.arc.gov/appalachian_region/CountyEconomicStatusandDistressedAreasinAppalachia.asp.

14. The University of Tennessee, Knoxville, "Experience Learning," accessed June 23, 2017, http://experiencelearning.utk.edu/.

engagement, the main goal falling under this objective was to introduce regional NPOs to resources at a large academic library that can help them achieve their goals. From delivering client programs to interacting with a board of trustees to reviewing volunteer applicants, evidence-based practices can affect an NPO's success and the lives of those it serves. So, the AAR workshop introduced ways to access evidence found in peer-reviewed articles, case studies, data sets, and so on.

In addition to facilitating university engagement with the community, the AAR workshop also supported the service learning aspect of the QEP. Though not tied to course credit, SIS students involved in the workshop helped organize the events and observed reference interview skills in the field, helping prepare them for LIS careers by observing and assisting in librarian-community interactions.

The workshop's second objective supported the library's scholarly communication efforts on campus: to create a program for OA Week that librarians considered worth the investment of their time and energy. Since 2009, many (mostly academic) libraries around the world celebrate OA Week in October to advocate for open access publishing as well as open archiving in repositories—including both disciplinary repositories, such as *arXiv* for physicists, and institutional repositories, such as the University of California's *eScholarship*.[15] While the number of libraries participating in OA Week has grown exponentially, the workshops, presentations, tabling, and other outreach efforts in which librarians invest significant time often result in a low return on investment.[16]

Despite low turn-out at OA events in past years, UT librarians' interest in offering an OA Week program remained high. After experimenting for several years with different styles of faculty engagement on OA issues, librarians decided to turn their attention from authors to readers. In doing so, campus authors might learn how a lack of access to research impacts people outside of academia in the words of those who

---

15. Heather Joseph, "The Open Access Movement Grows Up: Taking Stock of a Revolution," *PLoS Biology* 11, no. 10 (2013).

16. Ibid.; Paula C. Johnson, "International Open Access Week at Small to Medium U.S. Academic Libraries: The First Five Years," *Journal of Academic Librarianship* 40 (2014): 626-631.

directly experience it, rather than from second- or third-hand accounts, which research shows are less persuasive.[17]

The goals falling under this objective were:

- to interview participating NPOs about the lack of access to academic research journals,
- to record and incorporate their stories into a promotional campaign intended to influence and encourage campus researchers to publish or archive their research results openly, and
- to share the stories with liaison librarians, providing them anecdotes to include in outreach and reference interviews.

These objectives were designed to benefit all partners reciprocally. NPO staff gained continuing education in research skills and were introduced to librarians to add to their support network, regardless of whether they agreed to a recorded interview or not. The university and its library were seen as partners sharing resources to help community organizations and leaders improve the lives of vulnerable and disenfranchised East Tennesseeans. SIS students gained experience relevant to future careers, and librarians collected evidence of community research needs to support the case for open access.

Stakeholders

The scholarly communication librarian designed the workshop with the input and support of liaison librarians serving disciplines with a strong public service element: education, public health and nursing, and veterinary medicine. These liaisons often field questions related to open publishing and also advocate for open access, due in part to access-related questions they receive from former students who lose

---

17. Joanne R. Cantor, Herminia Alfonso, and Dolf Zillman, "The Persuasive Effectiveness of the Peer Appeal and a Communicator's First-Hand Experience," *Communication Research* 3 (1976): 293-310.

subscription privileges after graduation. Librarians considered the workshop an outreach approach worth exploring and recognized its potential to lead to greater engagement with the community.

Buy-in was needed from library administration and nonprofit agencies in the community. Librarians asked for the administration's support by tying the event to the library's then-developing five-year strategic plan. Amidst library-wide discussions about goals and priorities, the workshop supported several important initiatives, including advocating for open scholarship and improving community awareness of the library's (and university's) contributions to the region. Perhaps with these goals in mind, and following a long-standing tradition of community outreach from the library, library administration supported the program by providing space, staff resources, and lunch for workshop participants.[18]

Central to the workshop organizers' goals was shifting the notion of audience away from campus and towards the community. This required additional librarian preparation because workshop participants were community members working at and leading NPOs, with needs distinct from the library's typical audience of faculty and students. Preparation included anticipating the kinds of research findings NPOs would find most valuable (**Table 1**). The region struggles with interrelated issues commonly found throughout Appalachia: high rates of opioid abuse, greater incidences of lifestyle diseases (e.g., tobacco-related diseases), a lack of access to healthcare, levels of educational attainment below the national average, and so on. Thus, the involvement of the public health liaison and education liaison was key to a successful workshop.

---

18. Thura Mack, Ingrid Ruffin, and Nicole Barajas, "Beyond BOSS: A Blueprint for STEM Engagement, Student Recruitment and Outreach," *Tennessee Libraries* 64, no. 4 (2014), http://www.tnla.org/?page=TL64_4_STEM; Mark Patrick Baggett, Anne Bridges, Ken Wise, Sarah Tanner, and Jennifer Mezick, "Populating the Wilderness: Crowdsourcing Database of the Smokies," *Library Hi Tech* 32 (2014): 249-259; Barbara I. Dewey, "Through Any Means Available: Connecting People with Scholarship," *Journal of Library Administration* 49 (2009): 533-544.

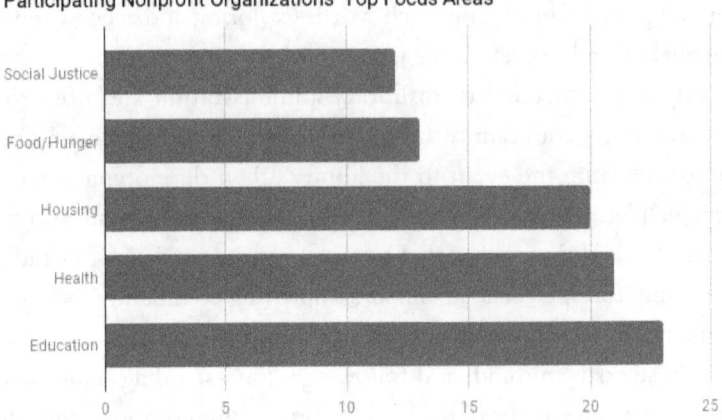

Table 1. Pre-Workshop Survey Responses: Organizational Focus

NPOs received invitations and promotional materials that emphasized the relevance of the workshop to finding research that could be applied to grant proposals, client services, and organizational management. This approach seemed to be effective, as evidenced by the number of participants at the workshop (see "Reflection").

Campus researchers were another group with potential interest in one of the workshop outcomes. Buy-in from this group remains uncertain. One hope is that exit interviews between librarians and NPOs, once shared with the researchers, will persuade authors to consider the relevance of their work to readers beyond institutions of higher education and, in turn, participate more often in open publishing or open archiving in repositories. Videos are currently in the editing phase and have not been distributed to campus.

Intervention

NPOs registered one or two staff members for the workshop, with spaces limited to the first twenty-four applicants. A total of three stand-alone workshops were offered over the course of a year. The first was a two-hour pilot program held in the afternoon. The second and third workshops lasted five hours each, starting in the morning with lunch provided.

Because most of the library's license agreements permit unaffiliated researchers to access subscription databases only while on campus from a library IP address, participants were encouraged to visit the library after the workshop. But the library also offered participants up to twenty articles delivered to individuals for their own research purposes in the six months following the workshop. This makes the pro-gram relevant as both an annual OA Week program and an annual Fair Use Week program. Since 2015, the Association of Research Libraries has encouraged week-long celebrations of Fair Use every February.[19]

Methods for inviting NPOs expanded over the course of the three workshops. Participants in the summer 2016 pilot were identified and invited through two umbrella organizations associated with the university's annual giving campaign, the United Way of Greater Knoxville and Community Shares. In the subsequent fall and spring, invitations were also sent via direct emails, announcements sent to the Alliance for Better Nonprofits (a local organization focused on training and supporting NPOs), and messages sent to local community networks through social networking sites, such as Facebook.

As part of the second and third workshops, attendees were invited to participate in an optional interview held directly after the workshop. (It should be noted that, as part of the registration process, participants were informed that photography may occur at the event and were thus more likely to participate in recorded interviews). Interviewing was strictly voluntary and not a condition for attending the workshop. Staff in The Studio, a media production lab in the library, helped record the interviews. Each interview lasted less than ten minutes.

Interviewees were asked the following questions:

---

19. Association of Research Libraries, "Fair Use/Fair Dealing Week," accessed June 23, 2017, http://fairuseweek.org.

- In a nutshell, what does your organization do?
- Does your organization have a need to access research? If so, for what purposes?
- Before today, how and where have you searched for research findings?
- Have you ever had trouble accessing research findings?
- Knowing that researchers have the option to publish openly, imagine that there is a professor listening to you right now. What would you want to say to that professor about open access publishing?

The resulting videos will be distributed as part of an open access awareness campaign in Fall 2017 and beyond.

Reflection

Attendance numbers suggest the workshop fulfills a continuing education need for training to find and access research. A total of twenty-five organizations and thirty-six individuals have participated over three workshops. Two participants that attended the second workshop sent another colleague from their organization to the third workshop.

Though open access was one aspect of the program, the demonstrated tools and research skills were not focused only on UT-subscription databases. This is notable because, by a show of hands, over half of the participants in each session were unfamiliar with the statewide library resource *Tennessee Electronic Library*, which provides access to some subscription databases free of charge to anyone with an IP address in the state. Furthermore, domain searches limited to state- and federal-government sources were also not known by a majority of participants.

Prior to the workshop, participants provided information about their organizations and their expected outcomes in the online registration process. After the workshop, librarians sent participants a post-workshop survey, which elicited feedback and quotes that 1) have helped improve the workshop and 2) may be used for OA advocacy in addition to the videos. Based on feedback, librarians have increased the time allotted for taking sample research questions from participants to demonstrate search skills and strategies to the group. Participants were also given several copies of a handout with a link to the library guide designed for them, and librarians have taught exclusively from the guide.[20] In ten months, the guide has been viewed nearly 600 times.

NPO participants reported that they were immediately able to put into practice what they learned in order to improve their organization's professional efficiency, services to clients, and grant proposals; however, only two participants have asked for copies of articles from librarians after the workshop, and four participants have reached out to librarians with additional questions. It is difficult to say if this means that NPOs are having success in their searches and in contacting authors directly for a copy of a research article, or if they are making do with what they find.

Survey responses (n=26) indicate that 69% of participants found the workshop's greatest value to be working with and learning from librarians directly, with 35% specifically mentioning the hands-on nature of the workshop or time for one-on-one consultations as the most valuable aspects. Also valuable was learning how to use tools other than a simple Google search to find resources and/or how to access these tools as non-UT-affiliated members of the community (38%). Former UT students, once with full access to university library resources, have been among the participants. Their responses indicate a new awareness that access to peer-reviewed research is not equitable. One participant (not a former student), wrote in an email to organizers that he is more aware of the issues involved in academic publishing as a result of the workshop and, "anything to help return control to the authors is worth time and effort toward accomplishing."

Six individuals participated in the optional recorded interviews (17%). Each one gave the library excellent material for videos promoting open access. Once the videos are distributed, authors' interest in openly archiving their research in the institutional repository, Tennessee Research and Creative Exchange (TRACE), may or may not increase as

---

20. University of Tennessee Libraries, "Accessing Academic Research: For East Tennessee Nonprofits," last modified May 23, 2017, http://libguides.utk.edu/nonprofits.

a result of the campaign. However, draft videos have been shared with liaison librarians, many of whom were not part of the workshop. The drafts have been well-received and equipped liaisons with both anecdotes and evidence about the importance of public access to research.

Participants also provided written quotes in their post-survey responses that could be useful in OA advocacy, such as:

- Access to research is "critically important for implementing effective prevention programming."
- "Researchers and authors need to [consider] where they place their potentially valuable and life-improving research and information.... We cannot use it if we don't have access to it!"
- "As a nonprofit, we want to utilize research to drive us to best practices. However, it is difficult if the research that applies to our work is hidden behind paywalls!"
- Open access "is so helpful for non-profits with few employees and low budgets, doing research for grants and presentations [to Boards] for new programs."
- "Grant applications using the most recent data and peer-reviewed best practices may have a better chance of approval. Access to this research also enables applicants to ensure they're on the right track with program planning."
- "Open access publishing is an opportunity for everyone to learn about the research you do."
- "Open access is helpful to allow communities to make real-world application of University research. Please help further open the doors to access."

The library may take some of these quotes and incorporate them into presentations and the homepage of the university's open repository, similar to Harvard's use of community feedback to promote Digital Access to Scholarship at Harvard (DASH), their institutional repository. Harvard Library's Office for Scholarly Communication asked readers who accessed an article or other research document in the repository to leave a comment about what access to scholarly research means to them (**Figure 1**).

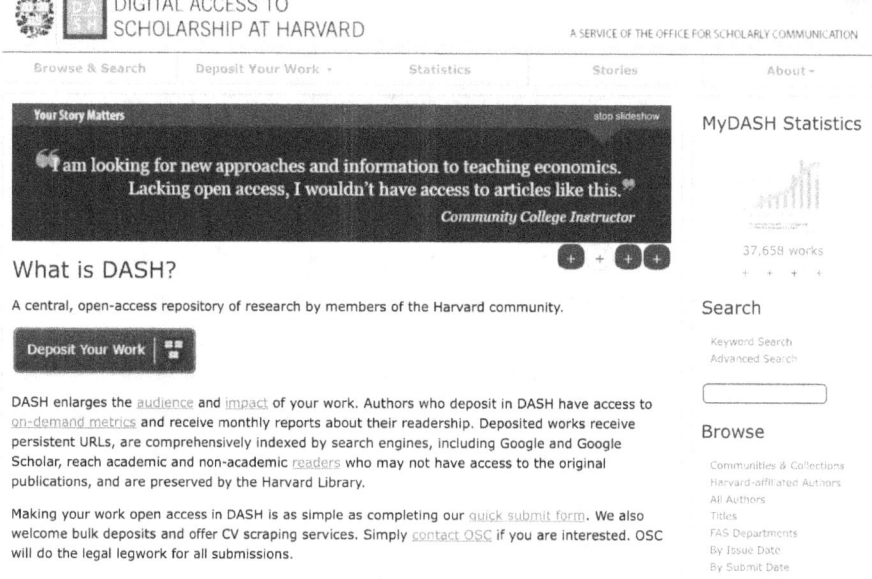

Figure 1. Homepage of Harvard University's institutional repository (https://dash.harvard.edu), featuring quotes from repository users.

Videos are compelling, easy to share, and the expected medium for advocacy in today's media-rich environment. By enlisting the expertise of staff at The Studio in the library, the librarians ensured that high-quality recording of comments was easy and quick for workshop participants willing to be recorded. However, capturing comments to promote open access as Harvard does might be more sustainable due to the effort involved in video post-production tasks.

In whatever way feedback is shared with campus in the future, the participants' enthusiasm for the workshops, and evidence that the workshop benefits the community and addresses a research need, have made the return on investment worthwhile to librarians who plan to continue the program for both OA Week and Fair Use Week for the foreseeable future. Though it is too early to know if there will be any change in campus authors' behaviors after hearing the NPOs' stories, the workshops have brought more of an audience to the library than any other single previous OA Week outreach effort. Furthermore, all survey respondents (100%) indicated that they would "definitely recommend" the AAR workshop to other NPOs, indicating both success and a potential future audience.

There are also early signs of campus support for the workshop's goals. The library was awarded a small internal grant in 2017 to support LIS student involvement. Librarians expect that a cohort of five to ten LIS students will commit to approximately twenty-five hours of involvement over the academic year, first observing, then shadowing, and finally leading drop-in sessions for NPO participants seeking individual research assistance after the workshop. Librarians will lead several training sessions for these students as part of the program.

Long-term assessment goals include measuring any impact of the training on services offered by NPOs, grants awarded, interactions with an NPO's board of trustees, and so on. After the NPOs' recorded interviews are shared on campus, the scholarly communication librarian will investigate possible correlations in the number of faculty research deposits to the institution's open repository, and the number of applications to the open access publishing fund (where faculty request the university to cover the article processing charges that some open access journals charge), before and after the campaign. Feedback from SIS students will also be collected to improve their experience. Finally, in preparation for upcoming workshops, librarians aim to implement best practices in adult learning to improve outcomes for workshop participants.

Bibliography

Appalachia Regional Commission. "County Economic Status and Distressed Areas per County in the Appalachian Region, FY 2017." Accessed June 23, 2017. https://www.arc.gov/appalachian_region/CountyEconomicStatusandDistressedAreasinAppalachia.asp.

Association of Research Libraries. "Fair Use/Fair Dealing Week." Accessed June 23, 2017. http://fairuseweek.org.

Baggett, Mark Patrick, Anne Bridges, Ken Wise, Sarah Tanner, and Jennifer Mezick. "Populating the Wilderness: Crowdsourcing Database of the Smokies." *Library Hi Tech* 32 (2014): 249-259. doi: 10.1108/LHT-11-2013-0150.

Cantor, Joanne R., Herminia Alfonso, and Dolf Zillman. "The Persuasive Effectiveness of the Peer Appeal and a Communicator's First-Hand Experience." *Communication Research* 3 (1976): 293-310. doi: 10.1177/009365027600300304.

Cargo, Russell A. "Made for Each Other: Nonprofit Management Education, Online Technology, and Libraries." *Journal of Academic Librarianship* 26 (2000): 15-20.

Crumpton, Michael, and Nora Bird. "Connecting Libraries and Learning with Community Organizational Needs." Paper presented at the Annual Meeting of the Association for Library and Information Science Education Conference, Atlanta, Georgia, January 18, 2017. https://libres.uncg.edu/ir/uncg/f/M_Crumpton_Connecting_2017.pdf.

Courtney, Nancy, ed., *Academic Library Outreach: Beyond the Campus Walls*. Westport, CT: Libraries Unlimited, 2009.

Dewey, Barbara I. "Through Any Means Available: Connecting People with Scholarship." *Journal of Library Administration* 49 (2009): 533-544. doi: 10.1080/01930820903090912.

Durbin, Roger, and Jo Ann Calzonetti. "Academic Meets Corporate: Science and Technology Library Services in the Corporate World." *Science & Technology Libraries* 24 (2003): 73-86. doi: 10.1300/J122v24n01_06.

Johnson, Paula C. "International Open Access Week at Small to Medium U.S. Academic Libraries: The First Five Years." *Journal of Academic Librarianship* 40 (2014): 626-631. doi: 10.1016/j.acalib.2014.07.011.

Joseph, Heather. "The Open Access Movement Grows Up: Taking Stock of a Revolution." *PLoS Biology* 11, no. 10 (2013). doi: 10.1371/journal.pbio.1001686.

Mack, Thura, Ingrid Ruffin, and Nicole Barajas. "Beyond BOSS: A Blueprint for STEM Engagement, Student Recruitment and Outreach." *Tennessee Libraries* 64, no. 4 (2014). http://www.tnla.org/?page=TL64_4_STEM.

Miller, William, and Rita M. Pellen, eds. *Libraries Beyond Their Institutions: Partnerships that Work* Binghamton, NY: Haworth Press, 2006.

Salinas, Romelia, and Richard Chabrán. "Preparing Ethnic Non-profits for the 21st Century." In *Libraries Beyond their Institutions: Partnerships that Work*, 121-136. Binghamton, NY: Haworth Press, 2005.

Scholarly Publishing and Academic Resources Coalition. "How Open Access Empowered a 16-Year-Old to Make a Cancer Breakthrough." Accessed June 23, 2017. http://www.openaccessweek.org/video/how-open-access-empowered-a-16-year-old-to-make-cancer-breakthrou.

Scholarly Publishing and Academic Resources Coalition. "International Open Access Week." Accessed April 24, 2017. http://www.openaccessweek.org.

Schneider, Tina. "Outreach: Why, How and Who? Academic Libraries and their Involvement in the Community." *Reference Librarian* 39 (2004): 199-213.

Simon Fraser University Library. "The Community Scholars Program." Last modified June 15, 2017, http://www.lib.sfu.ca/about/overview/services-you/community-scholars.

Stangl, Angela M. "Academic Library Outreach: A Framework." Paper presented at the Annual Meeting of the BOBCATSS Symposium, Barcelona, Spain, January 29-31, 2014. https://proceedings.bobcatsss2014.hb.se/article/view/302.

Tennessee. Department of State. "The Three Grand Divisions." In *Tennessee Blue Book 2013-2014*, 625. Nashville, TN: Secretary of State, 2013. http://www.tennessee.gov/sos/bluebook/.

University of Tennessee, Knoxville. "Experience Learning." Accessed June 23, 2017. http://experiencelearning.utk.edu/.

University of Tennessee, Knoxville, Office of Institutional Research and Assessment. "UTK 2016-17 Fact Book." https://oira.utk.edu/factbook/admissions.

University of Tennessee Libraries. "Accessing Academic Research: For East Tennessee Nonprofits." Last modified May 23, 2017. http://libguides.utk.edu/nonprofits.

West, Jillian, and Stephanie Chernitskiy. "Turning Research into Action: A Dialogue with Decision-Makers (Part One)." *Policies for Action* (May 16, 2017). http://www.policiesforaction.org/blog/turning-research-into-action-a-dialogue-decision-makers-part-one.

Case Study 9

COLLABORATING ON SCIENCE PROGRAMMING

Tracy Englert

Abstract

By partnering with informal science education agencies such as Public Broadcasting Service's NOVA ScienceNOW and Nanoscale Informal Science Education Network, I have been able to provide diverse and valuable learning experiences for university faculty, students, staff, and community, as well as promote and enrich the library's resources.

I have been successful in identifying, initiating, and forming new partnerships by looking to organizations outside of academia to enrich the opportunities available to those within academia and to create bridges that connect the university to the outside world in significant ways. Specifically, these partnerships have been with the nonprofit informal science education organizations: Public Broadcasting Service's (PBS) NOVA ScienceNOW, and The Nanoscale Informal Science Education Network (NISE Net). The missions of these non-profit agencies are akin to libraries; they foster public awareness, engagement, and understanding of science and strengthen scientific literacy.

Overview of Institution and Library

The University of Southern Mississippi (Southern Miss) has approximately 15,000 students and is classified by the Carnegie Foundation as a RU/H: Research University (higher research activity). I am primarily responsible for working as a reference and liaison librarian for the science and technology disciplines in the Joseph Anderson Cook Library. In my areas of job responsibility as the Science & Technology Librarian, I provide curricular and research support through library-based information literacy instruction, reference services, individualized research consultations, and collection development for the College of Science and Technology. This includes Southern Miss's departments of Biological Sciences, Chemistry and Biochemistry, Geography and Geology, Mathematics, Physics and Astronomy, and the schools of Computing, Construction, Criminal Justice, and Polymers and Higher Performance Materials as well as the Center for Science and Mathematics Education.

I am an accidental science librarian and do not have a science background. This has made outreach efforts to science departments particularly problematic and challenging. By partnering with informal science education agencies, I have been able to collaborate with STEM faculty and students in outreach and campus engagement opportunities. This has helped to create and cultivate strong, ongoing campus relationships.

Overview of Partner 1:
Public Broadcasting Service's (PBS) NOVA ScienceNOW

PBS is a private, nonprofit corporation founded in 1969, whose members are America's public TV stations. PBS NOVA is the most watched prime time science series on television, and it also produces and supports science programming. This includes producing programs such NOVA ScienceNOW, as well as supporting science cafés throughout the United States by sponsoring the sciencecafes.org website. My partnership with NOVA launched my own foray into science cafés. This successful, ongoing partnership started in 2010 when I was awarded a science café grant from NOVA ScienceNOW to start a science café series. Many of the "Cook Library Science Cafés" have incorporated NOVA ScienceNOW content into their presentations or lectures. I've also been able to enrich the library's resources through the partnership with NOVA by obtaining free NOVA ScienceNOW DVDs which have been added to the library's collection. Many scientific associations and societies sponsor science cafés and I encourage librarians to seek out collaborations with their STEM faculty in applying for grants and materials from these agencies.

During the cafés, held in a casual environment, students, staff, and community members engage in conversations with university faculty about their research and academic innovations. The cafés increase the relevance and visibility of the university in the community. They foster public understanding of and engagement in science and technological subjects. Science Cafés as a form of informal science education serve to enhance the teaching and learning experience of students and increase retention of scientific knowledge.

These events are an opportunity for the scientist to communicate to the public, gain potential students for their classes or labs, and can also serve as a vehicle to meet funding agencies' requirements for dissemination to broader audiences as well as provide evidence of synergistic activities. They are an opportunity for the librarian to link appropriate library and university resources with timely scientific topics and ongoing research at the university. They can also strengthen and support the academic curriculum. At Southern Miss, the science cafés at Cook Library are often listed as mandatory honors college forum events, as well as for extra credit assignments.

In May of 2011, I became a member of the Science Café Advisory Board at PBS NOVA sciencecafes.org. This advisory board was a core group of science café organizers who answered questions and offered feedback, as well as providing a sounding board role. This provided the opportunity to help in evaluation of the Science Café model as an effective mode of informal science education outreach. Our main project was redesigning the sciencecafes.org website and serving in an advisory role for that website, which is an important vehicle for science café information.

I have also taken part in several themed cafés through NOVA ScienceNOW. In 2012, NOVA ScienceNOW began recruiting organizers and speakers for the Innovation Cafés campaign. This was a national Science Café campaign inspired by Making Stuff with David Pogue. Cook Library Science Café was one of forty science cafés selected to host a Making Stuff themed café. Rock the Cafés was a national geology-themed Science Café campaign inspired by "Making North America" with host Kirk Johnson, a three-part television series that aired on PBS in the fall of 2015. Both of these DVD series were gifted to the library and added to the collection following the event. In addition to the DVD's, NOVA ScienceNOW provided promotional materials and door-prizes for the cafés such as themed t-shirts, hats, and coasters.

Overview of Partner 2: Nanoscale Informal Science Education Network (NISE Net)

NISE Net was a major National Science Foundation (NSF) initiative to form a national infrastructure that linked science museums and other informal science education organizations with nanoscale science and engineering research organizations to foster public awareness, engagement, and understanding of nanoscale science, engineering, and technology. It has now, as of February 2017, transitioned to a new, ongoing identity as the National Informal STEM Education Network. The new NISE Network is an informal national community of educators and scientists dedicated to supporting learning about science, technology, engineering, and math (STEM) across the United States.

I have collaborated with the Nanoscale Informal Science Education Network (NISE Net) on several diverse projects. In March of 2014 and 2015, Cook Library hosted a NanoDays Festival. NanoDays is a nationwide festival of educational programs exploring nanoscale science, matter, and engineering and its potential impact on the future. We were one of 250 sites awarded the NanoDays Physical Kit Award for both of those years.

These kits consisted of hands-on activities and programs to engage a public audience in nanoscale science and technology. During the festival, faculty, students, and volunteers provided a variety of hands-on activities from the kits such as exploring kinetic sand, exploring size, exploring materials-Ferrofluid, exploring tools-Dress Up Like a Nanoscientist, exploring materials-Stained-Glass Windows, exploring products-Computer Hard Drives, and exploring materials–Thin Films.

During the festival we also offered a presentation on "Nano Themes in Children's Literature." This was presented by a faculty member in the University of Southern Mississippi's School of Library and Information Science. In addition, colleague Xiaojie Duan and I developed an exhibit of NanoDay materials in the Cook Library Learning Commons Gallery. I hope to one day have these kits cataloged and available for check-out. Currently, I keep them in my office and faculty may request them as needed for outreach and educational purposes. I have also used the materials to facilitate, along with faculty and graduate students, STEM activities with underserved audiences at the local public library during the summer reading program.

In 2014, I further expanded my partnership with NISE Net, and was selected as one of eight participants in the NISE Net Sharing Science workshop (SSW&P), a professional development and training program in nanoscale informal science and education for early career researchers. This all-expense paid training seminar was held at the Museum of Science in Boston, MA, on November 14-16, 2014. I was the only non-museum educator and sole librarian at this event, and it was thrilling to work with students from MIT and Harvard. The best part was getting to interpret science on the floor of the Museum of Science in Boston!

In 2015, I collaborated with Southern Miss faculty from the Department of Chemistry and the School of Library and Information Science, in successfully applying for a mini-grant project ($3000) from NISE Net. The goal of this project was to bring awareness of and inspire interest in nanoscale science to school librarians, and children's book authors and illustrators in an effort to reach new audiences.

We presented a workshop entitled "Nano What?" at the Fay B. Kaigler Children's Book Festival in Hattiesburg, MS, on April 10, 2015. During the workshop, Dr. Guo and Dr. Pigza (Chemistry) presented an overview of basic nanoscience concepts. Dr. Creel, (Library and Information Science) and I discussed and presented appropriate materials, including NISE Net resources, to help school and public librarians develop their library collections and increase science programming with nano-related resources. We also facilitated hands-on activities, appropriate for libraries or classrooms, which helped participants engage with nano concepts.

I continued my collaboration with the chemistry faculty as well as bringing in fellow librarian colleagues on another grant from NISE Network for funds to support hosting a Sharing Science workshop and practicum. On April 15, 2016, NISE Network Sharing Science Workshop & Practicum participants, after receiving training and coaching on communicating to a broader audience, provided an educational activity program on nanoscale materials and properties to Mississippi middle and high school students, teachers, and parents at the Mississippi Science Olympiad. In addition, I fostered a very well-received partnership with the Southern Miss Speaking Center and worked with several doctoral and graduate students in communication studies on hosting the workshop and practicum event.

On September 7, 2016, we had a special science café that was funded in part by the NISE Net grant-funded Synthetic Biology project, which paid for speakers' honoraria and refreshments. This café consisted of a panel discussion about synthetic biology and genetic engineering and the related ethical and societal aspects. This café was held in the Polymer Science Auditorium at Southern Miss; it was the first café that was held outside Cook Library. "We Engineer the Mosquito" included Dr. Sarah E. Morgan, Professor of Polymer Science and Engineering; Dr. Joseph R. Lott, Assistant Professor of Polymer Science and Engineering; Dr. Donald A. Yee, Associate Professor of Biological Sciences; and Dr. Shahid Karim, Associate Professor of Biological Sciences.

The partnership activities that I have undertaken have required a lot of work. I've had to learn how to coordinate a variety of outreach and publicity activities such as booking venues and speakers, writing press releases, appearing on university radio newscasts, writing grant proposals, handling fund codes, writing and submitting grant reports, and dealing with a lot of logistics.

However, students, faculty, staff, and the general public greatly appreciate their experiences at these outreach and education efforts sponsored through Public Broadcasting Service's (PBS) NOVA ScienceNOW and the Nanoscale Informal Science Education Network (NISE Net). I also believe that the role that the University of Southern Mississippi plays in the community has been expanded by my efforts with these programs. The strong partnerships fostered are increasingly being expressed through more requests from faculty for letters of support from University Libraries on external funding proposals involving scientific outreach vehicles such as the science café series. I am certain that my career is substantially more gratifying because I have participated in these education and public outreach activities.

Case Study 10

LIGHTS! CAMERA! ACTION! LIBRARIAN COLLABORATION WITH A SCIENCE FILM FESTIVAL

Amani Magid

Abstract
This case study looks at Science and Engineering Librarian Amani Magid's involvement with the Imagine Science Film Festival Abu Dhabi, which takes place every year on the campus where the librarian works. It will detail the different roles the librarian has played in regards to the Imagine Science Film Festival. Readers will also gain insight through a critical analysis of the librarian roles and the collaboration.

Issues to Be Addressed
Magid was presented with a unique opportunity to become involved in a film festival with a science theme. Yet, how does one integrate involvement with a film festival, no less one with a science theme, with the profession of librarianship? The Science and Engineering Librarian seamlessly combined the two, thereby cementing a new type of collaboration for the library. Film festival involvement has also inspired the librarian to find more ways to incorporate film and videos into her liaison duties.

Overview of Library
New York University Abu Dhabi (NYUAD) is a degree-granting institution located in the city of Abu Dhabi in the United Arab Emirates.

Established in 2010, it is one of two portal campuses of New York University (NYU) in the United States, the other being in Shanghai. It is primarily a liberal arts undergraduate university where students can choose to study in four different departments: Arts and Humanities; Social Research and Public Policy; Science and Engineering.[1] With a current student population of approximately 1,000, this year NYUAD graduated its 4th class.

The NYUAD Library opened its doors the same year that the University began to teach classes, 2010. The library's mission is service to scholars, and this mission is carried out by the myriad programs and resources made available. The library houses 60,000 physical volumes, 100,000 e-journals, 1,135 databases, and over 1.5 million ebooks online. The NYUAD community also has access to over four million titles available at the New York campus of NYU. The computers in the library provide access to over fifty software programs, including statistical, audio and video, and data analysis. In addition, a Special Collections department collects rare and older materials unique to the Middle East, India, and other regional areas of interest. NYUAD is also a collaborator in Arabic Collections Online, which is "a publicly available digital library of public domain Arabic language content."[2]

The NYUAD library boasts a variety of services for its users. Instruction is a cornerstone of its services, as on offer are both standalone workshops on many topics, and in-class workshops specific to the needs of students enrolled in courses. The Center for Digital Scholarship serves the scholarly needs of the community via various technologies and software assistance including data services; geospatial data services; assistance with media used in courses and teaching, and media for preservation; and assistance with enterprise technology tools unique to NYU. In addition to the obvious service of book loans, users may also

---

1. Amani Magid, "'Patenting' a New Engineering Librarian at an American University in the UAE," paper presented at the 123rd American Society Engineering Education Annual Conference and Exposition, New Orleans, LA, 2016.

2. New York University Libraries, *Arabic Collections Online*, accessed June 15, 2017, http://dlib.nyu.edu/aco/.

borrow a variety of technology items including laptops, noise-cancelling headphones, cameras, and more.

Partner Overview: Imagine Science Film Festival Abu Dhabi

Who would believe that one person's frustration could lead to the establishment of what would become a global leader in science film festivals? Dr. Alexis Gambis was frustrated about the lack of access to films about science for the general public. A biologist by training, Gambis developed an interest in film while completing his Ph.D., as there were many visual elements in his study of neurons. He earned a Master's degree in film from NYU's Tisch School of the Arts. One might think that as a scientist, Gambis might be interested in making science documentaries. Although there is some interest in documentaries, his main focus as a filmmaker are films that focus on science, but which may bring a fictional aspect into it; for example, films about the personal life of a scientist along with the science that made them famous. Gambis was bothered by the lack of films that brought that aspect of science to the public. While working at Rockefeller University, he began to screen films to the community and, in 2008, founded the Imagine Science Film Festival in New York City.

Fall 2018 marks the Imagine Science Film Festival's 10th anniversary. It is headquartered in New York City, and many of the New York staff come to Abu Dhabi to set up the local film festival. When Gambis accepted a new position as a professor of biology at NYUAD, he saw a role for the film festival in Abu Dhabi and Imagine Science Film Festival Abu Dhabi was launched in 2015. In line with Gambis' interests, some of the films featured in the festival mix science with fiction, although this doesn't mean that it is science fiction. Other films may fall within the documentary genre or other genres. In addition to New York and Abu Dhabi, the film festival has expanded to Paris. Imagine Science also hosts many satellite film festivals around the world including: Warsaw, Poland; Athens, Greece; San Francisco, California; Quito, Ecuador; Hong Kong, and other locations.

Objectives

Some collaborations can be quite formal. The collaboration between Magid and the Imagine Science Film Festival was very organic, and the idea to collaborate came about in a conversation with Gambis regarding the library's services to the science and engineering community. Because of Magid's interest in video as a medium for teaching and learning about science and engineering topics, she was intrigued with the idea of a film festival focused on science, either as a topic or an underlying theme. Magid viewed this as an opportunity to get involved with an organization that shared similar views. Although no purpose or goal was set in place at the beginning of the collaboration, one goal of the librarian was to demonstrate to the film festival how library resources and the librarian's knowledge of those resources could be used to supplement the festival. This is further detailed in the intervention section.

Intervention

Magid's involvement with the Imagine Science Abu Dhabi Film Festival has varied over the years, starting with the inaugural season in 2015. Library administration has always encouraged librarians to form collaborations with other units on campus. Therefore, it was a natural fit for the Science and Engineering Librarian to team up with a biology professor who organizes a science film festival. Each of the Abu Dhabi festivals have also included an art exhibit with a focus on science. For the 2015 exhibit, Experimental Records, Magid collaborated with one of the (now former) Imagine Science staff from NY, Claire Watson, in creating an exhibit focused on the stereoscope, which is "an optical instrument with two eyepieces for helping the observer to combine the images of two pictures taken from points of view a little way apart and thus to get the effect of solidity or depth."[3] Stereoscopes are available in the UAE through the Dubai Moving Images Museum, which displays

---

3. Merriam-Webster, "Stereoscope," accessed June 15, 2017, https://www.merriam-webster.com/dictionary/stereoscope.

early images and photographic equipment belonging to a private collector. In collaboration with this museum, Magid and Claire Watson were able to display not only the stereoscope, but also stereoscopic images of the Middle East ranging from the late 19th century to the early 20th century, hand selected by the two. The Science and Engineering Librarian also worked with the then Special Collections Librarian in locating a copy of the book, *Book of the Ten Treatises of the Eye*, which was included as part of the art exhibit. Plans to acquire this book were already in motion before the film festival, so it was a win for both the library and the film festival.

At the conclusion of the film festival, Gambis was in search of an office for Imagine Science Abu Dhabi. In addition to the Science and Engineering Librarian, two of her library colleagues also played different roles in the inaugural festival. One helped in the procurement of the rare book mentioned above and one taught high school students how to create films. Because of the involvement of the library staff, Imagine Science Abu Dhabi Film Festival was allowed to establish an office in the library. This was facilitated by the fact that the university had moved to a new campus in 2014 and was still not functioning at full capacity. Even with the empty offices, library administration was not willing to offer its spaces to just any unit of the university that asked. However, Imagine Science was viewed as an organization which had already established working collaborations with three members of its staff, and therefore a move into existing empty office space was fully supported. This move into the physical space of the library also cemented the collaboration between the two organizations.

The librarian was also involved in the 2016 version of the festival in Abu Dhabi, albeit in different roles. Prior to each festival, researchers and faculty in the UAE are recruited to submit video clips and/or visualized data of research they are conducting that involves video, for example a video of cell division. These clips are compiled and shown in each festival, prior to the screening of the feature films for each day, in a segment called "Abu Dhabi Scenes."[4] Magid was tasked with recruiting scientists from NYUAD to submit their video clips and/or data visualization for Abu Dhabi Scenes. As the Science and Engineering Librarian is a liaison to the science and engineering community at NYUAD, she had previously made acquaintances with all of the potential recruits. In addition to emailing all faculty, she also highlighted the recruitment in her monthly newsletter, "Science Bytes," which is focused on the interests of the science and engineering community at NYUAD. She was successful in recruiting faculty to submit their videos. Magid also met with key individuals at other academic institutions in the UAE, ranging from Public Affairs representatives, to deans and heads of departments, all of whom shared an interest in having their researchers contribute to the film festival. Although only one video from outside of NYUAD "made the cut" to Scenes, the meetings also served to publicize the film festival to local universities.

The NYUAD Arts Center was established at the university and "offers NYUAD compelling programming that connects to the curriculum and illuminates the scholarly pursuits of students and faculty."[5] In the 2015-2016 academic year, the NYUAD Arts Center began to feature international artists, singers, and various festivals as part of the Arts Center performances open to the university community and the public. As the Imagine Science Film Festival Abu Dhabi is a recurring cultural event occurring on campus, the NYUAD Arts Center incorporated it into its annual lineup of events and performances. That same year, the NYUAD library began to create research guides for each of the performances. The research guides serve as a knowledge base for attendees to learn more about the artists or the fields which they represent, through the library's resources. Primarily tailored to NYUAD students, the guides also list freely available resources to appeal to the attendees of the performances unaffiliated with the university. Naturally,

---

4. Imagine Science, Abu Dhabi Scenes 2016, accessed June 16, 2017, http://imaginescience-films.org/abu-dhabi/year-2016/abu-dhabi-scenes/.

5. New York University Abu Dhabi, *The NYUAD Arts Center*, 2017, accessed December 15, 2017, http://www.nyuad-artscenter.org/en_US/about/.

the Science and Engineering Librarian created a research guide for the Imagine Science Film Festival.[6] The homepage of the guide includes an introduction to the event, including various media accounts. This is followed by a section on the Student Film Lab and Sci-Art Exhibit and library resources to learn more about science in film, and a section on news about this event. Finally, each guide contains sections about other events in the Arts Center, and an information section about the library.

Although in the past the librarian had only become involved in the "behind the scenes" work, 2016 marked the first time that she was at the forefront. Each year's Imagine Science Abu Dhabi Film Festival also includes a Student Film Lab, in which students from different high schools in the UAE are invited to spend two days with Gambis and his team in order to produce films around a specific theme. Students use their mobile phones to create the films. During the two-day filmmaking workshop, the students also learn from guest speakers about films and filmmaking, including speakers from NYUAD. Magid had an interest in using video and film to help students learn about science and had created a library workshop that was offered a couple of times during the academic year, starting in 2015, called Sci-Eng Vids. Gambis was aware of the workshop and excited that it was offered to the NYUAD community. When the next season of the film festival arrived, Magid was asked to present a student workshop on how to find reliable, trustworthy videos about science education online. In the time allotted, Magid taught the students how to find videos and about their importance in learning about science and engineering. She tailored the workshop to make it more engaging at a high-school level and included an element of humor, as well as eliciting participation from the students.

The librarian continued her volunteer efforts with Imagine Science Abu Dhabi Film Festival in 2017. Once again, she was invited to speak at the Student Film Lab, although the student population differed this time in that the students were middle-school aged rather

---

6. Amani Magid, *Imagine Science Film Festival Research Guide*, 2016, accessed June 17, 2017, http://guides.nyu.edu/imaginescience.

than high-school. As in the previous years, she produced a research guide specific to the festival.[3] The 2017 research guide differs from the 2016 version in that there is much more of an emphasis on distinguishing resources for the NYU Community, "Scholarly Analysis: NYUAD Library Resources," and resources for the local community, "Scholarly Analysis: Freely Available Resources." Changes were also made to all Arts Center research guides after hearing feedback from Arts Center faculty. The NYUAD Library started a tradition in the 2015-2016 academic year of creating a new book display each month which mirrors events occurring on campus. The librarian created a video display that showcases a sampling of the many DVDs on science topics available in the library for Imagine Science. During the 2017 film season, the video display was photographed by the Imagine Science team and this display was featured, along with the research guide, on their social media accounts.

Reflection

In retrospect, the collaboration has changed the approach of the Science and Engineering Librarian to teaching students and faculty about library resources. Attending the film festivals has made her realize the power of videos to relay information in a visually pleasing way, but also in a manner that facilitates learning. At the faculty and staff level, she has created Quicktime videos to demonstrate how to access journal articles from the library's homepage; in the past, she would have attached a numbered list of steps for finding a journal article. At the student level, she realized that her time in one-shot classes for engineering students, particularly in Design and Innovation where the students must create an original invention, was declining each year, so she created a video on how to search for patents using the United States Patent and Trade Office (USPTO) database. She also promotes the *Journal of Visualized Experiments*, a peer-reviewed journal of video articles and protocols, and other video resources, when appropriate for faculty, students, and staff. She has also purchased Engineering Case Studies for the library's collection, a database collection of documents and videos about major engineering failures and successes.[7] Magid is currently working on a publication about STEM videos. Her future goal is to create a series of videos on accessing various science and engineering resources.

The collaboration between the Science and Engineering Librarian and Imagine Science Film Festival Abu Dhabi has been successful, although to state that it was always a smooth one would be less than honest. Gambis is not on campus during fall semesters, and although distance should not serve as a hindrance in preparing for the festival, especially with the many communication technologies available, it was at first for Magid. However, Magid has learned to navigate the distance and concentrate on her contributions to the festival, however small or large they may be. This collaboration was the first for the Science and Engineering Librarian at NYUAD, and it has, in turn, instilled in her a culture of collaboration. This has led to collaborations with other groups both within the university, including the Office of Graduate and Postdoctoral Affairs, and outside the university in a new research collaboration with two professors of science and engineering who work in two different countries in Europe.

Although Magid set out on this partnership with no set goals, one of the underlying goals or themes that has emerged is to strengthen the librarian's and the library's roles in developing programming for the NYUAD community, and the UAE community at large. The NYUAD library's mission is "service to scholars," through access to scholarly resources and technologies that supports research and teaching. The collaboration with Imagine Science has, without doubt, supported the library's mission by publicizing videos available about science or those with science as an underlying theme at the resource level, and also highlighting the value of the librarian at the human level. There was a seamless integration of Magid's contributions, from research guides to video display to invited speaker, which fit not only the mission of the library, but also the faculty status of the librarians, who were all

---

7. Alexander Street Press. *Engineering Case Studies*, (2017) accessed June 18, 2017, https://alexanderstreet.com/products/engineering-case-studies-online.

promoted to faculty in 2016. The librarian is privileged to work with the Middle East's first science film festival and hopes that the partnership between her and Imagine Science will always be in a state of "Action!" and will grow and progress in the years to come.

Bibliography

Alexander Street Press. *Engineering Case Studies*, (2017). Accessed June 18, 2017. https://alexanderstreet.com/products/engineering-case-studies-online.

Imagine Science. *Abu Dhabi Scenes 2016*. Accessed June 16, 2017. http://imaginesciencefilms.org/abu-dhabi/year-2016/abu-dhabi-scenes/.

Magid, Amani. *Imagine Science Film Festival Research Guide*, 2016. Accessed June 17, 2017. http://guides.nyu.edu/imaginescience.

Magid, Amani. "'Patenting" a New Engineering Librarian at an American University in the UAE." Paper presented at the 123rd American Society Engineering Education Annual Conference and Exposition, New Orleans, LA, 2016.

Merriam-Webster. "Stereoscope." Accessed June 15, 2017. https://www.merriam-webster.com/dictionary/stereoscope.

New York University Abu Dhabi. *The NYUAD Arts Center*. 2017. Accessed December 15, 2017/ http://www.nyuad-artscenter.org/en_US/about/.

New York University Libraries. *Arabic Collections Online*. Accessed June 15, 2017. http://dlib.nyu.edu/aco/.

Case Study 11

PROJECT MYANMAR: EMPOWERING STUDENTS THROUGH MAKER EDUCATION

Michael Cherry

Abstract

Project Myanmar was a partnership between the Evansville Vanderburgh Public Library, Bosse High School, and Uncharted International in Evansville, Indiana. Uncharted International is a nonprofit organization whose globally-focused mission includes supporting and working with orphanages in Myanmar. As part of this collaboration, the Evansville Vanderburgh Public Library partnered with a life skills class at Bosse High School. Students in the class made soap that could be packaged and shipped to the orphanages overseas. Beyond learning how to make and package soap, students visited Uncharted International to learn about the orphanages. This situated or connected learning encouraged an understanding of local and global communities, in addition to a discussion about diversity. Instead of focusing primarily on craftsmanship or design, the project explored how maker education could be utilized to improve communities and empower students with disabilities. Furthermore, it examined how this type of learning could be taught in such a way that would promote life skills, vocational readiness, and civic engagement.

Introduction

Advocates of maker education argue that this type of learning could lead to discipline-specific skills and a focus on hands-on, experiential learning. Beyond making artifacts or experimenting with new tools and materials, students could harness these skills towards effecting change within one's own community. This broader understanding of "maker-centered learning" would encourage students to examine how social systems are designed and how the artifacts students create could improve the world around them.[1] This case study examines the role of maker education in a classroom with a primary focus on developing life skills. The case study demonstrates how maker education could be utilized to promote life skills and civic engagement for students with disabilities. This chapter describes a partnership between the Evansville Vanderburgh Public Library, Bosse High School, and Uncharted International, a nonprofit whose missionary work includes assisting impoverished communities.

Library Overview

The Evansville Vanderburgh Public Library (EVPL) provides a variety of resources and services to its community through its eight facilities. Its mission is to create experiences, opportunities, and an atmosphere for lifelong learning. The EVPL serves the 180,305 residents of Vanderburgh County, a southwestern Indiana county covering 233 square miles. It is the largest metropolitan area within a 100-mile radius. In addition to serving local charter and private schools, the EVPL provides educational services and resources to the Evansville Vanderburgh School Corporation, a public school corporation comprising thirty-seven different schools. Of the nine high schools, five of them offer a life skills curriculum to support young adults with disabilities. These students attend classes that foster independent living skills and provide instructional community activities.

---

1. Edward P. Clapp and Jessica Ross, *Maker-Centered Learning: Empowering Young People to Shape Their Worlds* (San Francisco, CA: Jossey-Bass, 2016).

In February 2017, youth librarians from the EVPL approached Sally Hale, a life skills teacher at Bosse High School, to explore a possible school and public library partnership. The library chose to partner with Bosse High School due to their existing relationship. Hale's class had visited the library on field trips and had recently organized a film screening for several EVSC life skills classrooms. In addition to the field trips and film screening, her students had volunteered at the library in the past.

Partner Overview

As part of the program, the EVPL also chose to partner with Uncharted International. Uncharted International is a nonprofit organization working in Myanmar, Central Asia, China, and Dubai. Central to Uncharted's missionary work is their commitment to assisting and supporting orphanages in Myanmar. Currently, Uncharted financially assists eleven orphanages in Myanmar while creating micro-finance programs and fair-trade retail opportunities. As young women graduate from the orphanages, they are employed at a Loom House and are provided sustainable incomes through creating blankets woven on looms and other handmade items, such as scarves, jewelry, and other products.

In addition to helping those in need of support, this culture of micro-financing and making became a catalyst for the project. It taught students that empowerment through the creation of one's material goods could lead to the improvement of one's community. Students participating in the project were tasked with the creation of handmade soap. This soap would be shipped to the orphanages as a means to improve the health of the community. Project Myanmar is described below and includes various activities designed to teach civic engagement and life skills.

Background

In her article, "Making Space in the Makerspace: Building a Mixed-Ability Maker Culture," author Meryl Alper states, "Analyzing maker culture requires us not only to look closer at materials, techniques, and activities that constitute making, but also the social context that surrounds participation in and exclusion from maker culture."[2] Alper advocates for a more equitable and ethical culture of making that would also encompass youth with disabilities.

Similarly, Megan Egbert's book, *Creating Makers: How to Start a Learning Revolution at Your Library*, contains a chapter called "Making for Everyone" which suggests that librarians design programs with accessible making in mind.[3] Egbert proposes a broader culture of equity that would include programs for students of all ages, abilities, and genders. In addition to these authors, a number of studies have advocated for learning opportunities that would include diverse youth within the maker movement.[4]

Case

Project Myanmar addressed many of these issues by providing learning experiences for students with disabilities. The project was designed with a service learning component that combined making with community service. Rather than focus exclusively on abstract knowledge, this approach allowed for a pragmatic understanding of learning objectives. Students worked collaboratively to achieve real objectives that benefited the Myanmar community.

Initially, Hale's class visited Uncharted International so that students could learn about the organization. The field trip to Uncharted International situated learning within the context of multicultural education. During the course of the field trip, students watched a video about

---

2. Meryl Alper, "Making Space in the Makerspace: Building a Mixed-Ability Maker Culture," (2013), https://teethingontech.files.wordpress.com/2013/03/idc13-workshop_meryl-alper.pdf.

3. Megan Egbert, Creating Makers: *How to Start a Learning Revolution at Your Library* (Santa Barbara, CA: Libraries Unlimited, 2016).

4. American Society for Engineering Education, *Envisioning the Future of the Maker Movement: Summit Report* (Washington, DC: American Society for Engineering Education, 2016); Shirin Vossoughi, Paula K. Hooper, and Meg Escude, "Making Through the Lens of Culture and Power: Toward Transformative Visions for Educational Equity," *Harvard Educational Review* 18, no. 2 (Summer 2016): 206-232; Angela Calabrese Barton, Edna Tan, and Day Greenberg, "The Makerspace Movement: Sites of Possibilities for Equitable Opportunities to Engage Underrepresented Youth in STEM," *Teachers College Record* XX, no. X (2016): 1-44; Intel Corporation, *MakeHers: Engaging Girls and Women in Technology through Making, Creating, and Inventing* (Santa Clara, CA: Intel Corporation, 2014).

Myanmar. They discovered how the orphans are raised and how young women graduate from the orphanages and are employed in the Loom House. This was important because many of the students did not understand the term "orphan," nor were they aware of the socio-economic differences between cultures.

As students explored the facility, they saw the many handmade goods that are produced in the Loom House and then sold at the organization's headquarters in Evansville, IN. These goods included clothing, blankets, small bracelets, and other artisan crafts. These items are available for sale at the headquarters' store with proceeds supporting the orphanages.

Additionally, students learned how Uncharted International's globally-focused mission seeks to address the needs of international communities. The organization's facility includes an impressive packaging and shipment room that houses all the donations and material goods that support human aid efforts in Myanmar. Witnessing these efforts firsthand reinforced the students' own actions towards civic engagement and community problem solving. The students' handmade soap would be packaged and shipped with these goods in an effort to provide assistance to those in need.

Furthermore, this type of situated learning borrows from many of the key concepts of connected learning. Connected learning is a pedagogical approach that explores how new knowledge is acquired across multiple spheres of formal and informal learning. This may include online environments that support peer-to-peer interaction, as well as learning environments that link learning to multiple settings such as school, home, and community. Advocates of connected learning write, "In many ways, the connected learning approach is part of a longstanding tradition in progressive education and research on informal learning that has stressed the importance of civic engagement, connecting schools with the wider world, and the value of hands-on and social learning."[5]

---

5. Mizuko Ito, et al., *Connected Learning: An Agenda for Research and Design* (Irvine, CA: Digital Media and Learning Research Hub, 2013), 33.

Soap Making

After the field trip to Uncharted International, students visited the EVPL's Central Library to make, seal, and package the soap. Students participated in two soap-making workshops that were facilitated by library staff. The workshops included various activities for students with diverse abilities.

During the first workshop, students used the melt-and-pour technique common to beginner soap making. This technique is different from the hot or cold processes familiar to specialty soaps. The latter technique uses lye, a liquid metal hydroxide, which can burn skin on contact. The melt-and-pour technique involves melting a pre-made soap base and pouring it into silicone molds. Librarians purchased a 25-pound brick of soap base with the goal of melting and pouring 100 bars of soap. In addition to the soap base, silicone molds were purchased and several others were donated by a student's parent. Silicone molds come in a variety of shapes and sizes and work well with the melt-and-pour technique. It is easy to remove the soap from the silicone rubber once it has cooled and solidified.

Initially students cut the soap base into chunks and placed them in a microwaveable container. This assured that the soap base would melt and return to a liquid form. The liquid could then be measured and poured into various molds.

In addition to melting, pouring, and measuring the soap base, students were tasked with adding fragrance and color to each individual bar. Using eye-droppers they measured the color and fragrance in teaspoons and tablespoons, much in the same way one makes simple culinary measurements. These math measurements are important to students with disabilities as they reinforce basic arithmetic and help to support independent living skills. They indicate that students are able to reason quantitatively and persevere in problem solving. Aside from the soap station, several other stations provided additional activities. Students with mobility impairments used spray bottles and water to moisten layers of colored tissue paper. Each layer of tissue paper was dampened with water and a new layer was added to the preceding one. The process was repeated until nearly twenty layers of tissue paper were thoroughly dampened and the colored ink began to bleed. As various colors blended together, the dampened layers created marbled tissue paper that could be dried and used to package the soap.

Elsewhere students prepared labels that could be attached to each individual soap bar. Much like the marbled tissue paper, the labels were marbled using copperplate paper and Suminagashi marbling ink. Suminagashi or "floating ink" is the process of marbling paper with water and ink. This process is very easy to do and only requires plastic tubs, small palettes, and paint brushes. Students float the colored ink on top of the water by touching the surface of the water with a paint brush. Once the desired pattern is created, they dip the paper onto the water and it absorbs the ink, much like a sponge. This activity works well with students who may have physical limitations that determine the extent to which mobile devices are used.

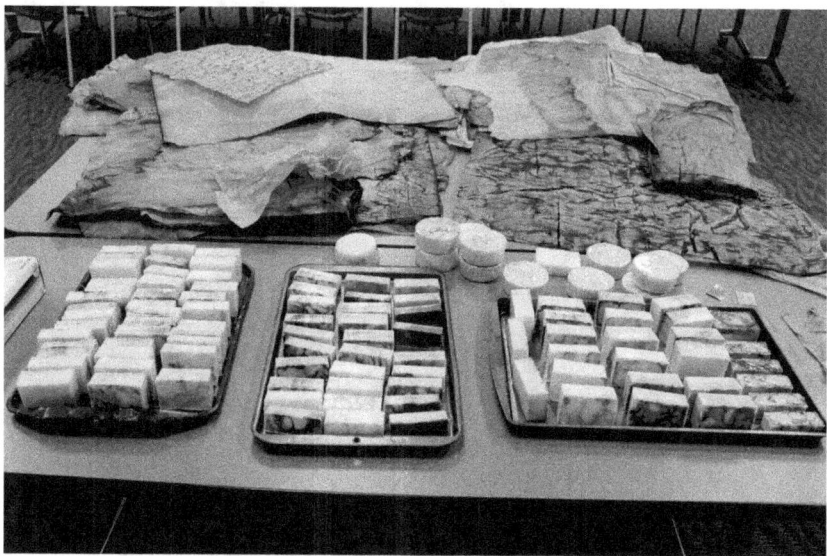

Figure 1. Soap and Marbled Tissue Paper, Unwrapped

Throughout the second workshop, students wrapped, labeled, and packaged the bars of soap. Much like the first day, various maker stations were set-up and students were matched to a station based on their abilities. For example, one group was tasked with shrink wrapping each individual bar. Students used shrink wrap, latex gloves, and hair dryers to carefully seal and preserve the bars. Once the bars were sealed, they were passed to another group of students who wrapped them in the marbled tissue paper. Other students cut the tissue paper into thin strips that would allow for ease when wrapping. Additionally, two other stations required students to cut the marbled Suminagashi paper into small squares. The squares were used to create labels for shipping and were stamped with natural patterns such as flowers and leaves. Altogether over 100 bars of handmade soap were packaged and shipped to orphanages in Myanmar. The soap was shipped in May 2017 as part of Uncharted International's mission to provide human aid to impoverished communities.

Figure 2. Soap with Marbled Tissue Paper and Labels, Wrapped

Assessing Learning

Perhaps one of the most challenging tasks for librarians is to assess learning over the course of a program. Often times the best way to measure this is to assess what students can do with their learning. Upon completion of the soap project, students returned to Hale's classroom to create candy and lotion for the orphanages. They used the same melt-and-pour technique required of soap making to create edible candies and hand lotion. This demonstrated that students could apply new knowledge across learning environments. Moreover, the students plan to create more handmade soap to sell as part of a fundraiser for their class. In addition to basic finance skills, this endeavor supports communication skills and the ability to organize events. Additionally, throughout Project Myanmar students exhibited various life skills that help to support independent living and vocational skills. For example, the activity stations were organized in a way that required coordination and collaboration amongst peers. While each student was matched according to his or her abilities, students were required to work together towards a common goal. These interpersonal skills are important because they demonstrate an ability to work effectively with others.

Furthermore, students exhibited a number of skills commonly referred to as "21st century skills."[6] These skills include global awareness, civic literacy, and productivity. In order to assess learning, librarians documented activities throughout the course of the project. This documentation included photographs of students engaged in learning, in addition to artifacts of learning, such as the soap and other handmade items. Additionally, several students were interviewed in a short video that discussed the project. The video includes commentary from students, the teacher, and a library board member, all of whom underscored the value of Project Myanmar. The video, titled "Critical Making," can be accessed via the library's Facebook channel under the videos tab.

Reflection

In Barbara Klipper's article, "Making Makerspaces Work for Everyone," the author states, "Accessible making at the library can enrich

---

6. Refer to the Partnership for 21st Century Learning at http://www.p21.org/.

the lives of people with disabilities in many ways, allowing them to create items to improve their world, have fun, and identify hobby and career possibilities."[7] As discussed in the preceding paragraphs, various studies indicate problems concerning accessibility and equity related to the maker movement. Project Myanmar was a partnership between the Evansville Vanderburgh Public Library, Bosse High School, and Uncharted International that sought to explore these issues in a way that would empower students with disabilities. Students participating in the project learned about orphanages in Myanmar and discovered the culture and community of this region. Through civic engagement and critical making, students sought to improve the lives of orphaned children. They utilized maker-centered learning not only as a means to create artifacts, but as an opportunity to shape global communities and to improve one's world.

Currently the EVPL is hoping to expand this partnership with additional life skills classrooms at the Evansville Vanderburgh School Corporation. A future project includes designing backpacks for the orphanages that would consist of silkscreened bags, in addition to various items that could be bundled in the backpacks. Each life skills classroom would be responsible for the creation of one artifact or the design of the backpack. Items could include toiletries that improve hygiene and health, as well as handmade journals and clothing. In conclusion, maker education brings with it new challenges that include issues of diversity and inclusion. Libraries can provide opportunities for maker-centered learning that seek to address these issues. These programs can be designed in such a way that problem-based, hands-on learning leads to the acquisition of life skills. Such programs would seek to define making beyond traditional arts and crafts and would place it within the context of larger social issues and civic empowerment. They would ultimately require students to think more critically about why they make and how their creativity could impact the world.

---

7. Barbara Klipper, "Making Makerspaces Work for Everyone: Lessons in Accessibility," *Children and Libraries* 12, no. 3 (2014): 5.

Bibliography

Alper, Meryl. "Making Space in the Makerspace: Building a Mixed-Ability Maker Culture." (2013), https://teethingontech.files.wordpress.com/2013/03/idc13-workshop_meryl-alper.pdf.

American Society for Engineering Education. *Envisioning the Future of the Maker Movement: Summit Report.* Washington, DC: American Society for Engineering Education, 2016. https://www.asee.org/documents/papers-and-publications/papers/maker-summit-report.pdf.

Barton, Angela Calabrese, Edna Tan, and Day Greenberg. "The Makerspace Movement: Sites of Possibilities for Equitable Opportunities to Engage Underrepresented Youth in STEM." *Teachers College Record* 119, no. 6 (2017): 1-44.

Clapp, Edward P., and Jessica Ross. *Maker-Centered Learning: Empowering Young People to Shape Their Worlds.* San Francisco, CA: Jossey-Bass, 2016.

Egbert, Megan. *Creating Makers: How to Start a Learning Revolution at Your Library.* Santa Barbara, CA: Libraries Unlimited, 2016.

Intel Corporation. *MakeHers: Engaging Girls and Women in Technology through Making, Creating, and Inventing.* Santa Clara, CA: Intel Corporation, 2014. https://www.intel.com/content/dam/www/public/us/en/documents/reports/makers-report-girls-women.pdf.

Ito, Mizuko, Kris Gutiérrez, Sonia Livingstone, Bill Penuel, Jean Rhodes, Katie Salen, Juliet Schor, Julian Sefton-Green, and S. Craig Watkins. *Connected Learning: An Agenda for Research and Design.* Irvine, CA: Digital Media and Learning Research Hub, 2013.

Klipper, Barbara. "Making Makerspaces Work for Everyone: Lessons in Accessibility." *Children and Libraries* 12, no. 3 (2014): 5-6.

Vossoughi, Shirin, Paula K. Hooper, and Meg Escude. "Making Through the Lens of Culture and Power: Toward Transformative Visions for Educational Equity." *Harvard Educational Review* 18, no. 2 (Summer 2016): 206-232.

Case Study 12

PARTNERS IN PRIDE: COLLABORATING WITH A COMMUNITY ARCHIVE TO DOCUMENT LGBTQ HISTORY

Anna Culbertson and Lisa Lamont

Abstract

Two librarians at San Diego State University (SDSU) Library have partnered with the Lambda Archives of San Diego (LASD) to create a digital resource documenting the LGBTQ Pride phenomenon in the San Diego and Northern Baja California region. Original materials, including photographs, ephemera, memorabilia, and oral histories, will chronicle the Pride movement from the small-scale protests of the early 1970s to the larger, crowd-drawing parades and festivals of the past several decades. SDSU and LASD are uniquely positioned to take on this partnership. SDSU has one of the first degree programs in the nation for LGBTQ studies and was ranked one of the top thirty LGBTQ-friendly campuses in the nation by the Campus Pride Index in 2016.[1] LASD is dedicated to collecting and preserving San Diego and Northern Baja California LGBTQ history and houses a broad range of original materials dating

---

1. "Campus Pride releases annual 'Best of the Best': top 30 list of LGBTQ-friendly campuses across the nation," Campus Pride, August 22, 2016, https://www.campuspride.org/campus-pride-releases-annual-best-of-the-best-top-30-list-of-the-lgbtq-friendly-campuses-across-the-nation/.

back to the 1930s.[2] The partners recognize numerous benefits to be gained by building a collaborative digital resource, not only by both organizations, but also by the broader research community. The resource will support and advance further study of the Gay Rights Movement and the LGBTQ community in Southern California and will preserve these documents for future generations. This chapter will discuss the background and progress of the project to date including grant-writing, technology, staffing, workflows, challenges, and plans for the future.

Introduction

In 2015, San Diego State University Library (SDSU) and the Lambda Archives of San Diego (LASD) embarked on a partnership to document and preserve local and regional LGBTQ history through the development of a digital resource. The authors of this chapter collaborated with SDSU Library's Special Projects and External Affairs Officer, Lynn Hawkes, and LASD's then-President Maureen Steiner and Head Archivist Jen La Barbera to develop a grant that would successfully fund these efforts. We were fortunate to have been the recipients of a Community Stories grant through California Humanities, a non-profit partner of the National Endowment for the Humanities. Upon its launch in the latter half of 2017, *OUT on the Left Coast: The Story of San Diego Pride* will document the emergence of the LGBTQ Pride phenomenon in the San Diego and Northern Baja California region. The original materials for the project, including t-shirts, posters, buttons, banners, photographs, and oral histories of early community activists, date from the late 1960s to the present and are housed at LASD. Our shared goal is to create an online discovery tool to provide enhanced access to this important historical collection. This chapter will discuss the background and progress of the project to date including grant-writing, technology, staffing, workflows, challenges, and plans for the future.

---

2. "Lambda Archives. Collecting, Preserving and Teaching LGBT History of San Diego," Lambda Archives, accessed June 2017, https://lambdaarchives.org/home/about/.

The Partners

The California State University system, which includes twenty-three campuses throughout the state, is committed to maintaining one primary library location on each campus to serve as a research hub and to consolidate collections and services. The mission of Library & Information Access at SDSU is to support "the information, curricular and research needs of the university's diverse community through the widest possible range of resources. We are committed to information literacy, lifelong learning, and creative endeavors in a welcoming environment."[3] As of October 2015, the library included over 6.6 million items, with over 216,900 journals, databases, and ebooks. At the time of writing this chapter, the library employed twenty-four library faculty, fifty employees in other classifications (administration, staff, and information technology) and over 120 student assistants. Library faculty provide subject expertise in ninety areas and liaison support to faculty and students affiliated with nearly all degree programs on campus. Innovative services and spaces in the library include a makerspace, a GIS lab, a science fiction reading room, a robust suite of digitization activities, and a digital humanities center, which is currently in development.

The mission of LASD is "to collect, preserve, and teach the history of lesbian, gay, bisexual, and transgender people in the San Diego and Northern Baja California region." The non-profit community archive houses a broad range of original materials dating back to the 1930s, although the majority of its materials date from the 1970s to the present.[4] The archive is governed by a volunteer board of directors and employs three part-time staff who manage a steady rotation of volunteers and interns. LASD actively maintains and develops archival collections, a reading library, exhibits, oral histories, and programming in support of its mission. They cultivate an extensive network of supporters and produce events to foster community involvement. Culbertson cur-

---

3. "Strategic Plan," San Diego State University Library, accessed June 2017, http://library.sdsu.edu/about-us/strategic-plan.

4. Lambda Archives, https://lambdaarchives.org/home/about/.

rently serves on the board and, in her capacity as a special collections librarian, leads a collections management sub-committee that revises and updates LASD policies and procedures as needed.

Purpose and Goals of the Partnership

Academic libraries have a long history of collaborating with community partners in innovative ways and "Out on the Left Coast" carries on the tradition. By the time we began to pursue the specific grant that would fund this project, we had been actively strategizing about ways to collaborate with LASD, as both parties recognized the mutual benefits of a partnership. We were in agreement that a cross-organizational digital resource was our ideal goal, since Lambda is not currently able to invest in its own digital asset management (DAM) system and SDSU library is always seeking unique resources to support its LGBT Studies degree.[5] Since the funding maximum for the grant we sought was modest, capped at $10,000, and the holdings at LASD so extensive, we agreed that we would need to focus our efforts on showcasing a specific collection, or thematic group of materials, with regional and historical significance.

As we embarked on writing the grant in 2015, we recognized that our efforts took place during a year that marked a monumental victory in the ongoing struggle for LGBTQ equality—the Supreme Court's decision to legalize same-sex marriage in the United States. California stakes an early claim in this history by becoming the second state to legally recognize same-sex domestic partnerships.[6] When the Stonewall Inn, a licensed gay bar in New York City's Greenwich Village and now a national monument, was raided by police in 1969, riots ensued, marking a turning point for the modern gay liberation movement. These events

---

5. The authors wish to note a distinction between acronyms used in this chapter. The degree program at SDSU is officially known as LGBT Studies, while for our own purposes, LGBTQ is used to refer to the broader topic. We also note that no acronym adequately summarizes the broad range of gender identities and sexual orientations that represent the human experience, while acknowledging the many distinct populations that have been marginalized therein.

6. "A Timeline of same-sex marriage in the US," Boston Globe, posted January 9, 2016, https://www3.bostonglobe.com/2016/01/09/same-sex-marriage-over-time/mbVFMQPyxZCpM2eSQMUsZK/story.html?arc404=true.

were commemorated the following year by a march that drew national attention and ushered in a new tradition of annual Pride marches all over the country. San Diego's first Pride event was held in 1974 by a community group that had established a Center for Social Services in San Diego's Golden Hill neighborhood.[7] The event included an informal, unpermitted march from the Center to the city's cultural epicenter, Balboa Park, and back. The following year, a permitted march of around 400 people marked the beginning of an annual Pride parade that has taken place every year since then, without fail (see **Figure 1**). The story of San Diego Pride represents a noteworthy regional manifestation of a national phenomenon, and through our partnership with LASD we had access to substantial, historically important collections for telling this story.

Figure 1: San Diego Pride Parade, 1978.
Courtesy of the Lambda Archives of San Diego

---

7. "About," San Diego LGBT Pride, accessed June 2017, https://sdpride.org/about/.

Foremost among the people involved in the formative years of San Diego Pride were two men whose preservation efforts made it possible to share the history of this Southern California social movement. Jess Jessop, a Vietnam veteran and alumnus of San Diego State University, was a community supporter and political organizer whose tireless activism helped shape in large part San Diego's enthusiastic acceptance of the LGBTQ community. Over the years, Doug Moore, a minister, community activist, and long-time Pride leader, compiled a massive collection of Pride-related items such as posters, buttons, t-shirts, programs, banners, and photos. Jessop and Moore assembled these materials and others to establish the Lesbian and Gay Archives of San Diego, now known as the Lambda Archives of San Diego. Today, the collections provide an extensive account of San Diego Pride history and illustrate an important milestone in the power of demonstration.

Lambda's collection of San Diego Pride materials, some of which are already digitized, seemed like the perfect starting point. The bright and colorful artifacts and photographs convey a positive and celebratory message that, combined with compelling community stories, will make an engaging Internet production. We were in agreement that a website with coordinated social media and promotional efforts would make this foundational piece of San Diego LGBTQ history accessible to the broadest audience possible. In order to encourage multimodal forms of learning, we envisioned the site combining the visual experience of browsing the photographs, ephemera, and memorabilia assembled by Jessop, Moore, and others, with opportunities to interact with personal narratives in the form of oral histories that LASD has produced over the years. The project seeks to communicate what it means and how it feels to not conform to mainstream ideas of sexuality and gender, and use these experiences to build a greater understanding of how California has come to be distinguished by its unique reputation for inclusivity.

Funding

The California Council for the Humanities (CCH) is an independent non-profit partner of the National Endowment for the Humanities, whose mission is "to connect Californians to ideas and one another in order to understand our shared heritage and diverse cultures, inspire civic participation, and shape our future."[8] Our institution had been successfully funded by CCH for a different project in the past and, being very satisfied with the results, our administration was eager to appeal to the funding agency with a new project. CCH seeks to support projects that promote and preserve the humanities with a view toward the betterment of California through the creation of "a state of open mind."[9] We were pleased to find that our project aligned with their current vision so well as to have been awarded funding. The process was highly competitive in its most recent cycle, both at the internal level—we were selected as the one application to represent the campus through a white paper process—and at the actual grant application level—twenty out of 109 applications (18%) were funded in this cycle.

Audience

A major audience for this project is the Southern California community, including high school students, college students, educators, and the general public. It includes anyone who would benefit from the opportunity to contextualize contemporary issues of social equality and human rights through this important historical movement. It also includes those members of the LGBTQ community who were a part of the movement, seeking to chronicle their own history and finally see it celebrated in their lifetimes. The resource will also be useful to the greater research community, based not only in California but internationally. The temptation to describe this project as a resource for digital humanities scholarship is difficult to resist, but it is important to think of its intended audience in more open and inclusive terms. As a multimedia resource available for use by scholars in a relatively young program on our campus (LGBT Studies), it undoubtedly poses unique

---

8. "Our Story," California Humanities, last modified 2020, https://calhum.org/about-us/history-mission/.

9. Ibid.

opportunities for the curation, visualization, and analysis of a piece of a much larger, important, and under-documented history. Our campus research emphasis on "Digital Humanities and Global Diversity" was implemented to explore the impact of the digital on diverse populations and make access to the resources and technologies dominated by privileged academics available to underrepresented and disadvantaged communities.

Impact

Many marginalized populations have been disserved by history due in part to a lack of organized documentation. This project could not come at a more crucial point in time, if for no other reason than the need to gather and preserve as many stories as possible while participants are still alive to document this era. Much of the early community has already been lost to AIDS-related illnesses in addition to age, including Jess Jessop (1939-1990). In addition, while many groups are able to pass stories down through children and grandchildren, LGBTQ individuals, particularly of this generation, are less likely to have descendants with whom to share these stories.

Outcomes

Since having been awarded the funds in January of 2016, Culbertson (Assistant Head of Special Collections) has overseen the grant's administration needs and works with the Research Foundation on the project budget and time reporting. The grant carries a 1:1 cost-sharing requirement, in both cash and in-kind contributions, which we have already met by 200% at the time of writing this chapter. Culbertson also continues to oversee a research assistant, who has worked variously on research, website text, and metadata, the latter supervised by Lamont and the department's metadata specialist.

For the project, the SDSU Digital Collections group photographed over 600 Pride related t-shirts, 250 buttons and pins, and twenty-six large banners (see **Figures 2** and **3**). The photography was at times difficult given the constraints of the location. We preferred to leave the materials at the archives and thus used the available lighting and arranged backdrops for the shirts and buttons. The graphics and logos are legible and clear, although some of the photography is inferior.

Figure 2: San Diego Pride T-shirt, 1996, an example of one of over 600 t-shirts photographed for the project.
Courtesy of the Lambda Archives of San Diego.

LASD has numerous Pride photograph collections and many were already digitized. This work had previously been done at LASD by unsupervised volunteers and the digital images required hours of clean up, color correction, and general quality control. Several LASD collections lost in a server crash several years ago were re-digitized by the SDSU group. The research assistant is still discovering additional Pride photographs in other collections and we expect the photograph collection to grow to well over 3,000 images. All of the digital images are available through the SDSU library's DAM running on iBase software.[10] Although the DAM holds far more images than will be needed for the *Out of the Left Coast* site, we intend to archive as much as possible. The DAM is searchable and accessible through Google and other search engines as well as through its own native interface. By storing the digitized images in two locations (LASD and SDSU) and providing multiple points of access, we aim to better preserve these collections.

Figure 3: Banner from the 1995 Pride Celebration in San Diego, one of twenty-four banners photographed for the project.
Courtesy of the Lambda Archives of San Diego.

LASD has primarily been responsible for contributing staff time towards the archival research and metadata, which is important to the completion of the project as they possess the institutional memory and community contacts that we lack. Further, non-profit community organizations with part-time staff and limited resources are not easily able to meet major academic institutions in the middle when collaborating on grant requirements. The true value of their involvement lies in the ability to benefit from their expertise, their community connections, and their extensive collections. In return we are able to help them by providing additional points of access, increasing their visibility and helping to preserve the collections.

Measuring Success

During Pride weekend in July of 2017, we will table with LASD and provide a "soft launch" highlighting the content we have digitized and

---

10. "Digital Collections," San Diego State University Library, accessed June 2017, http://bit.ly/2s8vScs.

a sneak preview of the website. Public feedback to the site and materials will be recorded. In the fall of 2017, we will also collaborate with LASD on creative programming to promote the site launch. We have begun planning an event to gather LGBTQ educators and scholars at LASD, in addition to hosting an opening reception on campus at SDSU.

Once we have launched the site, we will focus on a well-rounded assessment. Google Analytics will supply data on the number of visitors, the number of pageviews, and the length of time visitors remain on the site. Database reports will list the keywords users are searching, the success of their searches, and the most viewed materials. We can then use those results to modify our metadata so that users are successful in navigating the site and the materials. Additionally, the website will include an online survey asking viewers about the usability, quality, and value of the materials. We plan to solicit feedback on the materials in the DAM and encourage crowd-sourced identification of persons and events in addition to donated content. As the website will be an ongoing historical resource for users, we anticipate that the project will uncover more related stories and inspire additions and other collaborations. In short, we are designing the site with future growth in mind.

Physical attendance at events will be counted, and we will record social media and blog interactions relating to the site lecture series as well. In addition to meeting regularly to evaluate and maintain progress, we must also complete a comprehensive final evaluation and report for the funding agency. We will compile and analyze statistical data relating to both the website and the lecture series and gather summary information for each of the project phases to compile the final report, which we are expected to submit in December 2017.

Reflection

The challenges involved with the partnership were primarily resource-focused. At the start of the project, staffing at LASD was in transition and during the grant period, the then-President had completed a maximum term. LASD staff are professionals with many competing responsibilities, of which this grant was just one. On the SDSU side, this small grant involved a great deal more administrative oversight than seemed necessary. We spent a significant amount of time working with grant liaisons at the SDSU Research Foundation, and in hindsight we will give this aspect greater consideration for our next grant effort. The 1:1 cost-sharing requirement of the grant itself also posed an unanticipated time commitment in the form of in-kind project management. We have successfully managed to complete our work, but not without acknowledging how significant our in-kind contributions truly turned out to be in the end. All this aside, we do already consider this a successful partnership as we have provided increased access to materials that our faculty and students will use, in addition to providing increased access and visibility to the community. We view the collaboration as symbiotic and intend to continue working with future content from the archive's considerable collections.

Conclusion

As with any small grant, viewing such a project as a springboard offers numerous possibilities for growth. While we are still at work on our vision, we are excited to unveil the site, evaluate its impact, and pursue additional content and funding by the end of 2017. San Diego Pride 2017 will mark our first public viewing of the site, and the community feedback we obtain will be invaluable to our completion of the project. We anticipate an ongoing resource for which we can facilitate additional collaborations with other nonprofits, archives, museums and library collections in Southern California. We know now that we can continue to commit a reasonable amount of in-kind time and work towards such growth, and we endeavor to do so.

Bibliography

Boston Globe. "A Timeline of same-sex marriage in the US." January 9, 2016. https://www3.bostonglobe.com/2016/01/09/same-sex-marriage-over-time/mbVFMQPyxZCpM2eSQMUsZK/story.html?arc404=true.

California Humanities. "Our Story." Last modified 2020. https://calhum.org/about-us/history-mission/.

Campus Pride. "Campus Pride releases annual 'Best of the Best': Top 30 list of LGBTQ-friendly campuses across the nation." August 22, 2016. https://www.campuspride.org/campus-pride-releases-annual-best-of-the-best-top-30-list-of-the-lgbtq-friendly-campuses-across-the-nation/.

Lambda Archives. "Lambda Archives. Collecting, Preserving and Teaching LGBT History of San Diego." Accessed June 2017. https://lambdaarchives.org/home/about/.

San Diego LGBT Pride. "About." Accessed June 2017. https://sdpride.org/about/.

San Diego State University Library. "Digital Collections." Accessed June 2017. http://bit.ly/2s8vScs.

San Diego State University Library. "Strategic Plan." Accessed June 2017. http://library.sdsu.edu/about-us/strategic-plan.

Case Study 13

DOING GOOD: AN ACADEMIC LIBRARY AS A SOCIAL CHANGE AGENT

Judith Schwartz

Abstract

In 2014, a college library and a public school transition center established a partnership. The public school, P373K Brooklyn Transition Center, places students with developmental disabilities between the ages of eighteen to twenty-one in nonprofit worksite environments. When the library at Medgar Evers College, City University of New York, moved into its state-of-the-art facility, the partnership evolved into providing an ongoing worksite and also a digital literacy learning experience for the students. The partnership introduced multiple learning approaches such as integrating the students into information literacy classes with the general student population and then creating stand-alone workshops that focused primarily on learning information and visual literacy skills tailored to each student's special needs and disabilities. The author, an "embedded librarian" in the classroom, collaborated with the special education teacher to plan a yearbook project that enabled the students to participate in the library computer labs, where they learned digital literacy skills and graphic design terminology. The production of the yearbook resulted in a tangible product that, in addition to teaching students basic skills, helped to foster a better understanding between the two institutions. This chapter discusses the need for academic librarians to be involved in microactivism, to become social change agents, to volunteer, and to engage beyond the traditional library and classroom environments. It also considers how these actions can benefit the academic institution.

Introduction

There is an extensive literature pertaining to the ways in which libraries transform communities and function as social change agents, though the focus is primarily on public libraries. The American Library Association (ALA) states in its policy B.8.10 *Library Services to the Poor*: "It's crucial that libraries recognize their role in enabling poor people to participate fully in a democratic society, by utilizing a wide variety of available resources and strategies."[1] Libraries can provide a welcoming and inclusive environment to underrepresented or otherwise marginalized groups, embracing diversity in communities. In 2017 the ALA passed an amendment that adds issues of "equity, diversity, and inclusion" to their strategic plan.[2]

Many public libraries work to develop strong connections to communities and to expand the reach of library services. Some examples of how libraries are transforming communities include introducing "therapy dog reading programs" (literacy programs that involve children reading to dogs), implementing community approaches to homelessness by helping patrons to find housing and jobs and to apply for food stamps, repurposing transportation buses into mobile showers parked outside libraries, helping incarcerated adults read to their children, and conducting workshops for prisoners on how to conduct legal research.

In contrast, the literature pertaining to academic libraries partnering with nonprofits is far more limited. Some examples of this type of collaboration are academic libraries partnering with food banks to

---

1. American Library Association, *Policy Manual B.8.10 Library Services to the Poor* (Chicago: ALA, 2012). http://www.ala.org/aboutala/governance/policymanual/updated policymanual/section2/52libsvcsandrespon #B8.10.

2. American Library Association, *Final Report of the ALA Task Force on Equity, Diversity, and Inclusion* (Chicago: ALA, 2016), 1.

address the growing issue of hunger and homelessness that students on college campuses are faced with, and providing financial literacy workshops for students.

A social change impact report conducted by the Harris Poll contends: "Positive social change refers to involvement in activities that improve the lives of individuals and communities locally and around the world. It includes volunteering or service; donating money, goods or services; and educating others about a particular issue or cause."[3] It would be beneficial if more academic libraries explored partnering with nonprofit institutions to become social change agents.

Case

This case study describes a collaborative partnership between two academic organizations: the Charles Evans Inniss Memorial Library at Medgar Evers College, City University of New York, located in Brooklyn; and the P373K Brooklyn Transition Center, a New York City public school that works with adults aged eighteen to twenty-one who have developmental disabilities. The initial partnership was established in 1993 between the Transition Center and the Medgar Evers College Office of Services for the Differently-Abled. The purpose of the public school's involvement with the college initially was to provide opportunities for young adults with developmental disabilities to participate in structured volunteer work experiences on the college campus.

In 2014, the college's collaborative efforts with the public school significantly expanded. That year the school entered into a partnership with the Medgar Evers Library to provide the P373K students with information literacy development in a college learning environment and to offer these students the same access opportunities that are available to the wider community. The issues to be discussed in this chapter include barriers and challenges that young people with disabilities face that contribute to a digital divide.

---

3. Harris Poll, *Social Change Impact Report* (Minneapolis, MN: Walden University, 2014), 1.

The 2010 U.S. Census reported that close to 57 million people in the United States—nearly 19% of the population—have disabilities.[4] Significantly, data indicate that these individuals lag behind the overall population in terms of digital literacy. For example, summary findings from a 2009 Federal Communications Commission (FCC) survey reported that 56% of adults living with disabilities are Internet users, which is well below the national average of 78%. Further, 39% of all Americans without broadband (non-adopters) have some type of disability. Finally, 25% of people with disabilities cite a lack of digital literacy skills as a reason why they don't have broadband.[5] Clearly, a pressing need exists to extend digital literacy skills to this population.

It is important to acknowledge that a digital divide exists in our communities. Students in lower-income, traditionally-underserved communities don't have the same access to digital technologies or the Internet as do more affluent communities. A 2012 report for the Pew Internet & American Life Project concluded that the lack of access to and ability to use digital technologies creates major social and economic disadvantages.[6] Moreover, this problem is widespread. For example, the report contends: "Nearly a third of Americans have a low level of digital readiness."[7]

In 2006 the United Nations Convention on the Rights of Persons with Disabilities (CRPD) became the first human rights treaty to protect the rights of people with disabilities. The convention effectively "foregrounded disability as a human rights and equity issue."[8] Along

---

4. Matthew W. Brault, "Americans with Disabilities: Household Economic Studies," *Current Population Reports* (Washington, DC: U.S. Census Bureau, 2010), 4.

5. John B. Horrigan, "Broadband Adoption and Use in America: OBI Working Paper Series," no. 1 (Washington, DC: Federal Communications Commission, 2010), 24-27, http://hraunfoss.fcc.gov/edocs_public/attachmatch/DOC-296442A1.pdf.

6. John B. Horrigan, "Digital Readiness Gaps" (Washington, DC: Pew Research Center, 2016), 17.

7. Ibid, 6.

8. Jo Durham, Claire E. Brolan, and Bryan Mukandi, "The Convention on the Rights of Persons with Disabilities: A Foundation for Ethical Disability and Health Research in Developing Countries," *American Journal of Public Health* 104, no.1 (2014), 2037.

similar lines, Moni and Jobling state that "literacy learning for individuals with an intellectual disability has been viewed as a human rights and equity issue."[9] Although educational opportunities for individuals in this population have expanded, multiple barriers remain.

In addition to having developmental disabilities, the majority of the students in the library partnership are of African-American descent. Hughes-Hassell and Rawson contend that "Literacy instruction for African American youth is a critical social justice issue."[10] The library serves as a bridge to overcome the digital divide by providing the students with daily lab access and learning opportunities they otherwise may not have. The interaction of race, disability, and institutional inequities that confront this population make crossing over the digital divide even more difficult. Enhancing the students' skills and offering access to modern technologies help to ensure that they will not be left behind in the digital age.

Background

Medgar Evers College, City University of New York, is a senior college "named after the civil rights leader Medgar Wiley Evers that was established in 1970 in Brooklyn, New York, with a mandate to meet the educational and social needs of Central Brooklyn."[11] The Charles Evans Inniss Memorial Library at Medgar Evers College is an academic library that promotes educational resources for the college. One of the library's missions is to be open to the public, providing resources and Internet access to the underserved surrounding community.[12] The library strives to build a diverse and inclusive environment by supporting

---

9. Karen B. Moni and Anne Jobling, "LATCH-ON: A Program to Develop Literacy in Young Adults with Down Syndrome," *Journal of Adolescent & Adult Literacy* 44, no.1 (2000), 40.

10. Sandra Hughes-Hassell and Casey H. Rawson, "Literacy Education for African American Youth: A Social Justice Issue for Librarians," in *Libraries, Literacy, and African American Youth: Research and Practice*, edited by Sandra Hughes-Hassell, Pauletta Brown Bracy, and Casey H. Rawson (Santa Barbara, CA: Libraries Unlimited, 2017), 3-30.

11. "About," Medgar Evers College, http://www.mec.cuny.edu/about/.

12. Medgar Evers College, "About the Charles Evans Inniss Memorial Library," *Library Facts & Data Booklet* (New York: CEIML, 2014), 1.

students regardless of their experiences or their ability to conduct research.

The P373K Brooklyn Transition Center is a public school that describes itself as "a diverse educational community serving students identified with learning and intellectual disabilities, emotional disturbance, and autism."[13] The school places special needs students and staff in worksite environments in Brooklyn. These sites are usually nonprofit institutions located in the community such as schools, nursing homes, and hospitals. Students learn how to perform job-related tasks in these hosted worksites.

Project Overview

Beginning in the fall of 2014, when the Medgar Evers College library moved into its newly renovated state-of-the-art facility, Marc Parrella, the P373K special education teacher, approached the library department chair to discuss the possibility of giving his students the opportunity to use the library as a work-experience training site as well as providing the students with access to the library's computers. The chair agreed, thus marking the beginning of the partnership. P373K students began using the library, where they perform organizational and light custodial duties. They were also granted a regularly scheduled time to access technology in a computer lab.

In the ensuing years, the partnership between the library and the P373K students has evolved into an ongoing learning experience. Several librarians have participated in class instruction. The partners have introduced multiple approaches such as including students in regular information literacy classes, teaching technology literacy skills, and creating a yearbook project that would give the students a tangible takeaway. Each approach provided value to both students and teachers. As part of their community inclusion experience, students first participated in information literacy workshops in the library in a classroom

---

13. "Mission Statement," Brooklyn Transition Center, http://p373kbtc.org/mission-statement.

setting among college students, where they were introduced to databases and research terminology. Participating in college-level classes without adaptations to individual student learning characteristics can be extremely challenging for people with intellectual disabilities. To overcome these challenges, the special education teacher worked with the author/librarian to create a project-based learning approach tailored to the special needs students. Collaborating and working with the group in their own workshop setting seemed more appropriate because of each student's individual learning needs.

The author/librarian is an Adobe Education Trainer who currently teaches a series of visual literacy workshops in the library including basic design, infographics, and an introduction to the Adobe Creative Suite software including Photoshop, InDesign, and Illustrator. The P373K transition program special education teacher requested that the librarian teach Photoshop to his students. After obtaining the approval of the library department chair, she became the "embedded librarian" for this class. This was the first time she had worked with learners who have developmental disabilities. Twelve students and three P373K staff members were in attendance in the library's Mac lab. They met a few times a month throughout the semester and focused on digital literacy skills. In an article about the recent trend of "embedded librarianship," Shumaker advocates for the use of this term "because the librarian becomes a member of the customer community rather than a service provider standing apart."[14] The author immersed herself in the class and became a collaborative partner and project coordinator.

In this library partnership class, students learned a combination of interrelated literacy skills including visual literacy, information literacy, and digital literacy. The Association of College and Research Libraries (ACRL) defines visual literacy as "a set of abilities that enables an individual to effectively find, interpret, evaluate, use, and create images

---

14. David Shumaker, "Who Let the Librarians Out? Embedded Librarianship and the Library Manager," *Reference & User Services Quarterly* 48, no. 3 (2009), 240.

Figure 1. Schwartz, Judith. Yearbook Class, interior page. Photo: Clareese Hill, 2016.

and visual media."[15] It incorporates this concept under the umbrella of information literacy. The American Library Association's (ALA) digital task force defined digital literacy as "the ability to use information and communication technologies to find, understand, evaluate, create, and communicate digital information, an ability that requires both cognitive and technical skills."[16] The report states, "Twenty-first century digital literacy skills are basic to classroom performance and workforce readiness, as well as full participation in civic life."[17]

---

15. Association of College and Research Libraries, ACRL *Visual Literacy Competency Standards for Higher Education* (Chicago: ALA, 2011), http://www.ala.org/acrl/standards/visualliteracy.

16. American Library Association, *Digital Literacy, Libraries, and Public Policy Task Force Report* (Chicago: ALA, 2013), 2.

17. Ibid, 4.

Figure 2. Schwartz, Judith. Yearbook Class, interior page.
Photo: Dinley Leconte, 2017.

In a 2003 article, Chauvin describes literacy terminology as being interchangeable.[18] B. R. Harris contends: "The relationship between information literacy and visual literacy has been described as being intertwined."[19] He asserts that visual information and written text both require information literacy skills.[20] The visual literacy workshops fall under the umbrella of information literacy in the library. After careful consideration, the author and the special needs teacher identified what was actually being taught in the class as digital or technology literacy.

---

18. B. A. Chauvin, "Visual or Media Literacy?" *Journal of Visual Literacy* 23, no.2 (2003), 120-121.

19. B. R. Harris, "Blurring Borders, Visualizing Connections: Aligning Information and Visual Literacy Learning Outcomes," *Reference Services Review* 38, no.4 (2010), 524.

20. Ibid, 523.

Figure. 3. Schwartz, Judith. Yearbook, front cover.
Photo: Clareese Hill, 2016.

A recent ACRL report states that academic library partnerships "yield positive benefits for students." It concludes: "Collaborative academic programs and services involving the library enhance student learning."[21] The special needs students who participated in the Medgar Evers-P373K partnership were of college age. However, because they were not formally enrolled as matriculated students, there was no formal assessment of their performance. The library collaboration presented students with an opportunity to work within the college community in a library setting with college staff.

---

21. Kara J. Malenfant and Karen Brown, "Academic Library Impact on Student Learning and Success: Findings from Assessment in Action Team Projects" (Chicago: Association of College and Research Libraries, 2017), 2.

Figure. 4. Schwartz, Judith. Yearbook, front cover.
Photo: Marc Parrella, 2017.

The following semester the special education teacher suggested working on a yearbook. This endeavor would enable the students to learn digital literacy skills and apply them to an actual project. The partners collaborated with the students to plan and design a yearbook that would generate a tangible end product.

The first few sessions weren't highly structured. Rather, the students drove the class content by their comments and discussions. Students were given the opportunity to interact with a library professor and have their voices heard. Working on a book project is a collaborative undertaking. The students learned about the book-making process beginning with brainstorming sessions, researching yearbooks online, and compiling lists of ideas in order to make decisions concerning content and design. Throughout the semester, the P373K special education teacher compiled a design vocabulary list that was turned into a plain language lexicon for the students. There was a thumbnail page design session in which students collectively decided the content of each page, the final page count, and how the interior pages and cover would look. Students participated in a photo shoot and later in a photo-editing session. A production schedule was created and followed to meet the printer's deadline to ensure the books would be available before the end of the semester.

The following are examples of lesson themes:

- Basic Photoshop skills were introduced, using tools to manipulate and add effects to photos. This theme included examples and discussions of image-editing techniques and photo manipulation.
- Copyright infringement issues were discussed, as were the results of Google's advanced image search filters to find copyright-free, high-resolution images. Students received instruction on saving images from the web to the computer.
- Graphic Design file formats were explained. The lesson included examples of file resolution sizes, raster versus vector art, varying color and monitor display differences, and web versus print.
- Students received lessons on email, in which they learned to set up Gmail accounts and then practiced writing and sending emails. They also learned how to use a scanner, send files to their email, and open file attachments in Photoshop.
- Students learned about credible sources, fake news, accuracy, and where information comes from. They had the opportunity to work with several library databases.
- Students were introduced to vocabulary words related to design and production technology.
- Students were introduced to typography basics, particularly the difference between serif and sans serif font families.
- Students received an introduction to art direction, page layout, and InDesign.

Goals and Best Practices

The partnership goals were to provide the P373K students with information literacy development in a college learning environment and to offer them the same access opportunities that are available to the wider community.

The class was conducted utilizing the combined skills of the special needs teacher and the librarian, who uses the Adobe Education Training Model in visual literacy-related workshops:

"Motivation," a lecture and demonstration (10 minutes)
"Learning Activity" and "Guided Practice" (20 minutes)
"Independent Practice" (10 minutes)
"Wrap Up," lesson review (5 minutes)

The library classes enabled students to use computer technologies and to learn hands-on digital and information literacy skills, basic graphic design tools, layout, and vocabulary. Based on their experiences during the partnership, the author and the special education teacher recommend the following best practices for planning a project:
Plan and design a syllabus.

- Schedule the sessions and reserve the computer labs in advance.
- Begin the project early in the school year to encourage greater student collaboration and participation.
- Conduct regular meetings to discuss project goals and to create a production schedule with deadlines.
- Make detailed checklists of everything that needs to be done from initial planning stages, through design and layout, to the final printed product.
- Find a printing house, order paper samples, and negotiate prices and deadlines.
- Follow a production schedule based on the final book delivery date.

Reflection

The partnership has been very successful. To meet the project goals, both the special education teacher and librarian brought their individualized skill sets to the classroom. Marc Parrella, transition coordinator and special education teacher, observed, "Over the course of the past few school years, students and staff from P373K worked with Professor Judith Schwartz from the Library and Information Services Department to design, photograph, and assemble the yearbook. Our project is an example of what a thoughtful collaboration can produce for our students."

The special education teacher brought his understanding of how people with intellectual disabilities learn. He worked on adapting the language and ideas in a way that enabled the students to participate meaningfully in the planning and design process. The author previously had worked as an art director and design manager on numerous book projects for major educational publishers.[22] She has also taught university-level graphic design classes, is currently on the library faculty at the college, and teaches information literacy workshops to undergraduate students. The two partners work well together. Teaching hands-on technology to people with cognitive disabilities is a challenge due to their limitations in abstract thinking. Consequently, the teaching approach had to be adapted to the level of these special learners with different abilities. Although a lack of skills served as an obstacle in the physical bookmaking process, the partners aimed to encourage student involvement in the actual design process by having verbal discussions and making group decisions. The librarian would teach the class and follow the Adobe model. The special education teacher would then translate the materials and break things down to a more elemental level. The partners had to be flexible because the intended lessons could not always be followed and the classes frequently had to be improvised.

---

22. Mary J. Snyder Broussard and Judith Schwartz, "Visual Literacy Meets Information Literacy: How Two Academic Librarians Combined Information Science and Design in Their Careers," in *Skills to Make a Librarian*, ed. Dawn Wincentsen (Oxford, UK: Chandos Publishing, 2015), 146-147.

Parrella states, "Our students' time at Medgar Evers College is very important to their social, cognitive, and emotional development. Most of our students come to the college from 'self-contained' environments, school settings where all of the other students had disability classifications similar to their own. The effect that their experience at the college has on their integration into the larger community is significant. The college setting allows our students to experience an unsegregated environment throughout their entire school day."

The City University of New York has embraced the philosophy of corporate social responsibility (CSR), in which large institutions encourage their workers to volunteer or perform charitable works for the good of the community. For an academic faculty librarian in CUNY, one reappointment and tenure criterion is "Service to the Public" such as volunteer work in the community.

In an article about academic librarians and social justice, Lockman provides examples of how her university library is involved in a form of activism called microactivism, which is defined as the practice of engaging in small actions that will benefit the greater purpose.[23] She contends that academic librarians should start a social justice revolution in the course of their everyday work to make a difference.[24] It is important for academic librarians to become social change agents, to volunteer, and to engage beyond the library and classroom environments.

In the case study partnership, the Medgar Evers College library's role is to empower those students who have not had these opportunities in other settings, providing them with computer access and college-level guidance. Expanding beyond the traditional reach of the academic community and working with this diverse, special needs community is a form of microactivism; specifically, it is a small-scale effort of outreach and community building.

---

23. "Microactivist: Individuals Doing Little Acts That Collectively Create Massive Change," accessed June 10, 2017, www.microactivist.com.

24. Rachel Lockman, "Academic Librarians and Social Justice: A Call to Microactivism," *College and Research Libraries News* 76, no. 4 (2015), 193-194.

In the past, the author has participated in pro-bono graphic design work for nonprofit organizations. This is the first time she has volunteered to teach library information technology skills. She contends that it is essential to connect to communities, to be altruistic, and to share what she has to offer beyond the classroom and the college community. This is a form of microactivism, as well as a highly rewarding experience.

Conclusion

The partnership between an academic library and a NYC public school evolved over the course of several years. The Medgar Evers College library has provided an inclusive environment that is beneficial to both institutions. There are many benefits to the library. Helping this underserved population aligns the library with the school's mission to promote educational resources for the college and the surrounding neighborhoods of Central Brooklyn. It keeps the library connected to the community and demonstrates the feasibility of integrating other non-college school populations into the library's information literacy program. It also allows the library to serve as an example for other institutions that may wish to promote their services through microactivism. By experimenting with various teaching approaches, the partners in both academic institutions worked symbiotically to create a learning environment that is tailored to individual students' learning abilities. This approach has generated positive outcomes that will benefit the students in their future endeavors.

Bibliography

American Library Association. *Library Engagement Policy Manual B.8.10 Library Services to the Poor.* Chicago: ALA, 2012.

American Library Association. *OITP Digital Literacy Task Force Report: Digital Literacy, Libraries, and Public Policy.* Chicago: ALA, January 2013.

American Library Association. *Final Report of the ALA Task Force on Equity, Diversity, and Inclusion.* Chicago: ALA, 2016.

Association of College and Research Libraries. *ACRL Visual Literacy Competency Standards for Higher Education*. Chicago: Association of College and Research Libraries ALA, October 2011. http://www.ala.org/acrl/standards/visualliteracy.

Brault, Matthew W. *Americans with Disabilities Report, Current Population Reports Household Economic Studies*. Washington, DC: U.S. Census Bureau, 2010.https://www.census.gov/content/dam/Census/library/publications/2012/demo/p70-131.pdf.

Brewer, Bailey. "Libraries Transforming Communities." *American Libraries* 46, no. 1/2 (January 2015): 50-53.

Brooklyn Transition Center, in "Mission Statement," accessed April 2017. http://p373kbtc.org/mission-statement.

Broussard, Mary J. Snyder, and Judith Schwartz. "Visual Literacy Meets Information Literacy: How Two Academic Librarians Combined Information Science and Design in Their Careers." In *Skills to Make a Librarian*, edited by Dawn Lowe-Wincentsen, 137-53. Oxford, UK: Chandos Publishing, 2015.

Carlson, Tracy. "All in a Good Cause." *Meaningful Marketing ADMAP* (April 2012): 24-27.

Chauvin, B. A. "Visual or Media Literacy?" *Journal of Visual Literacy* 23, no. 2 (2003): 119-128.

Drewes, Kathy, and Nadine Hoffman. "Academic Embedded Librarianship:An Introduction." *Public Services Quarterly, Library and Information Science Source* 6, no. 2/3 (2010): 75-82.

Durham, Jo, Claire E. Brolan, and Bryan Mukandi. "The Convention on the Rights of Persons with Disabilities: A Foundation for Ethical Disability and Health Research in Developing Countries." *American Journal of Public Health* 104, no.11 (2014): 2037-2043. PMC. Web. 11 June 2017.

Harris, B. R. "Blurring Borders, Visualizing Connections: Aligning Information and visual Literacy Learning Outcomes." *Reference Services Review 38*, no. 4 (2010): 523-535.

Harris Poll. "Social Change Impact Report." Minneapolis MN: Walden University and Harris Poll, June 2014.

Horrigan, John. B. *Broadband Adoption and Use in America: OBI Working Paper Series No. 1*. Washington, DC: Federal Communications Commission, February 2012. http://hraunfoss.fcc.gov/edocs_public/attachmatch/DOC-296442A1.pdf.

Horrigan, John B. *Digital Readiness Gaps*. Washington, DC: Pew Rsearch Center, September 2016. http://www.pewinternet.org/2016/09/20/digital-readiness-gaps/.

Hughes-Hassell, Sandra, and Casey H. Rawson. "Literacy Education for African American Youth: A Social Justice Issue for Librarians." In *Libraries, Literacy, and African American Youth: Research and Practice*, edited by Sandra Hughes-Hassell, Pauletta Brown Bracy, and Casey H. Rawson, 3-30. Santa Barbara, CA: Libraries Unlimited, 2017.

Jaeger, Paul. T, "Disability, Human Rights, and Social Justice: The Ongoing Struggle for Online Accessibility and Equality." *First Monday* 20, no.9 (2015). http://firstmonday.org/ojs/index.php/fm/article/view/6164/4898.

Keogh, Kristina M., and Stephen A. Patton. "Embedded Art Librarianship: Project Partnerships from Concept to Production." *Art Documentation Journal of the Art Libraries Society of North America* 35, no.1 (2016): 144-163.

Lockman, Rachel. "Academic Librarians and Social Justice: A Call to Microactivism." *College and Research Libraries News* 76, no. 4 (2015): 193-194.

Malenfant, Kara J. and Karen Brown. *Academic Library Impact on Student Learning and Success: Findings from Assessment in Action Team Projects*. Chicago: Association of College and Research Libraries ALA, 2017.

Medgar Evers College in "Mission Statement." Accessed June 2017. http://www.mec.cuny.edu/about/

Medgar Evers College Library. "Charles Evans Inniss Memorial Library Facts & Data Booklet," About the Library." New York: CEIML, 2014.

Microactivist. "Individuals Doing Little Acts that Collectively Create Massive Change." Accessed June 10, 2017. www.microactivist.com.

Moni, Karen B., and Anne Jobling. "Latch-on: A Program to Develop Literacy in Young Adults with Down Syndrome." *Journal of Adolescent & Adult Literacy* 44, no. 1 (2000): 40-49.

Flannery, Mary Ellen, "A Growing Hunger." *NEA Higher Education Advocate* 35, no. 1 (2017): 5-6.

Shumaker, David. "Who Let the Librarians Out? Embedded Librarianship and the Library Manager." *Reference & User Services Quarterly, Library and Information Science Source* 48, no. 3 (2009): 239-257.

United Nations Educational, Scientific and Cultural Organization. *The Right to Education for Persons with Disabilities*. Paris: UNESCO, 2015. http://unesdoc.unesco.org/images/0023/002325/232592e.pdf.

Case Study 14

AGE MATES, PLAY GROUPS, AND THE COMMUNITY BUILDING BLOCKS OF LEADERSHIP FOR PUBLIC HOUSING RESIDENTS

Roland Barksdale-Hall

Abstract

This case study examines a collaboration between a public housing library and a nonprofit organization to provide preschool and afterschool arts, storytelling, civic, and healthy lifestyles programming to public housing residents. The library is the centerpiece of the community and integral to resident services. The librarian provides supervision and training of AmeriCorps members. Training modules offered by the library to AmeriCorps members include Cultural Competency and Skill-Building Workshops. Children's program highlights include anti-bullying, homework help, storytelling, and book giveaways. The library received the Coretta Scott King Book Donation Award in 2016.

Background

The Quinby Street Resource Center library located in the Mercer County Housing Authority's Malleable Heights community in Sharon, Pennsylvania is the centerpiece of a vibrant community with an active tenant's group and numerous events throughout the year.[1] In 2012 the Mercer

---

1. Mercer County Housing Authority, accessed July 27, 2017, http://www.mercercountyhousingauthority.com/web_communities/malleable_heights.php.

County Housing Authority (MCHA), which is one of 3,300 public authorities in the country, secured a commitment to a renewable grant from the Shenango Valley Foundation and hired a library director. The action taken during the initial phase of a five-year strategic plan was viewed as a step toward achieving the following goal: to enhance the quality of life for families who need affordable, safe housing choices and supportive services in well-maintained neighborhoods. This case study examines collaboration between a public housing library and a nonprofit with a youth focus to expand outreach through preschool and afterschool arts, storytelling, civics, and healthy lifestyles programming for public housing residents.

What outcomes can we anticipate by investing now in our youth? Book Rich Environment Initiative[2] (a partnership with U.S. Housing and Urban Development, the U.S. Department of Education, and other nonprofits) hopes to increase the educational success of boys and men through the promotion of reading.[3] Innovation allows the organization to reach traditionally underserved communities. Quinby Street Resource Center celebrates youth success in the public housing community. Public schools, through Twenty-First Century Community Learning Center federally-funded activities, offer expanded school library hours, provide tutoring, and increase outside school learning opportunities.[4] Participation in playgroup, after-school, and adult programs improve health, social interaction, and educational outcomes.

Parallels exist globally. Literacy is critical to progress in developing countries. For example, the African Library Project shows how books

---

2. Georgi Banna, "Book Rich Environment Initiative Launched," *NAHRO Blog: Legislative and Policy Updates from Washington, DC*, accessed July 27, 2017, https://nahroblog.org/2017/01/05/book-rich-environment-initiative-launched/.

3. Christina Vercelletto, "Libraries Join National Initiative to Transform Public Housing into Book-Rich Environments," *School Library Journal* (January 2017), accessed July 8, 2017, http://www.slj.com/2017/01/industry-news/libraries-join-national-initiative-to-transform-public-housing-into-book-rich-environments/#_.

4. U.S. Department of Education, accessed October 29, 2017, https://www2.ed.gov/programs/21stcclc/applicant.html.

changed the social fabric of rural communities.[5] The African Library Project, a literacy organization with a mission to "coordinate book drives in the United States and partner with schools" and communal networks, establishes libraries in Anglophone countries located in western, eastern, and southern Africa. The African partner provides "space, staff, and furniture for the library...trains teacher-librarians" and increases educational outcomes.[6] Dr. Martha Bruce, mentor and nontraditional community educator, taught teachers in Nigeria. As a visiting eductor, Dr. Bruce developed children's storytelling with dance, songs, and English lessons. She invited eight youth to her home in Nigeria and began a literacy program which met weekly and grew to 135 youths. Dr. Bruce explained the term "age mate," as a Nigerian peer group similar in age who through shared play or activities bonded, helped one another throughout life and later assumed proactive community leadership roles in building institutions. Her story-time mentees recognized benefits of the playgroup and its impact on leadership development.[7]

In the United States, innovation is also changing communities. Terry Bellamy "grew up in public housing," faced the false image of public housing residents as "lazy, unemployed by choice and scamming the system" and sought empowerment for "these hard-working families" seeking to better their situation.[8] In 2015, Bellamy, the former mayor of Ashville, was hired as the Asheville Housing Authority development's "first neighborhood outreach coordinator/communication specialist." He helped to establish a partnership between Big Brothers Big Sisters of Western North Carolina, Asheville development's Resident Councils, and Read to Succeed Asheville, a literacy nonprofit organization with a

---

5. Jason Alston, "The African Library Project is Changing Rural Africa One Library at a Time," *BCALA News* (Spring 2017), accessed July 27, 2017, http://bcala.org/Spring2017SpreadsInteractive/Spring2017SpreadsInteractive.html#p=48.

6. African Library Project, accessed November 5, 2017, http://www.africanlibraryproject.org/our-african-libraries/overview.

7. Aleah Jones, "Honoring Auntie Martha," *Pitt Magazine* (Summer 2012): 41.

8. Walton Beth, "Former Asheville Mayor Joins Housing Authority," accessed November 5, 2017, http://www.citizen-times.com/story/news/local/2015/04/27/former-asheville-mayor-joins-housing-authority/26474875/.

mission "to support the city and county schools in reducing the literacy achievement gap."[9] Thirty youth public housing residents participated in a "job readiness" program, "cleaned neighborhoods," and created book boxes to promote literacy and community empowerment at the Asheville development.[10] Barksdale-Hall presents a case study about genealogy and local history as play activity focused upon expanding outreach to various age mates and the development of a senior employment computer training at the Quinby Street Resource Center and Centennial Place development. The senior employment program is funded through a grant from the United States Department of Labor. He discusses best practices in partnering for development of adult programming in support of financial literacy and employment seeking as a case study on the Malleable Heights' Quinby Street Resource Center.[11]

Deborah J. Spiller and Michael Baker provide a model for library service planning in other public housing communities based upon needs assessment.[12] During the late 1980s, the Chicago Public Library hired Marketing Institute, a research company whose staff included a "librarian, a research specialist, and a staff member who had lived in a Chicago Housing Authority (CHA) development... worked for the CHA for ten years... [and] served as the community specialist and acted as the primary liaison with the community."[13] In consultation with the Public Library Association, they developed a pioneering study of the Robert Home Developments, one public housing site in Chicago. Twelve residents were hired to conduct three in-person interview surveys (a resident survey, library user survey, and a community leader survey) and

---

9. Read to Succeed Asheville, accessed November 5, 2017, http://www.r2sasheville.org/.

10. Beth Walton, "Mountain Causes: Books for Children," accessed July 8, 2017, http://www.haca.org/index.php/mountain-causes-books-for-children/.

11. Roland Barksdale-Hall, "Collaboration Fits the Bill for Best Practices in Programming for Public Housing Residents," In *The Libraries Role in Supporting Financial Literacy*. Ed. Carol Smallwood. (Lanham, MD: Rowman and Littlefield, 2016), 236.

12. Deborah J. Spiller and Michael Baker, "Library Service to Residents of Public Housing Developments: A Study and Commentary," *Public Libraries* (1989): 358.

13. Ibid., 359.

achieved an amazing 97% response rate. The unusually high response rate "underscored the importance of resident involvement."[14] Three out of four respondents reported using library services. The report identified several "critical factors" in the planning study:

- Active resident participation in the study was key to successful planning and implementation.
- The "uniqueness of service area" characterized as "physically, economically and socially isolated from the rest of Chicago."
- Residents' "sensitivity" to the "perceptions" by outsiders and some social stigma likely attributed to isolation.
- "Need to understand"…"education for all ages and services to children and young people" and "implication for materials, services and space."
- Importance of ongoing marketing and "networking with other agencies.[15]

Partnerships between public housing authorities and libraries are explored through service to underserved communities, cost saving, and resource sharing. Troy Lambert examines trends to reduce costs yet increase impact by highlighting contemporary case studies of collaboration between housing authorities and public libraries in Los Angeles, California; Milwaukee, Wisconsin; and Chicago, Illinois. In August 2013 a "joint project" between the Los Angeles Public Library, the Housing Authority of the City of Los Angeles, and Kids Progress Inc. (an organization formed by the housing authority in 2009) opened a satellite library at the Estrada Court development. The project lasted about a year, achieved some success and closed due to "lack of funding." Plans for revisiting this project remain under consideration for the future. The Milwaukee Public Library opened an automated and unstaffed branch at the Westlawn Gardens housing development. In 2018

---

14. Ibid., 360.

15. Ibid., 361.

Chicago Public Library plans to open three libraries: one on the ground floor of a senior site and the others in "mixed-income housing developments."[16]

Partner Overview

The Quinby Street Resource Center Library, located in Sharon's Malleable Heights multi-family public housing development, offers the following services: employment seeking, career planning, computer training, and community programs.

Quinby Street Resource Center serves approximately 1100 moderate-to-low income households, reaching over 600 youths. Service areas include public housing developments in Sharon, the neighboring communities of Farrell, Wheatland, Sharpsville, and outlying areas of Greenville and Mercer. In 2010, the population of Sharon was 14,038 and 5,111 in Farrell. 14.6% of the population in Sharon claimed African ancestry and 48.8% in Farrell. There exists moderate-to-high poverty and underemployment.

The resource center's collection consists of 4,000 books and 100 multimedia materials, along with six computers housed in a multipurpose meeting room. Resources support storytime for pre-k playgroups, after school study help, enrichment for ages 6-12, and adult programming at multi-family and senior sites.

Prior to 2012 a partnership existed between the MCHA and the Community Library of the Shenango Valley for several years. Through the partnership, Quinby Street Resource Center Library in the Malleable Heights complex of 88 multifamily brick townhomes operated as a satellite library. The housing authority provided the facility and maintenance. The public library reached a traditionally underserved community by providing materials and staffing. Yet the Quinby Street Resource Center lacked official branch status. Though the politics of

---

16. Troy Lambert, "Bringing the Library Home: Adding Libraries to Public Housing Developments Shares Resources and Costs," *American Libraries Magazine* (May 1, 2017), accessed July 1, 2017, https://americanlibrariesmagazine.org/2017/05/01/bringing-library-home-public-housing/.

this remains unclear, Quinby Street Resource Center faced closure due to a loss of funding from the public library.

As a result, Quinby Street Resource Center partnered with AmeriCorps, a voluntary service program supported by the U.S. federal government, foundations, corporations, and donors focused on engaging adults in public service work with a goal of "helping others and meeting critical needs in the community."[17] AmeriCorps members commit to full-time or part-time positions offered by a network of nonprofit community organizations and public agencies, to fulfill assignments in the fields of education, public safety, healthcare, and environmental protection. Cost share arrangements exist between MCHA and AmeriCorps. MCHA provides cash contributions to support programming at two learning centers, summer programming at various sites, and services to a rehabilitation garden site. MCHA offers a meeting place, access to various community building spaces for AmeriCorps programming, and assistance with purchasing certain supplies. AmeriCorps provides workers through a grant. Program offerings include a pre-k playgroup and afterschool at the Centennial site four days a week. AmeriCorps provides supervisory staff and provides a traveling summer program for MCHA family sites.

Purpose-Driven Living

The Quinby Street Resource Center assists families in their quest for self-sufficiency through education, job training, and culture. The library strategic planning committee included the library director, housing counselor, property manager, and resident initiative coordinator.

Quinby Street Resource Center identified planning, resident involvement, and partnering as critical to success. The library director developed a resident needs assessment and distributed it door-to-door. A gift card drawing was organized in an effort to increase response rates. Focus groups, program evaluations, and service requests provided data for

---

17. https://www.nationalservice.gov/sites/default/files/resource/Training_and_Retaining_ACMembers_Webinar_Description_of_audio.pdf.

development of goals, an annual program planning calendar, and a three-year plan. Focus group members included property managers and tenant's group leaders. A Resident Opportunities and Self-Sufficiency (ROSS) grant from the U.S. Housing and Urban Development agency made possible new computers, a photocopier, library furniture, and a children's rug. The ROSS grant provides for the hiring of service coordinators, promotes "development of local strategies" for service coordination of help with a combination of "private and public resources," and focuses upon "empowerment" of residents through financial literacy and "housing self-sufficiency."[18] A profile of a pioneer resident leader, Annabelle Wilder-Wright, included a social context for discussion of resident self-sufficiency, background on social change, and development of reading and after-school programming at Centennial Place, one of the MCHA sites in Farrell, Pennsylvania.

Measure of Success

The Quinby Center faced limited staffing, limited materials budget, and public perception as a high crime area. A need for information service delivery existed due to lack of transportation, isolation, and poor reading scores. The librarian solicited resident involvement, undertook a collection maintenance project, and sought materials through grants. The resolve of resident leaders to make the change happen was worthy of emulation.

Partnerships with nonprofits and active resident participation led to success in reaching goals. Shared goals include: to increase educational outcomes, to promote literacy, to provide equal employment opportunity, to build healthy, safe communities, and to foster empowerment and economic self-sufficiency for families. In 2016 I served as the graduation speaker for the playgroup. Students developed social skills, learned about health, and listened to storytelling. The Quinby Center gave away older and duplicate books to thirty-two

---

18. U.S. Housing and Urban Development, accessed November 6, 2017, https://www.hud.gov/program_offices/public_indian_housing/programs/ph/ross/about.

children during a Summer Youth Book Giveaway organized by the library's AmeriCorps and senior employment, and was later recognized with a 2016 Coretta Scott King Book Donation Award. AmeriCorps developed curriculum, demonstrated care for the community, and devoted 320 service hours to the Centennial Place playgroup and afterschool program. In August, the library, in collaboration with AmeriCorps, sponsored a "Back to School Bash," giving out backpacks with school supplies to almost fifty youth.

In 2017, in response to stated needs, the librarian developed and implemented a diversity training module for the AmeriCorps team members. The Cultural Competency and Diversity Building Bridges Workshop included various diversity speakers from a local Urban League chapter and various social service agencies. Training evaluation included questions designed to assess levels of satisfaction with the housing authority partnership. One AmeriCorps member stated, "It is a good partnership, both organizations have the passion of serving those in need," and "I think we work very well together." I facilitated a panel at the Keystone Smiles AmeriCorps Sharpsville Gardens Learning Center with a parent and family liaison from a local public school and the executive director from a local county mentoring program to address bullying.

Family-based programs aimed to improve safety, health and well-being, financial stability, and educational outcomes. AmeriCorps brought the Agricultural Safety Day summer program to community and after school activities with a focus on science, technology, reading, engineering, arts, and mathematics at housing development sites. Quinby Street Resource Center partnered with Greenville Literacy Council for homework help, GED classes, resume writing, and computer tutoring. Six-week life skills courses included an expanded Food and Nutrition Program in partnership with the Penn State Cooperative Extension as well as a parenting training and a financial literacy course in partnership with Quinby Street Resource Center Library, Mercer County Behavioral Health Commission, Prince of Peace Awesome Program, and Mercer County Community Action.

A partnership with Prince of Peace provided program participants with an incentive. Residents received a Prince of Peace Awesome Grant up to $125 dollars toward a life-sustaining bill (such as auto repairs, utilities, or rent) upon completion of each course. Program participation increased 300 percent. The AmeriCorps and Mercer County Housing Authority partnered to provide older youth with academic and work experience, renovated four houses, and created affordable low-income housing which residents purchased.[19]

In Pursuit of Excellence

The partnership with Keystone Smiles AmeriCorps fit well with the institution's vision and goals. *The Mercer County Housing Authority Strategic 5 Year Plan 2013-2018* included the following goals:

- Increase programming at center
- Establish a newsletter to market to and inform community
- Increase resident-supportive services

AmeriCorps members assisted in program development, maintained relational power, possessed compassion for youth, and became social change agents. In 2017, youth participated in the library's first Martin Luther King Cultural Day Challenge, learned about citizenship, and played Jeopardy. Afterschoolers enjoyed the competition and the battle of wits, and won trophies. The Martin Luther King Cultural Day Challenge program, AmeriCorps members, and the librarian were featured on an evening television news program. The Quinby Street Resource Center was named a 2017 Día Grant Winner from the Center for Multicultural Children's Literature. Respondents to the diversity training evaluation listed storytelling as the top future training topic. Día events included a storytelling program held at the Sharpsville Garden Keystone Smiles AmeriCorps Children's Learning Center, on one of the MCHA

---

19. Keystone Smiles AmeriCorps, accessed November 6,2 017, https://www.smilesamericorps.org/.

sites, followed by a storytelling training for AmeriCorps members the next day. The Quinby Center received a Día Award of thirty-nine new multicultural books.

The MCHA News, the newsletter of the housing authority, listed the following activities and new programs:

- Summer 2016—"Donations Support Youth Cultural Club and Collection at Quinby Street Resource Center"; "Celebrating Our Graduates and Awesome Kids" with coverage of keynote storyteller for playgroup graduation at Centennial Place, and successful high school graduates
- Fall 2016— "Grand People Our Children Love," story of the Grandparent's Day Celebration outreach with lesson on appreciation to playgroup and afterschoolers at Centennial Place; images of youth with the library director and AmeriCorps member from "Back to School" programs with book bags and school supplies at Quinby Street Resource Center, Centennial Place and Sharpsville Gardens Children Learning Center; "Community Notes" about "Stop Bullying: Love Your Neighbor" program at Sharpsville Gardens Children Learning Center in partnership with public schools, Mercer County Mentoring, AmeriCorps and Quinby Street Resource Center
- Winter 2016—"Friends and Families Enjoy Thanksgiving," story about Thanksgiving dinner outreach for families of playgroup and after-school at Centennial Place; announcement about intergenerational caroling with playgroup at McDowell Manor, one of the senior developments
- Spring 2017—job announcement seeking residents for summer AmeriCorps workers for housing authority developments; image from a bus activity at Diversity Training with AmeriCorps members
- Summer 2017—"Join in a Summer of Smiles" story about summer program offerings; 2017 Día event highlights.

Challenges in executing the partnership centered around meeting residents where they are. Building trusting relationships occurred over a series of transactions. Interventions included letter writing assistance for a stop sign at the Quinby Street Center to direct advocacy. AmeriCorps' commitment produced an impact.

Quinby Street Resource Center benefitted from active resident participation. Here are some profiles of our residents.

Resident Leader Profile I

"Ms. Annabelle…was a true champion, a former resident of the former Steel City Housing complex. She continued fighting for the next generation of children who would come out of the projects. She wanted the youth educated with hopes and dreams that they were somebody. She wanted better housing conditions to improve for the younger mother. She wanted reading and after school programs incorporated into the Steel City recreation center. At the time the center was being used for storage. She wanted the drugs and drug dealers out of the apartment complex; she felt that the drug dealers were a negative influence on the children.

Ms. Annabelle Wilder felt the children deserved better. She wanted the youth to grow and thrive in a better environment. Due to the latter, she worked closely with the Mercer County Authority…. She was a trailblazer, who was very instrumental in getting the implementation of Centennial Place. She constantly and consistently met with [the executive director]. She wrote letters to [the local newspaper] about the need to rid the complex of drugs and drug dealing in the community. She wanted the community to be a place where one could call home. At the time she was not fighting for herself but for the next generation of young people, who would emerge out of public housing."[20]

Resident Leader Profile II

In 2013 Marjorie, the first resident of public housing became an AmeriCorps member and served as a library assistant at the Quinby

---

20. "Our Housing Heroine for the Month of June and July," *Quinby Street Resource Center Newsletter* (May/Jume. 2015): 2.

Street Resource Center. A longtime resident leader, Ms. Paula tirelessly labored with youth programs at Quinby Center. Announcements about the dancercise class with Miss Marjorie leading it, Easter Egg hunt with Miss Paula, World Book Night event appeared in the March/April 2013 *Quinby Street Resource Center Newsletter*. Every inch of shelving was occupied with books, Marjorie recalled. "The adult fiction was the only thing with a semblance of order." She pulled up her sleeves, assisted with collection maintenance, book club, and youth programs. Feance, a former resident, donated books about African-American culture.[21]

Resident Leader Profile III

In 2016 Tisha, a resident, joined as an AmeriCorps library assistant in the Quinby Street Resource Center. Tisha lacked self-confidence and initially thought she would not succeed. Yet she developed confidence as she proceeded through this service project. She made beautiful frames from Popsicle sticks that children decorated for their grandparents that will be family heirlooms.

Tisha persuaded youth and adults to participate in programming. She was successful in contacting businesses and solicited donations for the Back to School Bash. Sponsors for the back-to-school bash included United Way, local health providers, pizza shops, bakeries and local pharmacy. She possessed skills in the media and culinary arts. She reached into her own pocket to make the change happen. She went beyond the call of service to make over a hundred cupcakes for youth.

Expressions of Gratitude

Lives literally changed. When I accepted resident requests for AmeriCorps assignment at the Quinby Resource Center I made a conscious decision to undergird the resident leadership role for all ages. Through a 2016 Coretta Scott King book donation award I promoted literacy. Playgroup members responded favorably to a reading of Kadir Nelson's

---

21. Roland Barksdale-Hall, "Collaboration Fits the Bill for Best Practices in Programming for Public Housing Residents." in *The Libraries Role in Supporting Financial Literacy* (Lanham, MD: Rowman and Littlefield, 2016): 237.

If You Plant A Seed. Children reflected upon the message of sharing, kindness, and cooperation and responded, "Now, that's a good book!"

Young males now are reading. Yesterday two youth came into the library. They had just been outside playing with squirt guns. One thirteen-year-old was so excited about the DVDs. He really likes Bruce Lee and Hell Raiser.

"What would you be interested in reading?" I asked.

"Jackie Robinson and Muhammad Ali. I like chapter books."

It was gratifying to know the youth knew of Jackie Robinson and Muhammad Ali. He was delighted to check out *Twelve Rounds to Glory: The Story of Muhammad Ali.* The thirteen-year-old male promised he would return the book in an hour.

His younger friend expressed amazement when he discovered I was an author and wanted to see the picture book I wrote. The younger patron selected *The Cat in the Hat.* The older reader returned *Twelve Rounds to Glory* with a great smile. I indeed am grateful for the smiles on youth's faces touched through our partnership with AmeriCorps.

The feeling of gratitude is mutual. AmeriCorps members were asked: How is the existing resource center storytelling and literacy program working for you? Responses included "Excellent," "Great! The Kids are very grateful as am I," and "Yes, I see the joy on the children's faces as Roland reads to them."

Due to collaboration and active resident participation, the Quinby Street Resource Center is a modern cultural center. As mentioned earlier, Marjorie was the first resident to serve as an AmeriCorps volunteer at the Quinby Street Center. She made a significant contribution to brainstorming, decision making, and program implementation. She later became senior employment program coordinator and approached me about a potential partnership with the senior employment service. I agreed to the role of trainer in a partnership with the senior employment service due to the success with AmeriCorps and prior work experience with Marjorie. Lorraine Whiteside, a daughter of Ms. Annabelle, one of the twenty senior trainees, serves as a senior library assistant volunteer and attends computer classes at the Quinby Street Resource Center.

Striking changes in materials, spatial arrangement, and cultural artifacts attracted positive attention for the library and as a result increased outreach.

I am thankful for Ms. Annabelle, Ms. Paula, Marjorie, and Tisha. Ms. Annabelle gave birth to the vision. Ms. Paula loved children and creative youth programming. Marjorie labored with me in a cramped library, later receiving a promotion to coordinator of senior employment training and provided training to senior library assistants. Tisha played a major role in the renovation and improved aesthetics of the Quinby Street Resource Center Library. Thank you to the Shenango Valley Foundation, Nannette Livadas, Holly Campbell, Joyce Fosdick, Nicole Potase, Mila Hiles, Fran McKenna, Renea Ingram, Sheila White, Stephanie Brenneman, Nichole Dora, Lorraine Whiteside, and Michelle Sparrow for support and encouragement.

Figure 1. Library

Figure 2. Group Shot at Storytelling Training

Figure 3. Back to School Bash, Sharpsville

Figure 4. Tisha Short, Resident, in Quinby Resource Center Library

Figure 5. Ms. Paula, Things from the Garden Program

Bibliography

Alston, Jason. "The African Library Project is Changing Rural Africa One Library at a Time." *BCALA News* (Spring 2017). http://bcala.org/Spring2017SpreadsInteractive/Spring2017SpreadsInteractive.html#p=48.

Banna, Georgi. "Book Rich Environment Initiative Launched." *NAHRO Blog: Legislative and Policy Updates from Washington, DC.* https://nahroblog.org/2017/01/05/book-rich-environment-initiative-launched/.

Barksdale-Hall, Roland. "Collaboration Fits the Bill for Best Practices in Programming for Public Housing Residents." In *The Libraries Role in Supporting Financial Literacy*, edited by Carol Smallwood. Lanham, MD: Rowman and Littlefield, 2016.

Bruce, Martha I. *Auntie's Paint Brush and Other Stories of African Children*. Hermitage, PA: Green Street Press, 2007.

Jones, Aleah. "Honoring Auntie Martha." *Pitt Magazine* (Summer 2012): 41.

Lambert, Troy. "Bringing the Library Home: Adding Libraries to Public Housing Developments Shares Resources and Costs." *American Libraries* (May 1, 2017). https://americanlibrariesmagazine.org/2017/05/01/bringing-library-home-public-housing/.

Spiller, Deborah J. and Michael Baker. "Library Service to Residents of Public Housing Developments: A Study and Commentary." *Public Libraries* 28, no. 6 (1989): 358-361.

Vercelletto, Christina. "Libraries Join National Initiative to Transform Public Housing into Book-Rich Environments." *School Library Journal* (January 2017). http://www.slj.com/2017/01/industry-news/libraries-join-national-initiative-to-transform-public-housing-into-book-rich-environments/#_.

Walton, Beth. "Former Asheville Mayor Joins Housing Authority." http://www.citizen-times.com/story/news/local/2015/04/27/former-asheville-mayor-joins-housing-authority/26474875/.

Walton, Beth. "Mountain Causes: Books for Children." http://www.haca.org/index.php/mountain-causes-books-for-children/.

Case Study 15

NETWORK TROUBLESHOOTING: CREATIVE PARTNERSHIPS IN DIGITAL LITERACY OUTREACH

Sarah McFadden

Abstract

In 2014, Cornell Cooperative Extension (CCE) of Rensselaer County launched a pilot program offering digital literacy training to communities underserved by high-speed broadband. With the broadly defined goal of increasing broadband adoption and no outlined curriculum or benchmarks to guide it, the program was poised to go in a multitude of directions, or nowhere at all. CCE partnered with area libraries to provide flexible, user-centered computer classes and tech support. This case study endeavors to examine the ways in which CCE and public libraries in New York State's Capital Region worked around the programming barriers typical among libraries and nonprofits to offer customized, empathetic digital literacy training to a diverse cross section of audiences. Early struggles to meet demand, as well as facility issues and unreliable technology were all decisive factors in shaping the collaborations, in many cases contributing to some of their greatest successes.

Issue: Tackling Rural Broadband Adoption in the Capital Region

Public library patrons need help getting online. Job seekers using public terminals to complete application materials, seniors toting recently unboxed mobile devices, and patrons of all backgrounds seeking access to trustworthy, helpful content and tools (which may exist increasingly in born-digital formats) frequently rely on their public libraries to bridge the divide between a lack of services in the offline world and the crucial tools of the web. For many of these patrons, the library is the sole location in their community where they can access the Internet. In New York State alone, the NYS Broadband Program Office (BPO) estimated that approximately 2.5 million housing units lacked access to high-speed Internet.[1] In 2013, the BPO awarded grant monies to broadband providers across the state through the Connect NY Broadband Program, an effort to expand reliable, high-speed Internet access and increase adoption of web-based services.

Cornell Cooperative Extension (CCE) of Rensselaer County participated in a Connect NY project as an adoption partner, a subcontractor to a Capital Region fixed wireless provider tasked with expanding broadband service in two mostly rural counties. As an adoption partner, CCE provided outreach and education to help communities take advantage of their new Internet connections through the efforts of a designated digital literacy educator. While CCE boasts an established network of educators and community partners, the creation of a digital literacy educator position and its focus on broadband adoption was an entirely new undertaking for the system. The position was designed to complement existing outreach and education efforts in agriculture, economic development, and family and consumer sciences. At its inception, the position was not imagined as a partner for libraries specifically, but as a liaison to rural communities in general.

CCE of Rensselaer County is a non-profit organization, one of fifty-six county-based CCE offices in New York State. Cornell University is New York State's land grant institution, with a large Extension system linking university research to local communities, as outlined in the mission of the Morrill Act of 1862. The organization and its educators work to combine research-based knowledge and local expertise

---

1. "The NYS Broadband Program Office," Broadband Program Office, accessed June 16, 2017, https://nysbroadband.ny.gov/.

to solve practical problems for New York State communities. With a CCE presence in each county, the individual offices are united in their ties back to campus, but function as local entities, reflecting the needs and socioeconomic concerns of specific regions. CCE offices partner with a variety of organizations, including senior centers, schools, county offices, and mission-adjacent nonprofits to expand programming to a number of populations. While CCE is most famous for its long-standing educational programs in 4-H youth development, agriculture, horticulture, and nutrition, individual associations often seek out grants and partnerships to pursue more targeted or experimental projects, as in the case of the digital literacy program.

In starting a digital literacy program from scratch, with no existing curricula or proven practices to grow from, it became essential for CCE to identify partnerships that could help bolster efforts in outreach, program design, and assessment, as well as provide for the kinds of sustained support that would best serve patrons in their efforts to get online. At the 2014 Broadband Summit, a conference organized by the NYS Broadband Program Office, Dr. Roberto Gallardo delivered a talk about the successes of the Mississippi State University Extension Service[2] in partnering with Mississippi libraries and librarians to deliver computer and Internet classes in local communities. CCE of Rensselaer County adopted this model as well, due to the digital literacy educator's background in librarianship, and the strength of the Capital Region library community.

Over three years, CCE partnered with twenty libraries across four counties to offer digital literacy classes. These libraries ranged from small rural outposts serving populations of 3,000 or less to city libraries with busy neighborhood branches. Facilities varied greatly across these libraries, especially with regard to public computer access. While larger libraries offered computer labs of around ten terminals, most libraries offered only three to five public access computers. While all

---

2. "Technology," Mississippi State University Extension, accessed June 16, 2017, http://extension.msstate.edu/community/technology.

partner libraries offered public wifi access, the reliability of these networks was uneven across municipalities. Many small, rural libraries are open limited hours each week, and are staffed by two to three library workers. However, in all participating libraries, the demand for digital literacy outreach and support was considerable.

Objectives

The aim of CCE's digital literacy pilot program was to encourage individuals to take advantage of newly available broadband connections by appealing to both practical needs and personal interests, all while helping to build the core skills necessary to be savvy Internet users. Prior to approaching any library partners, the CCE digital literacy educator drafted five core objectives on which to base all programming:

> I. Increase comfort levels with troubleshooting toward the development of digital confidence and a willingness to embrace new technology.
> II. Emphasize the importance of resource evaluation, especially as it relates to finding and using information on the web.
> III. Develop computer skills and behaviors that make efficient use of tools and resources.
> IV. Include thoughtful coverage of the ethical use of web-based information and work to develop an understanding of "netiquette" and its implications in the online community.
> V. Emphasize the importance of online safety and self-awareness, toward the development of cautious and discerning Internet users.

These objectives remain at the core of all outreach and education efforts, even as program logistics and training topics have shifted with patron demand.

In preliminary conversations with partner libraries, library staff reported patron interest in classes that addressed a range of topics and skills, including web browsing, mouse and keyboard skills, and mobile device basics. Requests for more advanced classes typically clustered around task-specific topics, such as applying for jobs, working with digital photos, and using services like Facebook and eBay. With many patrons seeking assistance with these topics, library staff were keen on growing library capacity to meet community need.

Planning in Detail

The digital literacy educator planned all curriculum and delivery, with considerable steering from the partner libraries. Lesson planning drew heavily on the resources made available by GCFLearnFree.org,[3] EveryoneOn,[4] and the New York State Digital Literacy curriculum.[5] Classes were also prepared around specific library resources and issues, including sessions on ereaders and library ebook platforms, and following the 2016 presidential election, a reworked version of an Internet Basics class that looked specifically at strategies for selecting trustworthy information sources and identifying fake news.

Partner libraries performed the majority of marketing tasks, both in the library and around the community. Librarians created messaging for print flyers and social media, and sometimes submitted press releases or calendar items to local newspapers and community websites. Library staff handled all program registration, but could refer patrons to the digital literacy educator for questions prior to the date of a program. If inclement weather forced the cancellation of a program, library staff were responsible for notifying registrants. At the conclusion of a program, evaluations were distributed to participants to solicit their feedback about the content and format of the class. The digital literacy educator designed and distributed the surveys and tabulated responses. Evaluation data was used primarily to inform future program planning and was also included in CCE's annual federal

---

3. "Technology," GCFLearnFree.org, accessed June 17, 2017, https://www.gcflearnfree.org/subjects/technology/.

4. "Campaign Materials," everyoneon, accessed June 22, 2017, http://everyoneon.org/campaign-materials/page/2/.

5. "Trainers," Digital Literacy in New York, accessed June 17, 2017, http://www.diglitny.org/index.php/trainers.

reporting. This data was shared with library staff for use in their own planning and reporting.

Defining the Target Audience(s)

The intended audiences for these programs were not especially well-defined beyond their geographic location in areas underserved by current broadband offerings. The vast majority of programs were designed for adult learners, with many specifically intended for senior populations. Most classes were offered during the evenings, though programming for seniors frequently took place in the morning or afternoons. A popular summer series of iPad classes offered weekly sessions in the library community room, and biweekly offerings in an affiliated senior center one town over.

The collaborations between CCE and the partner libraries did not envision a target participant but endeavored to bring about a service model that recognized and honored the widespread and varied experiences of community members attempting to accomplish essential and increasingly digital tasks in areas with little access to reliable Internet or the instruction and support often required to make use of it. Several workforce development series targeted job seekers, while later projects endeavored specifically to provide outreach and tech instruction to farmers and agricultural businesses interested in using social media to expand direct marketing efforts. However, most classes were intended to appeal to any patron with a pressing tech issue, curiosity, or aspiration.

Interventions

Offering computer help alongside other library services sends a powerful message that learning to use computers and the web is a worthwhile pursuit with ample support available to newcomers. Many patrons' resistance to getting online clustered along a mistrust of tech tools, a lack of perceived relevance, or general apprehensiveness around making irreversible or costly mistakes. Many patrons expressed feelings of abandonment or isolation against the rapid onward march of technology. Sense of community and the freedom to try new things are cornerstones of the public library. Places where community members are learning about seed saving, meeting with a games group, and attending family education programs should be places where they also feel comfortable getting help with password management, smartphone apps, and social media best practices. Messaging the value of broadband adoption is essential, as is broadcasting the availability of comprehensive and enthusiastically provided support for its use.

Early attempts at digital literacy programming could be difficult to plan for but endeavored to cast a wide net and be useful to learners with a range of expectations, backgrounds, and devices. While a one-and-a-half hour computer basics class proved too broad in scope to be universally effective (in large groups, participants were either bored or overwhelmed), they were useful in getting patrons in the door and in front of a computer and instructor. These classes also helped open doors into more specific topics for patrons to pursue. For example, many patrons were unaware that they could get recipes on an iPad, purchase engine parts on eBay and Craigslist, or create and share their own knitting patterns, essays, and photo projects online. After attending computer basics classes, patrons had the tools and vocabulary to seek out new uses for the web and could request corresponding workshops. Library staff worked to meet community tech needs by participating in digital literacy workshops alongside their patrons, on their own paths to seeking out new and exciting ways to use the web in service of their communities.

The ability to offer regular digital literacy programming and a continual presence in library spaces emphasized the message that tech literacy skills require repetition and practice, and some amount of failure and frustration. Reinforcing these ideas with regular classes, either as repeat instances or as part of a series, helped to build confidence in digital learners. At a minimum, it helped to craft a sense of safety and support for digital experimentation in library spaces.

Outcomes and Reflection

In the collaborations outlined above, the libraries acted as a kind of incubator for the CCE digital literacy program, a program that could never have flourished without these considerable contributions. The digital literacy program thrived on the strong foundations of community, constancy, and trust imbued in the libraries, combined with the flexibility and responsiveness of the CCE system and its commitment to filling gaps in learning wherever they occur.

The singular focus of the digital literacy educator's position afforded considerable nimbleness with regard to program design and scheduling. Classes could be scheduled when library traffic was expected to be high or when given audiences were available and willing to attend programs. Assessment data collected at the close of each class guided program design and delivery, as participants were asked to rate workshop delivery methods and suggest additional programming topics.

Public libraries are a natural partner for many kinds of extension programs, in that libraries are conduits and curators of human curiosity and expertise. Libraries and extension associations also share a reliance on detailed assessment and data-driven decision-making, and both are rooted firmly in local communities and traditions of hands-on learning. Public library Internet access is a multiplier, and in the right conditions, a kind of equalizer on par with extension's mission to disseminate the high-level knowledge of the land grant system to all kinds of local communities.

Though exceedingly successful in delivering digital literacy programming to communities across four counties, the digital literacy program was not without its specific challenges. Aging tech equipment, budget constraints, and limits on library staff and space were among the most notable challenges. While the grant funding the CCE digital literacy program laid out money for a mobile teaching lab, complete with laptops and projection equipment, funding issues delayed purchasing until the final weeks of the three-year grant. Instead, libraries often provided computer lab space and equipment, usually after hours. This equipment was often outdated and limited in quantity, or unable to perform high-bandwidth tasks. As a result, classes employed a bring-your-own-device model and were designed to accommodate as many device preferences as possible. Now that mobile lab equipment has been purchased, classes are still designed, where appropriate, to be device agnostic in order to encourage participation from the greatest number of potential learners, though the mobile lab equipment helps to increase program capacity and flexibility.

In the smaller rural libraries, library space for teaching was limited. Classes sometimes were held in the back corner of a library while non-participating patrons tiptoed around the rest of the library to go about their usual business. Purchase of the digital literacy lab equipment has afforded considerable flexibility in where library classes are held. The ability to provide laptops and tablets with long battery lives (many older libraries lack conveniently placed electrical outlets) in basement spaces or community rooms has opened up scheduling and programming options considerably.

Capital Region libraries address their patrons' need for tech classes in a number of ways. In many libraries, only one or two staff members are on duty at any given time. Some rely on volunteers to provide tech support, many of whom are students. This is an excellent community-building opportunity, and a creative solution to meeting considerable demand. However, there is an important message that is signified by the presence of a professional digital literacy educator. While this is absolutely a role that could be filled by a digital services or outreach librarian, the dedicated position within CCE, a hyper-local, community-embedded entity, signaled recognition of a local lived experience in the struggle to keep up with technological advancement and its influence on social and cultural mores. Patrons often expressed pleasant surprise at the existence of the digital literacy program and were even more surprised to learn that they would not be charged a fee for the service. The customizable, targeted nature of the program afforded patrons the time and space to stop, repeat steps, experiment, and embrace new ventures into computers and the Internet. Participants described classes as encouraging, inspiring, and uplifting.

As classes continue and program messaging reaches additional audiences, the opportunity for increasingly specific and creative programs grows as well. Changes in tech happen quickly, and those wishing to support rural and urban communities in their embrace of technology will be required to exhibit the kind of flexibility and personalization that made CCE and its library partners so successful in their endeavors. Though the designation of a full-time digital literacy educator is a considerable investment, it is the belief of the collaborators that this is a viable, reproducible model that could and should be put to work in a number of communities.

The partnerships outlined above were instrumental in building the capacity and reputation of the CCE digital literacy program. One direct result of this growth is CCE of Rensselaer County's recent success in seeking out and securing federal funding to double the life of the digital literacy program from three years to six years, and to grow outreach and training efforts from a two-county area to a seven-county area. Without question, the partnerships and benchmarks established in the first three years of the program were essential leverage in the grant-seeking process. The expanded program is expected to reach a much larger audience, and to offer more focused, in-depth instruction in social media and web marketing for agribusiness entrepreneurs, while continuing to build digital literacy skills for library patrons and rural communities at large.

Bibliography

"About Us." *Cornell Cooperative Extension of Rensselaer County*. Accessed June 16, 2017. http://ccerensselaer.org/about-us.

"Campaign Materials." *Everyoneon*. Accessed June 22, 2017. http://everyoneon.org/campaign-materials/page/2/.

"NYS Broadband Program Office." *Broadband Program Office*. Accessed June 16, 2017. https://nysbroadband.ny.gov/.

"Technology." *GCFLearnFree.org*. Accessed June 17, 2017. https://www.gcflearnfree.org/subjects/technology/.

"Technology." *Mississippi State University Extension*. Accessed June 16, 2017. http://extension.msstate.edu/community/technology.

"Trainers." *Digital Literacy in New York*. Accessed June 17, 2017. http://www.diglitny.org/index.php/trainers.

Case Study 16

GROWING ACCESS TO BOOKS: SUPPLEMENTING LIBRARY SERVICES TO RURAL STUDENTS

Tiffany Coulson and Barbara Peterson

Abstract

As of March 2013, the U.S. Department of Education reported that one quarter of all public school students attended rural schools.[1] Not only do these students face limited access to library materials within their schools, but often rural public libraries are also challenged in providing access to books due to decreased budgets, reduced hours, and staffing shortages.[2] With one of the fastest growing poverty rates in the nation, an average of one in four rural children lives in poverty.[3] In a small rural town in Washington state, located in a county with high childhood poverty rates and a high percentage of English Language Learners, access to books is crucial to the development of reading

---

1. United States, Department of Education, Institute of Education Sciences, National Center for Education Statistics, The Status of Rural Education, last modified March, 2013, https://nces.ed.gov/programs/coe/indicator_tla.asp.

2. Deanne W. Swan, Justin Grimes, and Timothy Owen, The State of Small and Rural Libraries in the United States, Institute of Museum and Library Services, 2013, https://www.imls.gov/assets/1/AssetManager/Brief2013_05.pdf.

3. United States, Department of Agriculture, Economic Research Service, Child Poverty, last modified September 2016, https://www.ers.usda.gov/topics/rural-economy-population/rural-poverty-well-being/child-poverty/.

skills.[4] An area non-profit organization, Northwest Learning and Achievement (NLA) Group, provides after-school programming to the elementary and middle schools in this district. As part of their out-of-school time literacy curriculum, NLA Group uses resources purchased through FirstBook.org by means of a federal grant establishing a 21st Century Community Learning Center at the school district. First Book is a non-profit organization that leverages their contact with publishers to provide low-cost books to children in need. This case study of K-5 students, parents, and staff in the school district will evaluate how an informal partnership between the non-profits of NLA Group and First Book is able to supplement local library services by providing access to books for students and their families. The ability of NLA Group to purchase multiple copies of literacy materials allows children access to high-quality new books in classes, during free reading, in after-school book clubs, and to check out and take home. The focus of First Book in stocking the latest award-winning books, and a large variety of less-available authentic multi-cultural selections means that supplemental programming designed by NLA Group is progressive and meets the needs of the school's culturally diverse population. Data collection examining the way books are used and their perceived value to participants was carried out using a mixed methods approach with observations, quantitative surveys, and qualitative interviews and focus groups with students, school staff, and parents at the elementary school over the course of a year.

Issues to Be Addressed

On a late March afternoon, almost two dozen Hispanic parents gathered in the sunny school cafeteria with their children for hot chocolate and Family Reading Night. The focus of the event was an award-winning bilingual children's picture book called *Grandma's Chocolate / El Chocolate de Abuelita*, written by Mara Price and illustrated by Lisa Fields.[5] The book

---

4. U.S. Dept. of Agriculture, Child Poverty.

5. Mara Price and Lisa Fields, *Grandma's Chocolate / El Chocolate de Abuelita*, trans. Gabriela Baeza

was chosen for its dual language narrative, its engaging informational content about Mexican history and culture, and the authentic presentation of a Hispanic family in a contemporary setting. Parents attending the event had children in the on-campus after-school club, facilitated by a federally funded non-profit, NLA Group. During a group read-aloud in both English and Spanish, families discussed a variety of ways of interacting with their children while reading the book, including talking about the pictures, sharing their own family stories, and asking their children open-ended questions rather than focusing only on the text.

The use of the book *Grandma's Chocolate / El Chocolate de Abuelita* addressed a number of issues important to the partnership between the non-profit afterschool provider and the school district.

1 - Parent Involvement

As part of their belief statement, the school district identifies parents as the "primary teachers" of students. They invite families to "cooperate with the school district to support, encourage, guide, nurture, and empower children through the learning and the education process." Assigning parents a role in the educational process is based on a variety of research which correlates student success with parental involvement.[6] Inviting parents to be part of the afterschool program also helps fulfill 21st Century grant goals that support the requirements of the federally identified Title I school (among those schools with students who struggle academically).[7]

2 - Extended School Day

Title I funding that supports academic programs also demands close monitoring of student progress through both formative and summative

---

Ventura (Houston, TX: Pinata Books, 2010).

6. Daphna Oyserman, "School Success, Possible Selves, and Parent School Involvement," *Family Relations* 56, no. 5 (2007): 480.

7. Office of Superintendent of Public Instruction, "21st Century Learning Program Guidance - Washington 21st Century Community Learning Centers," June 15, 2015, http://k12.wa.us/21stCenturyLearning/ProgramGuidance.aspx.

assessments. The school values the after-school partnership with NLA Group as it extends the learning day in creative ways by providing homework help and specific academic enrichment in math and reading. While individual student success is the educational goal of the district, data that shows improvement in grades and test scores is the primary lens through which the additional activities are measured for both the school and the non-profit after-school provider.

3 - Access to Books

With limited funding and staffing, the school library is open only during the day. The library staff provide access to books and a variety of literacy activities to all students on a weekly basis. This library access is important since statistics show a correlation between the number of books available to students and their success in reading.[8] Unfortunately, the library is not available for after-school reading, nor has there been a policy of providing out-of-school time access to parents in the district. Based on interviews with parents of after-school participants, it is also apparent that only about half of families use the public library.[9] This compares to studies by the Pew Center which show that eighty-three percent of U.S.-born Latinos say they use the public library while only sixty percent of immigrant Latinos say they have ever visited a public library or bookmobile in person.[10] The school being studied has a high immigrant Latino population that primarily speak Spanish at home.

4 - Value of Heritage Language

While only thirty percent of students in the school district are in the state's transitional bilingual program, over eighty percent of students

---

8. Lois Bridges, "Make Every Student Count: How Collaboration Among Families, Schools and Communities Ensures Student Success," *Scholastic Family and Community Engagement Research Compendium* (2013): 49-67, http://teacher.scholastic.com/products/face/pdf/research-compendium/Compendium.pdf.

9. Susana Bonis, "21st CCLC Report 2016," (third party evaluator internal report, NLA Group, 2016).

10. Anna Brown, "Public Libraries and Hispanics," Pew Research Center, http://www.pewhispanic.org/2015/03/17/public-libraries-and-hispanics/.

are Hispanic and most claim Spanish as the heritage language that is spoken to some extent at home. Not only is the school interested in using Spanish to communicate clearly with monolingual parents, they work in partnership with the after-school nonprofit in recognizing the importance of students' heritage language. Bilingual students who believe their heritage language is accepted and valued at school tend to show more interest in their studies and are more successful in school.[11]

5 – Culturally Relevant Programming

In an effort to establish connections between school and home through Spanish as a heritage language, exploration of related cultural content is important as well. Particularly in terms of literacy improvement, studies show reading enjoyment increases when students see stories that feature characters like themselves, and which include cultural cues that mirror their experience.[12] Federal Title I guidelines call for input from parents regarding program content.[13] Recognizing cultural funds of knowledge and presenting culturally familiar and relevant programming invite Hispanic families to contribute to student learning models even if they have not had the opportunity to specifically ask for this kind of inclusive content.

6 – Acknowledging Multiple Literacies

School standards for literacy activities are traditionally built around reading material. Culturally relevant programming recognizes that home literacy activities may include a variety of methods for developing

---

11. Corinne A. Seals and Joy Kreeft Peyton, "Heritage Language Education: Valuing the Languages, Literacies, and Cultural Competencies of Immigrant Youth," *Current Issues in Language Planning* 18, no. 1 (2017): 87-101

12. Melanie D. Koss, "Diversity in Contemporary Picturebooks: A Content Analysis," *Journal of Children's Literature* 41, no. 1 (2015): 32; John T. Guthrie, et al., "Increasing Reading Comprehension and Engagement Through Concept-Oriented Reading Instruction," *Journal of Educational Psychology* 96, no. 3 (2004): 403.

13. United States, Department of Education, "Improving Basic Programs Operated by Local Educational Agencies (Title I, Part A)," last modified October, 2015, https://www2.ed.gov/programs/titleiparta/index.html.

language use. The flexibility of after-school programming allows enhancement of multiple literacies that students may be more familiar with to augment traditional reading practices.[14] Use of collaborative reading, discussion, expanded storytelling, use of visual narratives, reading-related activities, and non-linear book exploration increase student affinity for reading and build new ways for them to use books to interact with their families at home.

Program Overview

The current partnership between the rural school district and the nonprofit NLA Group is based on implementation of a five-year federal grant creating a 21st Century Community Learning Center at the school. This type of grant is the only federal funding dedicated to after-school programs for students and their families. NLA Group's after-school program supports low income and struggling students by providing academic enrichment in math and reading, help with homework, and adult supervised social interaction. Activities supplement the school day with art, hands on science exploration, and access to books for pleasure reading. The program for students in kindergarten through fifth grade takes place after school Monday through Friday until five or six o'clock. To accommodate a waiting list of students, two groups of about fifty students are able to attend three days a week. Based on fifteen years of 21st Century program data, students who attend after-school programs regularly for two years show academic growth, improved grades, better school attendance, and less issues with behavioral problems than students who are unsupervised after school.[15] (While they are funded through the U.S. Department of Education, 21st Century Community Learning Center programs are administered at the state

---

14. JaNiece M. Terry, "Establishing Effective Home-School Partnerships by Building Capacity," (PhD diss. National Louis University, 2016), http://digitalcommons.nl.edu/cgi/viewcontent.cgi?article=1177&context=diss.

15. Afterschool Alliance, "Evaluations Backgrounder: A Summary of Formal Evaluations of Afterschool Programs' Impact on Academics, Behavior, Safety and Family Life," (January, 2013), 1-30, http://www.afterschoolalliance.org/Evaluations_Backgrounder_2013.pdf.

level. Annual data on anonymized student demographics, attendance, discipline, grades, and test scores are reported to the state annually by after-school providers in cooperation with school districts.)

Library Overview

A key aspect of the 21st Century program at the school district is the NLA Group Portable Library. The almost 3000-book library has been purchased over a three-year period and includes age appropriate children's picture books, chapter books, and graphic novels for grades kindergarten through twelfth grade. Books for the elementary school are usually purchased by NLA Group in sets of fifteen for partner reading, and whenever possible are hardcover editions. Many of the titles are bilingual editions that may be shared with families and half of the collection contains portrayals of individuals of diverse ethnicities and cultural backgrounds by diverse authors and illustrators. Some of the library is kept at the site for daily recreational reading time or for "checking out" to take home. Books also come to the after-school program in three-month thematic units, designed to be used twice a week. Units are rotated among other area 21st Century program sites with similar needs, all managed by NLA Group. The elementary schools within the grant or neighboring grants are spread across wide geographic distances. One grant has three elementary schools within a mid-sized rural town, while another grant serves three schools about thirty miles away from it. A third grant involves two elementary schools that are nearly 200 miles apart. All three grants share library resources. During monthly in-person administrative meetings or regional trainings for after-school site directors, books are boxed and exchanged by NLA staff to cut down on mailing costs. Rotating the books among sites ensures that students always have new, award-winning, engaging books that supplement their access to the school library collection.

Most of the NLA Group Portable Library has been purchased through an informal partnership with First Book, a non-profit organization that negotiates deep discounts from publishers on new, high-quality children's books with the intent of making them more accessible to underserved populations. First Book criteria for accessing their services is that the organization serves populations where at least seventy percent of children are eligible for free or reduced lunch.[16] After applying on the FirstBook.org web site for permission to access their resources, NLA communicated with First Book administrators to ensure sets of books were being used as intended by the non-profit organization. While the goal of First Book is to get more books into the homes of low-income students, the organization also recognizes the importance of books in determining academic success. They are committed to helping close the achievement gap for low-income students by providing popular and award-winning books that motivate kids to read and include them in the larger population of young readers. The role of NLA in giving students out-of-school access to books, allowing them to take books home, and rotating books among schools actually maximizes the impact of First Book by extending the use of each book.

Partner Overviews

Northwest Learning and Achievement (NLA) Group is a federally funded non-profit organization committed to supporting education in Washington state. NLA Group creates tools and strategies that are designed to inspire academic achievement among students from isolated and low-income rural environments. Since 1999, NLA has been transforming the lives of rural learners in seventy schools in twenty-seven districts across eight rural counties, using innovative strategies that inspire students of all ages to believe that they can excel academically and achieve ambitious life goals. Supported by funding partners such as GEAR UP, 21st Century, and the Gates Foundation, NLA develops and delivers effective after-school programs and educational resources to schools, colleges, and community organizations so that students from low-income families will be able reap the benefits of higher education[17]

---

16. First Book, "Registration FAQs," https://www.firstbook.org/receive-books ?id=439.

17. NLA: Inspiring Learning and Achievement, http://nlagroup.com/.

The home office for NLA Group is located in Wapato, Washington but has employees in the field throughout central Washington. Governed by a Board of Directors, the Executive Director and two Associate Directors of NLA Group live in rural areas of central Washington as do the office staff, and thirty-six site directors and their staff who oversee programs in various elementary, middle, and high schools.

The school district being studied is one of ten elementary schools served by NLA Group through 21st Century federal funding. The elementary school is located in central Washington state, about twenty-five miles from the nearest large town. It is part of a small school district with only about 1000 students enrolled in kindergarten through twelfth grade and almost 500 children in the K-5 elementary school. When the grant was first implemented, the school reported eighty-seven percent of elementary students were eligible for free and reduced lunch. The majority of students struggle academically, with less than forty percent meeting the most recent state requirements for math, reading, and science.

The surrounding community is agricultural, with a student population that is over seventy percent Hispanic. Twenty-five percent are considered migrant. The elementary school reports that close to fifty percent of students are in the transitional bilingual program, meaning most students speak Spanish as their first language. This area represents part of statistics which showed, at the time of grant implementation, that Washington state ranked third in the nation behind Alaska and New Mexico for the highest percentages of English Language Learners in rural districts.[18]

There are thirty certified teachers employed at the elementary school; twenty percent of them are Hispanic. The average years of experience among teachers is in the single digits, at only seven years. Although no longer a federal requirement, all teachers meet the ESEA (Elementary and Secondary Education Act) highly qualified (HQ) definition.[19]

---

18. United States, Department of Education, "Rural Education."

19. United States, Department of Education, "No Child Left Behind: A Tool Kit for Teachers

Because of the small student population, the entire school district is housed on a single campus. The number of students and smaller class sizes mean that students and their families are known personally by staff members over a long period of time. The single campus also provides an ideal environment for district administrators to be directly aware of how schools are operating on a daily basis.

Objective(s)

The partnership between NLA Group and the elementary school coordinated the mutual objective of seeing academic improvement reflected in student data from grades and test scores. From the perspective of school district administration, extending the school day and instructive practices provided more time for struggling students to engage with math, reading, and science. As an out-of-school time educational resource, NLA Group was able to bridge gaps needed for academic improvement under new state standards by reinforcing the requirements of the district while bringing in new material, methods, and activities that would keep students engaged in learning at the end of the very long school day. In terms of literacy programming across contexts, not only extension of the school day, but access to books and including families by valuing heritage language, diverse cultures, and acknowledging multiple literacies that support reading were all objectives that were intended to contribute to academic improvement. In this case study, the authors focus on how key elements of literacy programming developed reading improvement through the use of an innovative portable library to bring engaging books to students in the after-school program.

Stakeholders

Perhaps the most interesting part of the partnership between the elementary school and NLA Group was the inclusivity of stakeholder involvement. Not only were both formal and informal educators

---

— Archived," last modified August, 2009, https://www2.ed.gov/teachers/nclbguide/toolkit_pg6.html.

involved in writing to obtain grant funds and monitoring the awarded grant, but community members, parents, and students themselves were continuously consulted in building meaningful interventions that met needs beyond academic improvement. Highlighting the way in which program implementation addressed the needs of stakeholders is an ethnographic case study undertaken by the authors over a one-year period from the summer of 2016 to 2017. Participant observations during after-school activities; focus group interviews and surveys with students and parents by an independent evaluator; student, administrator, and informal educator interviews; and publicly available community and school district data were studied in the specific context of literacy interventions implemented in the after-school program. This data was used to report yearly academic progress among children in the after-school program, changes in children's reading habits over time, and also to collect statements relevant to program objectives that would indicate value to program participants and their parents.

Interventions – Actions That Made a Difference

The non-profit organization First Book operates on the premise that access to books is an important determiner of academic success. "Access to books and educational material is the single biggest barrier to literacy development in the United States and beyond. If we can solve the problem of access, we will be well on the road to realizing educational parity—a goal which has eluded this country for generations."— Susan B. Neuman, Ph.D. University of Michigan, Ctr. for Improvement of Early Reading Achievement.[20] As part of their mission they cite a study that showed in middle-income neighborhoods there are approximately thirteen books in the home for every child. In low-income neighborhoods, the number is only one book for every 300 children[21].

---

20. First Book, "First Book Statistics: Literacy in America," https://www.firstbook.org/images/pdf/Statistics-on-Literacy.pdf.

21. First Book, "Literacy."

With limited access to books outside of school hours, the most important reading strategy undertaken by NLA Group was putting new, engaging books in the hands of students. In an informal partnership, the after-school non-profit NLA Group was able to purchase discounted books from First Book to make regular access to books outside of school an important part of the reading programming. Books were given away during family literacy events, collected for after-school recreational reading, made available for take-home loans, used in after-school reading groups, and purchased for thematic summer enrichment activities to engage students in reading. Over the course of the first three years of the grant, over 2000 new, high quality books were added to the NLA Group library for use by students.

While NLA recognized that access to books was one thing holding students back from making progress in reading, it was also apparent that a variety of strategies had to be employed to create positive reading experiences for many of the school's struggling students. In an effort to align with reading instruction happening during school, the after-school program was asked to ensure that students were completing a compulsory fifteen minutes of reading before they went home. Often students were unmotivated to read the books they brought with them from school, and after-school facilitators struggled with getting students to read.

NLA Group began using age-appropriate picture books in sets of fifteen to involve after-school students in interactive partner reading activities. This group reading design builds on the idea that situational interest motivates students to read. Situational interest involves four aspects of design: providing choice, giving students the opportunity to collaborate, providing engaging texts, and incorporating hands-on activities or real-world connections related to a book.[22] For example, as part of a themed reading unit on multicultural art, students read the book *Magic Trash: A Story of Tyree Guyton and His Art* as a group in

---

22. John T. Guthrie, et al., "From Spark to Fire: Can Situational Reading Interest Lead to Long-Term Reading Motivation?" *Literacy Research and Instruction* 45, no. 2 (2005): 91-117.

partnered pairs.[23] The book is about how an African American artist used discarded items to transform part of his community into a work of art to encourage pride in the neighborhood. Interaction surrounding the book was designed so that students played collaborative games to help them understand the idea of communities. They discussed the story in the context of their own communities. Then working in small groups, they prepared discarded items to be used in creating their own works of art for an activity later in the week. During a Family Literacy Activity, students presented their artwork to visiting adults.

Rather than focusing only on the text of the book, the experience of reading *Magic Trash* became an opportunity to draw on and develop existing 21st-century literacies more comfortable to the students; cultural competence, creativity, critical thinking, and collaboration were all used in two days of literacy activities that accompanied the book.

NLA Group adopted a practice in which each encounter with the text in a picture book was completed in less than fifteen to twenty minutes, then added upon using the text to give struggling students a positive experience with reading. In 2003 Kong and Pearson noted the significance of allowing students alternative literacy experiences:

> First, students must have plenty of opportunities to engage actively in the meaningful literacy practices of a given community—even before they have mastered those practices. Second, students must receive support and scaffolds as they gradually move toward full participation and independent control of those practices. As they learn to participate in literature discussions, students need calibrated opportunities to master new ways of talking and thinking about books.[24]

During a summer school collaboration between NLA Group and the small rural elementary school, literacy enrichment activities were incorporated into the school day. This arrangement provided the opportunity

---

23. J. H. Shapiro, and Vanessa Brantley-Newton, *Magic Trash: A Story of Tyree Guyton and His Art* (Watertown, MA: Charlesbridge, 2015).

24. Ailing Kong and P. David Pearson, "The Road to Participation: The Construction of a Literacy Practice in a Learning Community of Linguistically Diverse Learners," *Research in the Teaching of English* (2003): 85-124

to directly align with the school district's academic goals, while using the situational interest model that had been practiced after school. In three days of one-hour units, students partner-read a short space-themed picture book. Poetry, biography, fiction, and non-fiction books were used. Short videos provided background vocabulary and concepts in the abbreviated time frame and students participated in literacy and science activities that built on the content of the books. At the end of the seven weeks of enrichment activities presented as "Summer in Space," students were asked to share their favorite book from the unit, their feelings about partner reading, and their favorite activity.

Overall, there was a consensus that partners made the reading process less intimidating, and all of the students who participated from kindergarten through fourth grade were enthusiastic about the reading activities.

Another focus of book purchases for the after-school program was on finding books that were culturally relevant to the large majority of Hispanic students and their families in the after-school program. In the initial stages of the after-school literacy program, the school district expressed interest in seeing more diverse books introduced to students and in adding these kinds of books to their own school library collection. In recent years there has been growing recognition that only a small percentage of the publishing industry for children's books includes people of color and other diverse groups.[25] The non-profit organization "We Need Diverse Books" has lately used their growing influence to partner with Scholastic, one of the largest distributors of children's books to teachers and students, to bring more diverse literature to the school market.[26] Smaller independent publishers like Lee & Lowe are committed to publishing books by diverse authors and illustrators.[27] The non-profit First Book not only negotiates affordable

---

25. Koss, "Diversity."

26. Scholastic News Room, "Scholastic & We Need Diverse Books Announce Expanded Partnership," accessed May 22, 2017, http://mediaroom.scholastic.com/press-release/scholastic-we-need-diverse-books-announce-expanded-partnership.

27. Lee & Lowe Books, "About Us," accessed May 22, 2017, https://www.leeandlow.com/about-us.

pricing to make books more accessible to low-income communities, but sometimes commits to buying the first 10,000 copies of original books with bilingual or diverse content to encourage publishers to take a risk on more uncommon topics of diversity or on less-known diverse authors.[28] NLA Group took an active role in purchasing books for their library by Hispanic authors and illustrators, about Hispanic culture, characters, and families in everyday contexts. It is interesting that the narrow practices of the publishing industry contributed to creating a school library collection where students were exposed to little that reflected the majority culture in their small community. Culturally relevant reading not only leads to the sharing of family stories that build upon traditional literacy practices, but it gives students the opportunity to explore their own identity within and outside their community.[29]

While some studies have shown students don't necessarily choose books that mirror their ethnicity, it is important to recognize that these books spark conversations associated with their culture and community. Students are more likely to enjoy reading when they see characters like themselves represented in the books they read. Supporting these efforts by making diverse books a priority makes students feel valued and motivates reading, making a difference to students personally and academically.[30]

The use of bilingual books and books that include Spanish words and phrases is another way of acknowledging the culture of Hispanic students. Students who are able to bring their knowledge of their

---

28. First Book Press Releases, "First Book's Stories for All Project Addresses the Lack of Diversity in Children's Books, Bringing Classics and Diverse Books to Kids in Need," accessed May 22, 2017, https://www.firstbook.org/about-first-book/media-center/press-releases/370-first-book-and-harpercollins-childrens-books-introduce-first-ever-bilingual-edition-of-goodnight-moon.

29. Koss, "Diversity"; Laura May and Gary Bingham, "Making Sense with Informational Texts: The Interactive Read-Aloud as Responsive Teaching," *Talking Points* 27, no. 1 (2015): 21.

30. Renee I. Ting, "Accessibility of Diverse Literature for Children in Libraries: A Literature Review," *SLIS Student Research Journal* 6, no. 2 (2017): 4; Kathleen AJ Mohr, "Children's Choices: A Comparison of Book Preferences Between Hispanic and Non-Hispanic First-Graders," *Reading Psychology* 24, no. 2 (2003): 163-176.

heritage language to the reading experience feel that their culture and language are valued by educators.[31] Creating a connection between school literacy practices and family literacy practices promotes a sense of inclusion in the learning community.

It is intuitive for school districts to think about modeling family reading after instructive classroom practices, rather than drawing upon literacy practices already in place in the home. As noted by Baker et al., "Although storybook reading is widely regarded by educators as an important means by which parents prepare their children for school, an absence of storybook reading does not necessarily mean that children are growing up without exposure to literacy practices."[32] As part of shared academic goals, the school district and after-school non-profit, NLA Group organized evening activities on a quarterly basis that invited parents to the school. Called "Family Reading Nights," these evening activities included games, art activities, reading activities, and refreshments. Based on evidence that the culture and language of students should be represented by staff, both the after-school site director and tutors assisting with program events were Spanish-speaking individuals from the local community.[33] Hiring Hispanic staff as informal educators for the after-school program not only made communication with parents easier, but also facilitated exploration of literacy activities outside of strictly academic contexts that invited parents to use practices with which they were already comfortable, like sharing stories from their childhood.

During a Family Reading Night in which parents were invited to participate in a group discussion about the book, *Grandma's Chocolate / El Chocolate de Abuelita*, families were encouraged to discuss a bilingual book using short passages, non-linear reading, and even pictures as

---

31. Nicola Friedrich, Jim Anderson, and Fiona Morrison, "Culturally Appropriate Pedagogy in a Bilingual Family Literacy Programme," *Literacy* 48, no. 2 (2014): 72-79; Seals and Peyton, "Heritage Language Education."

32. Elsa Auerbach, "Deconstructing the Discourse of Strengths in Family Literacy," *Journal of Reading Behavior* 27, no. 4 (1995): 643-661.

33. Auerbach, "Deconstructing Discourse."

prompts. The family interactions surrounding the book were designed to value parents for their prior knowledge rather than assigning them prescriptive reading models with their children.[34] Bilingual reading alone exposes children to words outside their spoken heritage language and can start conversations that make non-English-speaking parents the experts in the sometimes-unfamiliar territory of book reading. Both practices of discussion and bilingual reading were meant to include families that speak Spanish as their heritage language as participants in the literacy process. In parent focus group interviews, families expressed that they liked that the literacy night was in a mix of English and Spanish, because many are trying to teach their children Spanish also. Parents enjoyed having interaction with their children and the instructors at the event. Some said that they had tried to replicate the activities at home. One woman shared that it "...was inspiring to have my child show me how we should read the book. I had a better understanding of what my child needed to do for reading. We learned about activities that we could then do at home."[35]

As a partnership, the association of one small rural school district with NLA Group validated efforts to bridge school and family involvement for the benefit of students. As previously mentioned, grades and test scores were both important measures of the combined success of in-school and after-school literacy efforts. Students in the after-school program did show higher reading achievement on state assessments and in their language arts grades.[36] However, it is also important to note that children's participation in literacy activities and attitudes toward reading are also known measures of literacy engagement that are important to sustained progress in reading. [37]

In a poll of First Book network members, eighty-seven percent report an increase in reading interest after children received books from First

---

34. Terry, "Establishing Effective Partnerships."
35. Bonis, "21st CCLC Report."
36. Bonis, "21st CCLC Report."
37. Guthrie, "Increasing Reading Comprehension."

Book.[38] This is consistent with the experience of the after-school collaboration with NLA Group since, during year one of the grant in 2015, only thirty percent of focus group participants said that they liked to read. At the end of year two in 2016, eighty percent of participants said they did.[39] According to a third-party program evaluator, things children said they appreciated about the after-school program were being introduced to new books and having access to a variety of books of different genres, different lengths, and different reading levels. Also appreciated were books that had pictures, either in the more traditional picture book format or as graphic novels or comic books.

> I found my favorite author here. I was reading Percy Jackson and found a similar book here by same author.

> I found good books and authors that I can share with friends and family.

> I enjoyed the books in the program. I thought we'd be reading regular, normal books like in school. We got to look at fun books like comic books. If we don't like a book, we can sometimes change it. I love the books that we read in this program.

Many students valued not having to read alone, but having the teacher read a book, reading with partners, or taking turns in small group reading. Having a caring "read aloud partner" was reported as making a real difference to students (see **Figure 1**). Children saw a distinction between being read to by their classroom teacher and being read to by their after-school program instructor.

> Honestly, I don't like reading at all, but when (the instructor) reads to us, she makes it interesting. She gives each character its own voice and she explains what is going on in the story. If we don't understand a word, she will explain it to us. She keeps trying to help us. I don't like reading, but here the instructor inspires me and the books we read are

---

38. Samantha McGinnis, "Increase Your Students' Interest in Reading," First Book Research (blog). First Book, July 21, 2015, https://blog.firstbook.org/2015/07/21/increase-your-students-interest-in-reading/.

39. Bonis, "21st CCLC Report."

fun.

Several children liked the activities tied to books, particularly those related to science and history. But in interviews children also expressed a desire to see more games and puppets/drama as activities. Those children who said they did not like the activities often had other concerns not tied to the literacy program, e.g., being tired or hungry by the time of day when the program was offered.[40]

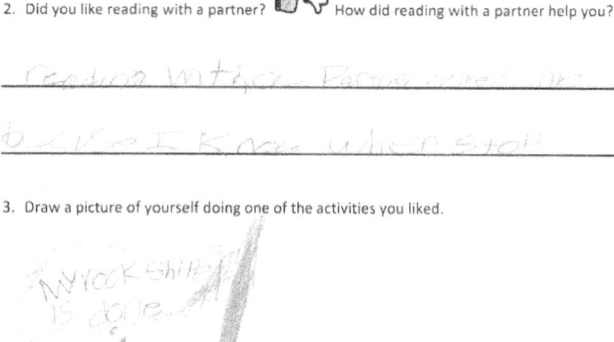

Figure 1. First Grade Student Feedback, Summer in Space, NLA Group, Washington State, 2015.

Reflecting on the use of the NLA Group portable library highlights some missed opportunities in encouraging interaction between students and books. While NLA Group was able to fulfill part of the First Book mission to increase student access to books, there is still a need to get more books into their homes. Sets of popular bilingual picture books were put in clear plastic bags with handles along with flyers displaying activities and discussion prompts in Spanish and English, but few of these resources were ever used by families. More conversations need to happen to determine whether the method of promoting the books was too prescriptive, if parents were not aware of the

---

40. Bonis, "21st CCLC Report."

opportunity to take the books home, if they did not have time for at home reading, or if students were simply not interested in the books because of content or lack of familiarity with written Spanish.

Additional partnerships with funding sources that would support more frequent book give-a-ways to students and their family members would support the mission of First Book, NLA Group, and the school district in getting more books into the homes of low-income families.

The use of the portable library needs to be expanded to make books used for group instruction available for recreational reading. Added to this collection should be reading material requested by students such as illustrated novels and shorter chapter books as well as easy-to-read graphic novels. The inaccessibility of school and public libraries makes the after-school library essential in ensuring that students are engaged with a variety of book choices on a daily basis.

Finally, while it is apparent that NLA Group has taken the opportunity to fill gaps opened by a lack of library access in the community, it would be productive to consider partnerships with the school and public library to highlight the importance of their services and make the availability of reading resources in the community a sustainable priority to students and their families.

Bibliography

Afterschool Alliance. "Evaluations Backgrounder: A Summary of Formal Evaluations of Afterschool Programs' Impact on Academics, Behavior, Safety. and Family Life." (January, 2013): 1-30. http://www.afterschoolalliance.org/Evaluations_Backgrounder_2013.pdf.

Auerbach, Elsa. "Deconstructing the Discourse of Strengths in Family Literacy." *Journal of Reading Behavior* 27, no. 4 (1995): 643-661.

Bridges, Lois. "Make Every Student Count: How Collaboration Among Families, Schools and Communities Ensures Student Success." *Scholastic Family and Community Engagement Research Compendium* (2013): 49-67. http://teacher.scholastic.com/products/face/pdf/research-compendium/Compendium.pdf.

Bonis, Susana. "21st CCLC Report 2016." (Third party evaluator internal report, NLA Group, 2016).

Brown, Anna. 'Public Libraries and Hispanics." *Pew Research Center.* http://www.pewhispanic.org/2015/03/17/public-libraries-and-hispanics/.

Cruz de Quirós. Ana M., Rafael Lara Alecio, Fuhui Tong, and Beverly J. Irby. "The Effect of a Structured Story Reading Intervention, Story Retelling and Higher Order Thinking for English Language and Literacy Acquisition." *Journal of Research in Reading* 35, no. 1 (2012): 87-113.

First Book. "First Book Statistics: Literacy in America." https://www.firstbook.org/images/pdf/Statistics-on-Literacy.pdf.

First Book. "Registration FAQs." https://www.firstbook.org/receive-books?id=439.

First Book Press Releases. "First Book's Stories for All Project Addresses the Lack of Diversity in Children's Books, Bringing Classics and Diverse Books to Kids in Need." Accessed May 22, 2017. https://www.firstbook.org/about-first-book/media-center/press-releases/370-first-book-and-harpercollins-childrens-books-introduce-first-ever-bilingual-edition-of-goodnight-moon.

First Grade Student Feedback. Summer in Space. NLA Group. Washington, 2015.

Friedrich, Nicola, Jim Anderson, and Fiona Morrison. "Culturally Appropriate Pedagogy in a Bilingual Family Literacy Programme." *Literacy* 48, no. 2 (2014): 72-79.

Guthrie, John T., Allan Wigfield, Pedro Barbosa, Kathleen C. Perencevich, Ana Taboada, Marcia H. Davis, Nicole T. Scafiddi, and Stephen Tonks. "Increasing Reading Comprehension and Engagement Through Concept-Oriented Reading Instruction." *Journal of Educational Psychology* 96, no. 3 (2004): 403.

Guthrie, John T., Laurel W. Hoa, Allan Wigfield, Stephen M. Tonks, and Kathleen C. Perencevich. "From Spark to Fire: Can Situational Reading Interest Lead to Long-Term Reading Motivation?" *Literacy Research and Instruction* 45, no. 2 (2005): 91-117.

Kong, Ailing, and P. David Pearson. "The Road to Participation: The Construction of a Literacy Practice in a Learning Community of Linguistically Diverse Learners." *Research in the Teaching of English* (2003): 85-124.

Koss, Melanie D. "Diversity in Contemporary Picturebooks: A Content Analysis." *Journal of Children's Literature* 41, no. 1 (2015): 32.

Lee & Lowe Books, "About Us." Accessed May 22, 2017. https://www.leeandlow.com/about-us.

May, Laura, and Gary Bingham. "Making Sense with Informational Texts: The Interactive Read-Aloud as Responsive Teaching." *Talking Points* 27, no. 1 (2015): 21.

McGinnis, Samantha. "Increase Your Students' Interest in Reading." *First Book Research* (blog). First Book. July 21, 2015. https://blog.firstbook.org/2015/07/21/increase-your-students-interest-in-reading/.

Mohr, Kathleen AJ. "Children's Choices: a Comparison of Book Preferences Between Hispanic and Non-Hispanic First-Graders." *Reading Psychology* 24, no. 2 (2003): 163-176.

NLA: Inspiring Learning and Achievement. http://nlagroup.com/.

Office of Superintendent of Public Instruction. "21st Century Learning Program Guidance - Washington 21st Century Community Learning Centers." June 15, 2015. http://k12.wa.us/21stCenturyLearning/ProgramGuidance.aspx.

Ogle, Donna, and Amy Correa. Kovtun. "Supporting English-Language Learners and Struggling Readers in Content Literacy with the 'Partner Reading and Content, Too' Routine." *The Reading Teacher* 63, no. 7 (2010): 532-542.

Oyserman, Daphna, Daniel Brickman, and Marjorie Rhodes. "School Success, Possible Selves, and Parent School Involvement." *Family Relations* 56, no. 5 (2007): 479-489.

Price, Mara and Lisa Fields. *Grandmas Chocolate / El Chocolate de Abuelita*, trans. Gabriela Baeza Ventura. Houston, TX: Pinata Books, 2010.

Scholastic News Room. "Scholastic & We Need Diverse Books Announce Expanded Partnership." Accessed May 22, 2017. http://mediaroom.scholastic.com/press-release/scholastic-we-need-diverse-books-announce-expanded-partnership.

Seals, Corinne A., and Joy Kreeft Peyton. "Heritage Language Education: Valuing the Languages, Literacies, and Cultural Competencies of Immigrant Youth." *Current Issues in Language Planning* 18, no. 1 (2017): 87-101.

Shapiro, J. H., and Vanessa Brantley-Newton. *Magic Trash: a Story of Tyree Guyton and His Art.* Watertown, MA: Charlesbridge, 2015.

Swan, Deanne W., Justin Grimes, and Timothy Owen. *The State of Small and Rural Libraries in the United States.* Institute of Museum and Library Services. 2013. https://www.imls.gov/assets/1/AssetManager/Brief2013_05.pdf.

Terry, JaNiece M. "Establishing Effective Home-School Partnerships by Building Capacity." PhD diss., National Louis University, 2016. http://digitalcommons.nl.edu/cgi/viewcontent.cgi?article=1177&context=diss.

Ting, Renee I. "Accessibility of Diverse Literature for Children in Libraries: A Literature Review." *SLIS Student Research Journal* 6, no. 2 (2017): 4.

United States, Department of Agriculture, Economic Research Service. *Child Poverty.* Last modified September 2016. https://www.ers.usda.gov/topics/rural-economy-population/rural-poverty-well-being/child-poverty/.

United States, Department of Education. "Improving Basic Programs Operated by Local Educational Agencies (Title I, Part A)." Last modified October, 2015. https://www2.ed.gov/programs/titlei-parta/index.html.

United States, Department of Education, Institute of Education Sciences, National Center for Education Statistics. *The Status of Rural Education.* Last modified March, 2013. https://nces.ed.gov/programs/coe/indicator_tla.asp.

United States, Department of Education. "No Child Left Behind: A Tool Kit for Teachers – Archived." Last modified August, 2009. https://www2.ed.gov/teachers/nclbguide/toolkit_pg6.html.

Afterword

Tatiana Bryant and Jonathan O. Cain

"A community is born when people begin to act together."—Absalom Jones

Libraries as institutions approximate the collective structure that associations and mutual benefit societies have filled historically. In his writing about libraries and their importance for preserving and serving contemporary democracy in the United States, Scott Cohen says "Libraries are critical resources in our service-oriented, brain-based economy. They fit well into the Millenials' movement towards a 'sharing economy.' In a digital age, using scarce apartment space for a book collection seems to make less sense than borrowing books and returning them after you read them."[1] Cohen hits on the adaptive role of the library, and how it shapes itself to fill an explicit or passive need expressed by a community. This is concretized in his example of a public library "making sure their WIFI was strong enough that people could use the internet on the library's steps even when the facility was closed."[2] Libraries 2016, a Pew Research Center study, confirms that "Public libraries, many Americans say, should offer programs to teach people digital skills (80% think libraries should definitely do this) and help patrons learn how to use

---

1. Steve Cohen, "America's Public Libraries: A Democratizing, Positive Product of Our Coummunites," https://blogs.ei.columbia.edu/2018/10/29/americas-public-libraries-democratizing-positive-product-communities/.

2. Ibid.

new creative technologies like 3-D printers (50%). At the same time, 57% of Americans say libraries should definitely offer more comfortable places for reading, working, and relaxing."[3]

The responses illustrate how users respond to economic and educational change using the tools and services offered by community organizations. Users identify a need for reliable, safe, comfortable, and accessible spaces for learning and working—reflecting changes to education and employment models (such as online learning and remote working). Users request tools to learn new technologies and for access to cutting-edge (and often cost-prohibitive) technologies that allow them to participate in contemporary culture and economies. Bearing these data in mind, our case study authors have embraced the traditions of adapting to meet the needs of their community (regardless of library type). Libraries operate as third spaces[4] in communities and nonprofits fill service gaps not provided by government and the private sector. Both serve as entities entrusted to provide community-enhancing services. These collaborations come from an observed or expressed need from a community that sparks a great idea, and from the talented, skilled, and determined individuals that turn that into a solution—be it a project, event, or service.

Fernandez, Nichols, Culbertson and Lamont, and Harada describe libraries and library workers collaborating with marginalized or minoritized communities to preserve their cultural heritage and memory. The library has taken on the charge of helping to preserve those histories. Public historian David Rotenstein has written about the importance of recording the contributions of a community to a place as it changes through time, age, gentrification, or other factors. In "Fragile History in a Gentrifying Neighborhood" he highlights the importance institutions

---

3. John B. Horrigan, "Libraries 2016," September 9, 2016, Prew Research Center, https://www.pewresearch.org/internet/2016/09/09/libraries-2016/.

4. Ray Oldenburg, *The Great Good Place: Cafés, Coffee Shops, Community Centers, Beauty Parlors, General Stores, Bars, Hangouts, and How They Get You Through the Day* (New York: Paragon House, 1989).

play in preserving and surfacing that history.[5] Barksdale-Hall's "Age Mates, Play Groups, and the Community Building Blocks of Leadership for Public Housing Residents" highlights how the library transforms into a community center by responding to community needs and driving service creation and delivery in partnership with public and nonprofit actors. Lenstra's "Partnerships for Physical Activity: Libraries as Active Spaces" reports how a small public library stepped up to fulfill a local request for a space for healthy lifestyle activities, and the ways that the institution negotiated with local government and collaborated with nonprofit organizations to meet those needs.

The key to coordinating diverse public programs is first to find or create the opportunity. The Foundation Center (http://foundationcenter.org) is a great resource to locate nonprofit organizations with impactful missions. Libraries can begin to partner with them by offering gratis space and marketing for new initiatives, publications, or strategic plans that align with the goals of your institution. Work with the resources at your disposal, and acquire sponsors at your institution or within your community who can provide gratis space, childcare, and catering. No or low-cost tickets, food and accessible scheduling are crucial considerations for community-centered nonprofit organizations that hold public events interested in attracting larger and economically diverse audiences. Request the time needed to coordinate across distance; nonprofit organizations follow different calendars than libraries. Establish a marketing plan to promote events via social media channels, public notice boards, and local media outlets to encourage participation. Plan the event around the space available at an accessible time and find speakers who can provide relevant context. Oftentimes nonprofit organizations can identify and coordinate experts, scholars, and others in the area who are knowledgeable about the organization, issues, and community. Let the nonprofit organizations drive the content and public

---

5. David Rotenstein, "Fragile History in a Gentrifying Neighborhood," March 20, 2015, National Council on Public History, https://ncph.org/history-at-work/fragile-history-in-a-gentrifying-neighborhood/.

participation. Make sure to capture and archive the event to make it freely available online.[6]

This volume captures a snapshot of the variety and ingenuity that library and nonprofit partnerships deliver. Hopefully, readers are inspired by the frameworks and ideas contained here, and they will spark the necessary imagination and will to develop their own library and nonprofit collaboration.

Bibliography

Bryant, Tatiana and Jonathan O. Cain. "Coordinating Diverse Public Programs in the Library." *OLA Quarterly* 21, no. 4 (2016): 36-38.

Cohen, Steve. "America's Public Libraries: A Democratizing, Positive Product of Our Coummunites." https://blogs.ei.columbia.edu/2018/10/29/americas-public-libraries-democratizing-positive-product-communities/.

Horrigan, John B. "Libraries 2016." September 9, 2016. Pew Research Center. https://www.pewresearch.org/internet/2016/09/09/libraries-2016/.

Oldenburg, Ray. *The Great Good Place: Cafés, Coffee Shops, Community Centers, Beauty Parlors, General Stores, Bars, Hangouts, and How They Get You Through the Day.* New York: Paragon House, 1989.

Rotenstein, David. "Fragile History in a Gentrifying Neighborhood." March 20, 2015. National Council on Public History. https://ncph.org/history-at-work/fragile-history-in-a-gentrifying-neighborhood/.

---

6. Tatiana Bryant, and Jonathan O. Cain, "Coordinating Diverse Public Programs in the Library," *OLA Quarterly* 21, no. 4 (2016): 36-38.

About the Contributors

Melanie Allen is the health sciences librarian for the University of Tennessee, Knoxville Libraries. Melanie supports Nursing, Audiology and Speech Pathology, Nutrition, and Public Health. Melanie is a Provisional Member of the Academy of Health Information Professionals and serves as President-Elect for the Knoxville Health Sciences Library Consortium.

Roland Barksdale-Hall currently serves as the library director at the Quinby Street Resource Center in Sharon, Pennsylvania. He is the author of *Leadership Under Fire: Advancing, Communicating, Teaching & Setting Communities at Liberty* (Amber Books, 2016). He has signed entries on "The Black Family in the Colonial Era," "Daisy Lampkin," and "Entrepreneurs" in *The Encyclopedia of African American History*, edited by Paul Finkelman (Oxford University Press, 2005) and a chapter, "Collaboration Fits the Bill for Best Practices in Programming for Public Housing Residents," appearing in *The Library's Role in Supporting Financial Literacy for Patrons*, edited by Carol Smallwood (Rowman & Littlefield, 2016). He has served as managing editor of *QBR the Black Book Review*, vice president of *The Buckeye Review*, interim executive director of Southwest Gardens Economic Development Corporation, and on the executive committee of the Black Caucus of the American Library Association, and on the editorial board of *Information, Society and Justice*. He served as a Twenty-First Century Community Learning Center teacher-librarian and has a chapter, "Librarian Writer Supports Courageous Conversations,

Critical Multiculturalism and Communal Networks" in *Library Partnerships with Writers and Poets* (McFarland, 2017). He credits a combination of professional employment, personal family background as residents in public housing, and community recognition as celebrated author of *Farrell* (Arcadia, 2012) for his current leadership role in community building and his passion "to rebuild walls and restore ruined houses" (Isaiah 58:12). Roland can be contacted at barksdalehall@gmail.com.

Tatiana Bryant is the Research Librarian for Digital Humanities, History, and African American Studies at UC Irvine. She holds an MPA in International Public and Nonprofit Administration, Management, and Policy from New York University, an MS in Information and Library Science from Pratt Institute, and a BA in History from Hampton University. She works with nonprofits, cultural heritage organizations, and academic institutions. She teaches courses in Black digital humanities, Global Studies, and information literacy.

Jonathan O. Cain is the Associate University Librarian for Research and Learning at Columbia University. He holds an MS in Information and Library Science from Pratt Institute, an MA in Africana Studies from New York University, and a BS in Anthropology from the College of Charleston. He works on issues of diversity, equity, and inclusion in data education, statistical literacy in libraries, and supporting digital library initiatives.

Rachel Caldwell is the scholarly communication librarian at the University of Tennessee, Knoxville Libraries. Rachel's background as an instruction librarian informs her current role as a campus advocate for open access publishing, open educational resources, and library publishing partnerships.

Michael Cherry was formerly the teen and youth librarian at the Evansville Vanderburgh Public Library (EVPL). Michael received his Master of Library and Information Science from the University of Pittsburgh.

Prior to working for the EVPL, he worked at the Crafton Public Library and Andy Warhol Museum in Pittsburgh, PA. He is the author of "A Picture is Worth a Thousand Words: Teaching Media Literacy" in *Critical Literacy for Information Professionals* (Facet Publishing, 2016) and "Animation Programs at the Evansville Vanderburgh Public Library" in *How to STEM: Science, Technology, Engineering, and Math Education in Libraries* (Scarecrow Press, 2014).

Tiffany Coulson is Associate Director of Programming, Northwest Learning and Achievement Group. She holds a Master in Library and Information Science from the University of Washington. She is an active member of the American Library Association and REFORMA (The National Association to Promote Library and Information Services to Latinos and the Spanish Speaking). Tiffany lives in rural Washington State and has over ten years of experience working in rural schools.

Anna Culbertson, MA, MSLIS, is a librarian specializing in rare books and special collections. She provides instruction and reference for primary source research and curates the library's speculative fiction and zine collections. Her research interests include feminist science fiction and comics, radical feminist movements (especially lesbian separatism), alternative reproductive health, and ideas of utopia in speculative fiction and alternative religious movements. Anna also co-chairs SDSU Library's Diversity Task Force and serves on the Board of Directors for Lambda Archives San Diego. Anna can be contacted at aculbertson@mail.sdsu.edu.

Tracy Englert is associate professor and Science and Technology librarian at the Cook Library at Southern Miss (University of Southern Mississippi). She is the recipient of several grants focusing on science and technology and is the creator and coordinator for a successful Science Café series at Cook Library, which are open to the community and the university. Tracy can be contacted at tracy.englert@usm.edu.

Natalia Fernández is an associate professor and the Curator and Archivist of the Oregon Multicultural Archives (OMA) and the OSU Queer Archives (OSQA) at the Oregon State University Special Collections and Archives Research Center. Fernández's mission for directing the OMA and the OSQA is to work in collaboration with Oregon's African American, Asian American, Latino/a, Native American, and OSU's LGBTQ+ communities to support them in preserving their histories and sharing their stories. Her scholarship relates to her work as an archivist, specifically best practices for working with communities of color. Fernández has published in the *Oregon Historical Quarterly*, *Journal of Western Archives*, *American Archivist*, *Multicultural Perspectives*, and *Archival Practice*. Fernández holds an MA in Information Resources and Library Science from the University of Arizona (U of A). She graduated from the U of A Knowledge River Program, a program that focuses on community-based librarianship and partnerships with traditionally underserved communities. Natalia can be contacted at natalia.fernandez@oregonstate.edu.

Violet H. Harada is a professor emeritus with the Library and Information Science Graduate Program at the University of Hawaii. Violet can be contacted at vharada@hawaii.edu.

Korey Jackson has been the Gray Family Chair for Innovative Library Services since 2013. He has explored digital publishing initiatives, whether through the adoption of new platforms or new formats. Given his role to explore new forms of publishing and library publishing services, he co-leads a partnership between OSU Libraries and CALYX to implement the National Endowment for the Humanities grant-funded project from to digitize their backlist.

Jill R. Kavanaugh, MLIS, AHIP is the librarian for the Center on Media and Child Health in the Division of Adolescent and Young Adult Medicine at Boston Children's Hospital. Jill provides research support, assists in creating and writing content for the Center's various tools, and reviews research on topics related to youth, media, technology, and health. Jill can be contacted at Jill.Kavanaugh@childrens.harvard.edu.

kYmberly Keeton is the African American community archivist at Austin History Center in Austin, TX. She began her career in librarianship at Lincoln University, Missouri. In 2014, she received a Master's in Library Science degree and a Graduate Certificate in Digital Content Management from the University of North Texas. She completed her Graduate Practicum Studies at the Hirsch Library, The Museum of Fine Arts Houston, and The Houston Museum of African American Culture. The artistic librarian serves on the ACRL Framework Information Literacy Advisory Board, founded & published the online Hip Hop LibGuide, and is the Art Editor and Creative Director of ART library deco. She is also a founding member of the Hip Hop Librarian Consortium. Keeton is a member of the ALA Emerging Leader Class of 2016 and Alumni of the 2016 ACRL (AiA) Assessment in Action Program. She is a mentee participant in the 2016-2017 LLAMA Mentoring Program | Library Leadership & Management. Her scholarship about Hip Hop Information Literacy is featured in Librarians With Spines, published by Hinchas Press, her research about African American G.L.A.M (Galleries, Libraries, Archives, and Museums) will be published in the forthcoming book by McFarland, *Expanding Relevancy: Innovation to Meet Changing Needs*, and she penned an article about the legacy of Prince Rogers Nelson in the *Journal of African American Studies*. Keeton is the 2018 Convener for the ACRL-African American Studies Librarians Interest Group. kYm can be contacted at kreativelibrarian@gmail.com.

Jane Kurahara is a staff associate with the Japanese Cultural Center of Hawaii. Jane can be contacted at jmklib@aol.com.

Lisa Lamont, MA, MLIS, is the digital collections librarian at San Diego State University. She has been the project manager of numerous digital collections including the University Archives Photograph Collection, the Student Newspaper Collection, the Works Progress Administration

Mural Collection, and many others. She has published and presented on her research concerning assessment and evaluation of digital collections. Lisa can be contacted at mlamont@mail.sdsu.edu.

Kristelle Lavallee, MA, is the content strategist at the Center on Media and Child Health at Boston Children's Hospital. Kristelle oversees the Center's outreach initiatives and translates scientific research into actionable advice, practical health resources, and curricula that promote children's healthy and developmentally optimal creation and consumption of media.

Noah Lenstra is an assistant professor of library and information studies at the University of North Carolina at Greensboro. He received his PhD from the University of Illinois Graduate School of Library and Information Science. His research and teaching focus on community engagement in libraries and archives. Noah can be contacted at http://www.noahlenstra.com/ and njlenstr@uncg.edu.

Amani Magid earned a degree in Integrative Biology with a minor in Arabic from the University of California, Berkeley. In her career as a scientist, she has worked as a researcher in Pharmaceutical Chemistry and managed biology lab classes at a community college. She soon realized her passion was in finding and locating science information and earned her Master's in Library and Information Science at University of Pittsburgh while interning at the Bayer Material Science Library. She worked in Qatar for over five years as a Medical Librarian prior to her present position as associate academic librarian for the Sciences and Engineering at New York University, Abu Dhabi. Amani can be reached at amani.magid@nyu.edu.

Sarah McFadden is a librarian and technology trainer in upstate New York. For the last four years, she has been a Cooperative Extension educator working to develop engaging digital literacy trainings for rural communities and library patrons. Sarah received her MSIS from the University at Albany, State University of New York in 2011, and has been helping people use the Internet ever since.

Alejandra Nann has been the electronic resources and serials librarian since February 2013. Her research interests include: electronic resource assessment and development, ebook acquisitions, and open educational resources. Alejandra manages the procurement, licensing, and management of all electronic resources and serials. She is also the liaison to Architecture. Alejandra holds a BA in Art History from the University of California, San Diego and an MLIS from San Jose State University. Alejandra can be contacted at ajsnann@sandiego.edu.

Jane Nichols is the Head of Teaching and Engagement and an academic librarian at Oregon State University Libraries & Press. She has worked in several areas including information literacy, emerging technologies, digital humanities/publishing, and as a subject librarian for the humanities and social sciences. She pairs her work with service; she has served as a board member for CALYX Press, Inc. a non-profit feminist press that nurture's women's voices through art and literature. She co-leads a partnership between OSU Libraries and CALYX to implement the National Endowment for the Humanities grant-funded project to digitize their backlist. Jane can be contacted at jane.nichols@oregonstate.edu.

Barbara Peterson serves as the Executive Director of the Northwest Learning and Achievement (NLA) Group, an education nonprofit that she co-founded in 1999 in the rural central Washington community of Wapato, where she lives. She earned an EdD in Leadership for Learning from the University of Washington. Her published work includes her extensive experience with STEM education for rural students. NLA works with low-income school districts throughout central Washington state, bringing auxiliary college outreach and afterschool programs.

Judith Schwartz is an assistant professor and librarian in the Department of Library and Information Services at Medgar Evers College, The City University of New York. She teaches Information and Visual Literacy workshops and designs marketing materials and posters for exhibits in the library as well as the college's Archives and Special Collections. She earned a BFA from the Cooper Union School of Art, an MA in Advertising and Communication Design from Syracuse University, and an MSLIS from Palmer LIU School of Library and Information Science. She has also worked as an art director for many prominent publishing houses and has expertise in all forms of visual-design communication. Judith can be contacted at jude.schwartz@gmail.com.

Ann Viera is the veterinary medicine librarian at the University of Tennessee, Knoxville Libraries. Supporting veterinary medicine, a small community of practice with a huge mandate, Ann has been active in identifying scholarly communication tools and publication options that fully support the land-grant university mission. http://orcid.org/0000-0003-3718-4803.

Alan Wallace is the education librarian at the University of Tennessee, Knoxville Libraries. In addition, he is liaison to the Cinema Studies and Psychology Departments. Alan provides expert searching and consultation to these areas. He has also taught for the UT School of Information Sciences program for many years.

INDEX

21st Century Community Learning Center, 218, 222-4
21st century skills, 149, 229

A
academic libraries, 39-41, 53, 103, 105-6, 108-9, 156, 168-9
academic librarians, 40-1, 104, 107, 181
academic presses, 60-1
accessibility, 14-5, 21, 53, 66, 83, 98, 144, 150, 158, 223, 231, 242-3
Adobe Education Trainer, 173, 179-80
advisory board, 55-6, 125
advocacy, 5, 20, 25, 39, 42-6, 48-9, 108, 114, 116-7, 198
afterschool programs, 187-8, 193, 195, 219, 227-8, 252
African American[s], 54, 75, 171, 199, 229
   in Oregon, 69-70, 72-3, 79-80, 83
African Library Project, 188-9

agriculture, 90, 206-7, 210, 214, 225
American Library Association (ALA), 2-4, 168, 174
AmeriCorps, 187, 193, 195-200
archival collections, 89, 155
art exhibit[s], 134-5, 137
articles, peer-reviewed, 15-6, 104, 106, 109, 113, 138
arts programming, 30, 53-6, 136, 150, 187-8, 195
assessment, 33-4, 81, 118, 163, 176, 190, 193, 207, 212
Association of College and Research Libraries (ACRL), 173, 176
authors, 59-61, 63-7, 104-5, 109, 112, 115-7, 127, 200, 223, 230-1, 234

B
Bayside Community Center, 39, 42-44, 47-49
BiblioVault, 64, 67

bilingual books, 218, 223, 231-33, 235
bilingual programs, 220-1, 225
blog[s], 14, 98, 163
board of directors, 63, 69, 72-83, 116,
  149, 155-6, 225
board of trustees, 109, 118
Bosse High School, 141-43, 150
Boston Children's Hospital, 11, 12
broadband, 170, 205-8, 210-1

C
California Council for the Humanities (CCH), 158
Calyx Press, 59-60, 62
Carnegie Mellon, 60
Center for Digital Scholarship, 132
Center on Media and Child Health (CMCH), 11-17, 19-21
Charles Evans Inniss Memorial Library, 169, 171
civic engagement, 91, 141-43, 145, 150
civil rights, 5, 78, 91, 94, 171
communication skills, 149
community archive[s], 71, 72, 153, 155
community center[s], *see also* Bayside Community Center
  libraries as, 3, 26, 35, 243
community garden, 25-28, 32, 33, 35
community outreach, 11-2, 17, 77, 111

computer access, 41, 45, 172, 181, 207, 211
computer classes, 167, 200, 205, 207, 211
connected (situated) learning, 141, 145
continuing education, 3, 17-19, 110, 114
Coretta Scott King Book Donation Award, 187, 195, 199
Cornell Cooperative Extension (CCE), 205-08, 210, 212-14
critical thinking, 150, 229
Cultural Competency Workshop, 187, 195
curriculum resources, 70, 80, 85, 91-2, 94-9, 195

D
digital divide, 169-71
digital humanities, 155, 159-60
digital literacy, 167, 170, 173-4, 177, 205-9, 211-4
digitization of texts, 60-2, 67, 155
disabilities, students with, 141-2, 144, 146, 150, 167-73, 180
discrimination, 69, 94
diverse books, 230, 231
diversity, 7, 56, 66, 141, 150, 168, 231
DVDs, 124, 138, 200

E
eBay, 208, 211
ebooks, 43, 60, 64-67, 132, 155

educational programs, 42, 89, 126, 207
educators, 13, 18, 91, 98, 126, 159, 163, 206, 226, 232
embedded librarian[s], 12, 15, 22, 167, 173
empathy, 95, 97, 205
English Language Learners, 217, 225
environmental sustainability, 95
equity, 144, 150, 168, 170, 171
evaluation
　of information, 92, 208
　of programs, 125, 163, 193, 195-6, 209
Evansville Vanderburgh Public Library, 141-2, 150, 246-7
experiential learning (hands-on), 92, 115, 108, 126-7, 142, 145, 150, 179-80, 212, 222, 228

F
Facebook. 32, 113, 149, 208
Fair Use Week, 113, 117
fake news, 11, 178, 209
family literacy, 228, 229, 232
Federal Communications Commission (FCC), 170
feedback, 16, 20, 45, 49, 81, 93, 98, 103, 114, 116-8, 125, 138, 163-4, 209, 235
feminist literature, 60-2, 64
feminist press/publishing, 59, 64-5
field trips, 143-4, 146

financial literacy, 169, 190, 195
First Book, 218, 223-4, 227-8, 230, 233, 235-6
food security, 43, 46, 49
funding, lack of, 56, 191, 194
fundraising, 54, 73-4, 77, 95
Friends of the Governor's Mansion (Jefferson City, MO), 54-56

G
Gay Rights Movement, 154
Google, 115, 162
Google Analytics, 169
Google Docs, 49
Google Scholar, 45, 106
grant[s], 17, 60, 62, 116, 118, 125, 194, 207, 223
graphic design, 167, 178-80, 182

H
Ham, F. Gerald, 71
HathiTrust, 64, 67
Hawaii Department of Education (DOE), 91, 93-95
HBCU institutions, 53, 54
health programming, 14, 18-9, 22, 30, 188, 194-5
healthcare professionals, 17, 18
healthy lifestyles, 32, 35, 187-8, 243
Hispanic parents, 4, 218-21, 227, 232, 233, 235
homelessness, 65, 168-9
homework, 187, 195, 220, 222

Honouliuli Internment Camp, 88, 90, 92, 96, 99
human rights, 5, 97, 159, 170, 171

I
Imagine Science Film Festival Abu Dhabi, 131, 133, 136, 139
Immigrants, 87, 220
InDesign, 173, 178
Information literacy, 40, 124, 155, 167, 169, 172-75, 179-80, 182
insurance, 29, 35
Internet access, 171, 206, 212
interviews, 71, 97, 103, 106, 110, 112-3, 115, 118, 218, 220, 227, 233, 235

J
Japanese American incarceration, 85-7, 91-5
Japanese Cultural Center of Hawaii (JCCH), 85-94, 96-100
Jessop, Jess, 158, 160
job readiness/training 172, 190, 193,

K
K-5 students, 218
K-12 schools, 48, 80
kits (discovery boxes), 92-3, 126-7

L
Lambda Archives of San Diego (LASD), 153-58, 161-63

land grant institutions, 62, 66, 80, 108, 206, 212, 252
language, heritage, 220-22, 226, 232-3
leadership skills, 39, 42-4, 46-7, 54, 189, 199
learning standards, 91-2, 221, 226
LGBTQ history, 153-4, 158
LGBTQ Pride, 153-4
library and information science (LIS) students, 107, 118
library databases (or databases?), 106, 178
library resources, 40, 46, 48, 115, 134, 137-8, 209, 223
life skills, 141-43, 149, 150, 195
low-income students, 222, 224, 227, 236

M
maker education, 141-2, 150
maker movement, 143-4, 150
marketing (materials)? 61, 63, 74-5, 191, 209, 210, 214, 243
math, 126, 146, 220, 222, 225-6
Medgar Evers College, City University of New York, 167, 169, 171-2, 181-2
media and health, 11-15, 18-22
mental well-being, 11, 13
mentoring, 55, 195, 197
Mercer County Housing Authority, 188, 192-4, 196-7

INDEX 257

microactivism, 168, 181-2
mission, 11-3, 20-22, 39-40, 42, 47, 55, 62, 66, 72-6, 81, 83, 89, 108, 132, 139, 141-2, 145, 148, 155, 159, 182, 189-90, 206-7, 212, 227, 235-6
Moore, Doug, 158
museums, 18, 54, 70, 79, 93, 126, 164
Myanmar, 141, 143-45, 148-50

N
Nanoscale Informal Science Education Network, 123, 126, 129
National Endowment for the Humanities (NEH), 60, 62, 63, 154, 158
National Informal STEM Education Network (NISE Net), 123, 126-29
National Park Service, 87-8, 96, 99
National Science Foundation (NSF), 126
New York University Abu Dhabi (NYUAD), 131-33, 136-39
newsletter[s], 105, 136, 196-7, 199
Northwest Learning and Achievement (NLA) Group, 208, 224, 247
NOVA ScienceNOW, 123-26, 129
nutrition, 13, 44, 46-7, 195, 207

O
Obama, Barack, 88
open access, 48, 62, 63, 103-6, 104, 108-10, 114, 116-18
opioid abuse, 1, 2, 111

oral histories, 89, 153-55, 158
Oregon Black Pioneers (OBP), 69-70, 72-83
Oregon Historical Society (OHS), 73, 75, 78
Oregon Multicultural Archives (OMA), 73, 77, 80
Oregon State University Libraries and Press (OSULP), 60, 62
orphanages, 141, 143, 145, 148-50

P
P373K Brooklyn Transition Center, 167, 169, 172, 173, 176, 177, 179, 180
Pearl Harbor, 86, 88, 95-6
photography, 113, 160-1, 178
Photoshop, 173, 178
physical health, 11, 13
playgroup[s], 188-9, 192-95, 197, 199
policy makers, 18, 19
poverty, 192, 217
preschool programming, 187-8
presentations, 12, 14-22, 47, 72, 109, 116, 124
primary sources, 64
project management, 61, 164
Public Broadcasting Service (PBS), 123-26, 129
public housing, 187-92, 198, 243
public libraries, 1-2, 4, 25, 28, 34-36, 71, 168, 191, 205, 206, 212, 217, 236, 241
public schools, 19, 90-1, 188, 197

publicity, 95, 128

Q

Quinby Street Resource Center library, 187, 192, 195, 201

R

race, 62, 64, 171
racism, 86, 95, 99
reading, partner, 223, 228, 230, 234
reading promotion, 64, 188
recreation centers, 30, 31, 198
research
    guides, 137-8, *see also* subject guides
    monitoring, 15
    scholarly, 69, 104, 117
    skills, 45, 46, 48, 107, 110, 114
Rhode Island Family Literacy Initiative, 4
Roosevelt, Franklin, 86
royalties, 63, 65
rural communities, 30, 189, 206, 214
rural libraries, 208, 213

S

San Diego Pride, 154, 157-8, 161, 164
San Diego State University (SDSU) Library, 153-56, 162
science café, 124-26, 128, 129
science film festival[s], 131, 133-37, 140
science programming, 123-4, 127
scientific knowledge, 14, 125

scholarly communication, 61, 109
Scholarly Publishing and Academic Resource Coalition (SPARC), 104
school librarians, 85-6, 91, 95, 127
secondary sources, 93-4
senior center[s], 32, 35, 36, 210
senior citizens, 205, 210
service commitment, 76, 81
service learning, 81, 109
soapmaking, 141, 143, 145-49
social change, 168-9, 181, 194, 196
social justice, 66, 95, 97, 171, 181
social media, 12, 14, 19-21, 45, 138 158, 163, 209-11, 214, 243
STEM, 124-27, 139
storytelling, 187-89, 194, 196, 197, 200, 202, 222
subject guide[s], 40, 46, 49 *see also* research guides
survey[s], 49, 112, 114-16, 118, 163, 170, 190, 209, 218, 227

T

tai chi, 25, 28-30, 35, 36
time commitment, 41, 76-7, 82, 164
Tokioka Heritage Resource Center, 89, 92, 98
training, 45, 47, 85-6, 92, 96, 105, 113-4, 118, 127-8, 187, 208, 214, 223, 251
    computer, 190, 192
    digital literacy, 167, 205-9, 211
    diversity, 195-7
    job, 141, 149, 172, 193, 196, 201

Tuchina, Natalia, 26, 27, 33

U
Uncharted International, 141-46, 148, 150
underserved communities, 170, 188, 191, 248
United Nations Convention of the Rights of Persons with Disabilities (CRPD), 170
U.S. Housing and Urban Development (HUD), 188, 194
University of San Diego, Copley Library, 39, 42, 43, 45-49
University of Southern Mississippi (Southern Miss), 123, 125, 127-29
University of Tennessee (UT Libraries, 103-5, 108-9

V
videos, 90, 103-4, 112, 114-7, 131, 136-9, 149, 230
visual literacy, 167, 173, 175, 179

W
Walkertown Branch Library, 26, 27, 31, 33, 34, 36
walking, 25, 31, 32, 34
WIFI, 208, 241
workshops, 12, 14, 17, 39-40, 44-46, 96-98, 103, 105, 107, 109, 112-14, 117-8, 132, 146, 167-69, 172-3, 175, 179-80, 187, 211

Y
yearbooks, 167, 172, 174-77, 180
YMCA, 32-3, 35
yoga, 25, 29-31, 34-36

www.ingramcontent.com/pod-product-compliance
Lightning Source LLC
Chambersburg PA
CBHW070827300426
44111CB00014B/2481